Public Expressions of Religion in America

Conrad Cherry, Series Editor

Published in cooperation with the Center
for the Study of Religion and American Culture
Indiana University–Purdue University at Indianapolis

UNCIVIL RITES

UNCIVIL RITES

American Fiction, Religion, and the Public Sphere

•

Robert Detweiler

University of Illinois Press
Urbana and Chicago

This book is printed on acid-free paper.

Library of Congress Cataloging-in-Publication Data
Detweiler, Robert.
Uncivil rites : American fiction, religion, and the public
sphere / Robert Detweiler.
Includes bibliographical references and index.
ISBN 0-252-01932-6 (acid-free paper). —
ISBN 0-252-06580-8 (pbk. : alk. paper)
1. American fiction—20th century—History and criticism.
2. Religious fiction, American—History and criticism.
3. United States—Religion—History—20th century.
4. Fiction—Religious aspects. 5. Religion in literature.
I. Indiana University–Purdue University at Indianapolis.
Center for the Study of Religion and American Culture.
II. Title. III. Series.
PS374.R47D48   1996
813'.5409382—dc20   95-41735
CIP

Contents

Appendixes

Acknowledgments

Many people have helped me in this study. I am very grateful to Conrad Cherry for asking me to write this book as one of the projects of the Center for the Study of Religion and American Culture. I am thankful to Paul Levine, William Doty, Ann-Janine Morey, Gregory Salyer, David Jasper, Mark Ledbetter, Daniel Zins, Allen Tullos, Amanda Porterfield, Alice Benston, Kerry Soper, Janet McAdams, Patricia Hilden, Carolyn Jones, and Dirk Detweiler for bibliographical information and/or critical readings of my study in progress. My thanks go to Hans Bungert from the University of Regensburg, to Cristina Giorcelli from the Center for American Studies in Rome, to Hortensia Marcu from the United States Embassy in Vienna, to Kirsten Nielsen from the University of Aarhus, and to the students in my seminar on American fiction and religion at the University of Copenhagen for providing me occasions to present early versions of some chapters to European audiences. I am grateful also to the students in my Emory University seminar on American fiction, religion, and the public sphere for what they taught me about many of the texts I have addressed in this book. It is a pleasure to acknowledge my debt to my research assistant Heidi Nordberg, who not only found reams of information for me but also read the whole study along the way and helped me see and say so much that I would have missed otherwise. And finally, of course, Sharon, who still surprises me.

The author and publishers gratefully acknowledge permission as follows:

From *Religion and American Culture: A Journal of Interpretation,* to print chapter 3, "*The Book of Daniel:* The Fatally Exposed Family," as a version of an article that appears in that journal under the title "Carnival of Shame: Doctorow and the Rosenbergs."

From Ron Hansen to quote the materials in Appendix 1.

From Elizabeth Dewberry to quote the materials in Appendix 2.

From Philip Caputo to quote the materials in Appendix 3.

From Pantheon Books to reprint, as Appendix 4, Dick Fool Bull, "The Ghost Dance at Wounded Knee," from *American Indian Myths and Legends,* edited by Richard Erdoes and Alfonso Ortiz (New York: Pantheon Books, 1984), 481–84. Copyright © 1984 by Richard Erdoes and Alfonso Ortiz. Reprinted by permission of Pantheon Books, a division of Random House.

UNCIVIL RITES

Introduction: Fictions of Public Realms

If there is any legacy of the Reagan years, it is to have devalued completely the importance of the public realm and to
have raised dramatically the value we place on the private
realm, so much so that the public realm has almost ceased
to have meaning.

—Paul Goldberger

The public sphere celebrated by Habermas, in which there was
"no authority beside that of the better argument," was found-
ed . . . on the authority of patriarchy (and we should add class,
privilege, racism, and colonialism). That is, the "public" pre-
supposed a sphere of privacy rooted in the patriarchal conjugal family. On this account, the novel emerged as the aesthet-
ic form that publicly represented subjectivity as "the innermost
core of the private."

—George Yúdice, "For a Practical Aesthetics"

This is a study of three bodies—not individual physical bodies, although
many of these play key roles, and not even of bodies as corporate entities, although a number of these are involved as well. The three bodies
exist only in relation to public discourse; or, better said, one of them exists there while the others are about to because I have created (or at least
appropriated) them for that purpose. The existing body is the familiar—
although never well-defined—body politic. The two I have recreated are
the body erotic and the body apocalyptic. These bodies can be thought
of as locales of public discourse, shaped in part by works of fiction, where
urgent matters such as the nurturing of a just state, responsibilities of
reproduction, and the conditions for human survival are expressed. My
examination of the shaping fiction, particularly as it articulates religious
concerns, seeks to show how that fiction, perhaps paradoxically, makes
these bodies real as communal projections (not always conscious) of who
we are and what we live for.

My study picks up where an earlier one left off in which I interpreted novels and stories, most of them written during and after the sixties, as texts about persons seeking meaning for their lives through some sort of community: family, clan, church, club, military unit, mental institution, or expedition.[1] I argued, among other things, that these communities cohered—when they did—through articulating and living out narratives of belief and commitment that their members inherited or created. I did not, however, examine in any depth the nature of these communities or how they inspired or discouraged belief and commitment. *Uncivil Rites* has given me the chance to do that. The invitation from the Center for the Study of Religion and American Culture to write this book on fiction as one sort of public expression of religion in America appealed to me because it provided the impetus and occasion to return to the subject of fiction, religion, and community in a more focused effort. My "assignment" was to concentrate my study on the United States and to align it to the notion of the public sphere or public realm. This I have done, although surely not in any definitive way.

I saw three possible approaches to the task. One was to offer a historical overview of the interactions among fiction, religion, and the public realm from the beginnings of the United States as a colony through its growth into a world superpower, paying attention to the impact of novelists and their texts on a broad readership. This would have meant addressing the inspirations and receptions of such widely read religious romances of the nineteenth and twentieth centuries as Elizabeth Stuart Phelps's *The Gates Ajar* (1868), Charles Sheldon's phenomenally popular *In His Steps* (1896), or Taylor Caldwell's *Dear and Glorious Physician* (1959); assessing the influence of literary-political phenomena and their religious dimensions, such as Harriet Beecher Stowe's *Uncle Tom's Cabin;* tracking the impact on popular religious culture of apocalypticists like Hal Lindsey and Frank E. Peretti; and attempting somehow to measure the broad influence of serious, religiously oriented novelists such as Flannery O'Connor and Frederick Buechner. To a degree, I will struggle with the last of these, but I am not an adept literary or cultural historian and did not feel moved to adopt this approach as my general strategy. There is also the fact that some of this ground has already been covered expertly by studies such as Ann-Janine Morey's *Religion and Sexuality in America* and R. Laurence Moore's *Selling God: American Religion in the Marketplace of Culture.*[2]

A second possibility was to develop a theoretical approach and attempt a definition of the elusive concept of the "public realm" through exploring the interplay of literature, religion, and political expression in America. This was a more tempting avenue; indeed, I had dealt briefly with differences between the public and private in the context of reading fiction "religiously" in my earlier book, and I considered expanding the argument via the influential work of Jürgen Habermas in texts such as *The Structural Transformation of the Public Sphere*, of John Rawls in *A Theory of Justice*, of Iris Marion Young in *Justice and the Politics of Difference*, and of Jean Bethke Elshtain in *Democracy on Trial*.[3] Above all, I was fascinated by the challenge of a collection entitled *The Phantom Public Sphere*, in which various contributors question whether the concept of the public sphere, at least according to Habermas's liberal agenda, has any utility in the postmodern world—or, in the words of the volume's editor Bruce Robbins, "If one recognizes the political importance that culture and media have acquired, both in identity politics and more generally, then one can no longer buy into Habermas's comfortably apocalyptic scenario of the rise of the mass media as the decadence of the public."[4]

At the same time, it seemed to me that a theory-oriented study would appeal mainly to a small number of specialist readers and might also inhibit the interpretive potential of some fairly irascible novels I already had in mind. Thus I decided not to engage comprehensively theoretical aspects of the public sphere, although I am guided by and will describe a concept of what the novel (and drama and film) can do in a "postbourgeois" society, and I have constructed basic theoretical scaffolding in each of this volume's three parts and twelve chapters (plus a conclusion).[5]

The third possibility, and the one I chose, was to undertake close readings of selected American works with a particular accent one way or another on public life and to allow those readings to illuminate a variety of ways in which public spheres can be thought to exist and manifest themselves religiously. This approach is cautiously aligned to the thinking introduced in my prefatory quotation by George Yúdice and practiced as well by Nancy Fraser. Yúdice continues his assessment of the role of the novel in a post-Habermas context by declaring:

> The grounding for the public/private divide has, of course, changed. And the novel, an art form rooted in bourgeois institutions, is no longer the form through which the hegemonic totality of the social formation is inscribed in the constitution of subjectivity. On the contrary, the novel, like autobiography and the diary, is used by subaltern groups to construct particular rather than overarching hegemonic identities. It is not the entire social formation that reads Zora Neale Hursten or Ed Vega or Paula Gunn Allen, nor has a latter-day, multicultural Lukács emerged to argue that "the complex, capillary factors of development of the *whole* society" are embodied in the particularity of the subaltern rather than the "higher consciousness" of the "world historical Individual."[6]

Fraser also refers to subaltern groups, arguing that "multiple publics" exist and stressing the role of *"subaltern counterpublics . . .* [which] are parallel discursive arenas where members of subordinated social groups invent and circulate counterdiscourses, so as to formulate oppositional interpretations of their identities, interests, and needs."[7] The texts I interpret not only represent such "subaltern counterpublics," but they also show problems in theorizing about where and how the novel functions amid multiple publics. The novel, although "rooted in bourgeois institutions," never was the unadulterated voice or efficient instrument of the hegemony; it criticized its own social-political conditions from the very start. Novelists from "subordinated social groups," such as Paula Gunn Allen, a Native American, even while they "invent and circulate counterdiscourses" also through their involvement in the politics and economics of commercial publishing, participate necessarily in creating and producing majority discourse. Further, by their sympathetic dramatizations of religiously oriented situations and characters, some of "my" authors who are not from subordinated social groups offer fictional discourses that challenge the secular assumptions of the commercial book reviewing and academic critical majority.

In other words, the language of postbourgeois theory about the public realm is not adequate to treat the complications of the relationship of literary (and dramatic and cinematic) fiction to public discourse, and my readings of the fiction, although borrowing from the theory, also expose its flaws. My approach thus raises more questions than it answers, a strategy that, I hope, troubles those who read this book as little as it troubles me. I believe that good fiction always unsettles more than it comforts, that the best novels upset dogmas and challenge prejudices of all kinds, and that one job of the critic is to stress and enhance this radical interrogatory reflex of fiction rather than attempting immediately to subdue it.

Subversive Texts

Thinking in that vein, I chose works emphasizing events and situations in American life marked by lack of closure—a condition that tends to turn the writing of narrative fiction against itself; traditional narrative, at least, always seeks some definitive end. Looking for examples of fiction in conflict with itself that embodies a deeply conflicted society, I found them mostly in recent writing, in so-called postmodern texts that capitalize not only on a lack of closure but also on absences of many kinds—of reliable narrators, of dependable realisms, of common symbolisms, and even of accurate historical orientations.[8] I tend toward such texts in any case— the sort that, as Toni Morrison says, subvert the reader's traditional comfort—because much of my profession involves teaching the "uncomfortable" narrative fiction of recent decades.[9] I have selected texts that exemplify such problematic conflict in three broad areas that identify the three parts of my study: politics, sexuality, and aggression—a trio with considerable interaction, as the news media and experience inform us daily.

It was convenient to focus the interpretation of the first part on politics on a specific midcentury event, the Rosenberg "affair" that culminated in the 1953 execution of the spy couple for treason, for the case inspired two first-rate novels, E. L. Doctorow's *The Book of Daniel* and Robert Coover's *The Public Burning,* while the communist hysteria of the late forties and fifties provoked Arthur Miller's composition of his durable play *The Crucible.* I argue that particularly the two novels, when provided with religion-oriented readings (Miller's play has received more of these), suggest how a nation can quickly sacrifice its rationality and self-confidence, as well as its sense of justice and mercy and endorsement of decent behavior, and indulge prurient rituals of victimization that produce no catharsis but rather a pervasive sense of shame disguised and expressed as a triumph over an alien evil.

The novels purposefully distort the historical dimensions of the Rosenberg case, but that fictional distortion relays truthfully the distortion of justice that the American body politic not merely permitted but encouraged and even demanded. The point is not whether the Rosenbergs were guilty of passing information on nuclear weaponry to the Soviets (if I had to choose, I would say that they were) and, if so, whether they deserved to die as their punishment (a sentence I consider deeply wrong and immoral), but what the public lust for that punishment conveys about us. It bears little relationship to the crime, assuming a crime was committed, but it does reveal the frightening power of the drive to find victims who are assigned the guilt of society and whose punishment seems, for a time, to set things straight. To state it like that is to articulate an ancient religious comprehension, one dramatized in later puritan dress in Miller's play about witchcraft. It is also precisely the comprehension that these fictions portray as operating in the contemporary American public realm.

I reflect on this comprehension in the first part through a concentration, in interpreting the three texts, on the dynamic of public accusation and confession, on the conditions created for understanding and responding to evil and goodness, and on the sociopathology of public exposure. Things are not as orderly in the second part, where I turn to the body erotic, a term that is less conventional than the "body politic," which *The American College Dictionary* defines as deriving from political science and meaning "a people as forming a political body under an organized government." I use "the body erotic" in a somewhat analogous way to designate a communal awareness of and participation in sexual and familial relationships, what some critics mean by the term *sexual politics,* and I choose this term over sexual politics in order to emphasize the corporeal significance of these relationships against the religious traditions and theologies that ignore, minimize, or denigrate the role of the body.

In projecting something like a public sexuality I risk misunderstanding, for we regard sexual relationships mainly as private matters, as, for example, the venerable American protest against the government's "invasion of the bedroom" suggests. But there is far more involved than the bedroom or the kitchen or, now, the home computer office. We now have, for instance, a decades-long pitched battle over reproduction rights and another one over equal rights for homosexuals, both of which have emphatic public and political aspects. We also endure from the news and entertainment media a barrage of erotic stimuli—some of it occasionally even useful and pleasant—that helps to make sexuality a national obsession.

I have identified no crucial public event such as the Rosenberg affair to focus my readings of the body erotic but propose instead that an archetypal sequence persists in American sexual practice that everyone recognizes and that informs our narratives, just as the narratives nurture the archetype. The sequence is found in the pattern of seduction, abuse, and abandonment that stands as an auxiliary formation to our still-flourishing (against the evidence) anticipations of romantic courtship, happy family life, and lifelong fidelity. This sequence is at work, in a complicated way, in the political and personal fortunes of the Rosenbergs, but in this second part of this volume I show how it underlies six powerful novels that evolve plots of women struggling corporeally and religiously, struggling to align their bodies with their faith, in oppressive contexts. Taking my cue from Morey's discussion of passion as a confusion of religious and erotic emotion in Americans' love relationships, I argue that our conflicted expressions of sexuality are closely connected to our efforts to learn and feel what it is that we believe. I identify four concepts—shame, pain, awe, and mystery—as representative elements of the body seeking to believe and the mind seeking to be loved.

That these novels all feature women as main characters was not something I intended; it was rather that these six seemed best to serve my purposes and happened to have female protagonists. But the coincidence does suggest that, among other things, women's awareness of corporeality in creating community offers a dimension of the body erotic, of the sexual public sphere, that the Habermasian understanding of the public realm does not—perhaps cannot—embrace.

In the third and final part of this book, I invent (I think I invent) the notion of the body apocalyptic to designate three things: the power of the American lust for revelation, the violence that usually accompanies American revelatory quests and creates victims, and the destruction of the environment that permeates our revelatory adventures. My interpretation of "the body apocalyptic" counters Harold Bloom's claim that the American desire to know, above all for self-knowledge, at all costs is an overwhelming gnosticism.[10] The American rage to know is radically corporeal, so much so that we are ready—even on occasion eager—to experience self- and world destruction as the necessary price to pay and that in this sense our rage to know is profoundly apocalyptic. To study this impulse I have selected two traumatic national events and their aftermaths: the 1890 massacre of Lakota Indians at Wounded Knee and the Vietnam War. As my texts I have chosen a film, *Apocalypse Now,* and two novels: Philip Caputo's *Indian Country,* which is on the Vietnam War, and Louise Erdrich's *Tracks,* which concerns Native Americans.

My juxtaposition of white American treatment of Native Americans and the trauma of the Vietnam War suggests a connection between the two, and I try to establish such a connection—one that some readers may find scandalous. I do not believe that this connection can be demonstrated convincingly in a causal-historical manner, but I do think that it exists "prophetically" in the sense that the drive to conquer the threatening Other on his and her own grounds that marked the Indian wars as well as the Vietnam venture is now being recognized, if still dimly, as part of the moral and physical blight that attacks our spirits, our bodies, and our landscape. I try to show this through redeploying my archetype of the second part, the seduction-abuse-abandonment sequence, and transposing the four elements I used there into four related ones. Shame, pain, awe, and ecstasy modulate into paranoia, trauma, simulation, and melancholy, a quartet of apocalyptic "survivance" strategies.[11]

If assigning such weight to the fate of Native Americans seems overdone, I can only report my agreement with historian David Stannard, who states that the decimation of American Indians by European invaders constitutes the worst act of genocide in human history.[12] If this study as a whole seems unduly bleak, I confess that, for the most part, I see things that way. It is true that serious fiction writers tend to stress the negative; they contrive their plots, after all, from conditions of conflict, and I am no doubt strongly influenced by decades of interpreting stories about lives and whole societies gone wrong. At the same time, I share a certain conviction with some of the novelists I study here who are religious believers: If human existence is harsh, unjust, and in need of redemption, it also offers, precisely in the heart of suffering, a compassion beyond comprehension.

Because this study addresses the public realm, I have done certain things I would not have done otherwise. First, I have included considerable attention to reviews of the novels, plays, and film, as well as to author interviews published at the time the various works first appeared. In this way I hope to convey a sense of the reception of the works and an impression of how they might have influenced public discourse. Further, three of the novelists whose fiction I interpret, Philip Caputo, Elizabeth Dewberry, and Ron Hansen, composed responses to my chapters on their work, which appear as appendixes, and thus helped me to engage in a conversation between author and critic of the sort that rarely happens. I am very grateful to them.

Among the many things my study lacks are two that I regret much: attention to gays and lesbians and attention to the AIDS epidemic. I had intended to comment on both of these through a reading of Tony Kushner's *Angels in America*, both Part One, *Millenium Approaches*, and Part Two, *Perestroika*. Although I read the scripts of both, I was unable to see productions of either, and it seemed pointless, after discussing the plays with those who had seen them, to attempt an interpretation of drama so crucially dependent on its performance.

Notes

1. Robert Detweiler, *Breaking the Fall: Religious Readings of Contemporary Fiction* (London and San Francisco: Macmillan and Harper and Row, 1989).

2. Ann-Janine Morey, *Religion and Sexuality in American Literature* (Cambridge: Cambridge University Press, 1992); R. Laurence Moore, *Selling God: American Religion in the Marketplace of Culture* (New York: Oxford University Press, 1994). See especially Moore's Chapter 1, "Moral Sensationalism and Voracious Readers: Religious Strategies in the Antebellum Book Market," for a fine sketch of the rise of fiction writing and reading in the colonies and the new republic in relation to religion.

3. Jürgen R. Habermas, *The Structural Transformation of the Public Sphere: An Inquiry into a Category of Bourgeois Society,* trans. Thomas Burger with the assistance of Frederick Lawrence (Cambridge: MIT Press, 1989); John Rawls, *A Theory of Justice* (Cambridge: Harvard University Press, 1971); see also Rawls's *Political Liberalism* (New York: Columbia University Press, 1994); Iris Marion Young, *Justice and the Politics of Difference* (Princeton: Princeton University Press, 1990); Jean Bethke Elshtain, *Democracy on Trial* (New York: Basic Books, 1994).

4. Bruce Robbins, ed., *The Phantom Public Sphere* (Minneapolis: University of Minnesota Press, 1993), xx. For a very helpful critique of Habermas's concept of the public realm see Nancy Fraser, "Rethinking the Public Sphere: A Contribution to the Critique of Actually Existing Democracy," in *The Phantom Public Sphere,* ed. Robbins, 1–32.

5. Readers who care to look will also find a running conversation on theory as a subtext in the notes to individual chapters: for example on the nature of

shame and public exposure; on the meanings of incarnation for the bodies politic, erotic, and apocalyptic; on hegemony and otherness, mainly in relationships of oppressors and victims; and on simulation, technology, and "postmodern reality."

6. George Yúdice, "For a Practical Aesthetics," in *The Phantom Public Sphere,* ed. Robbins, 218–19.

7. Fraser, "Rethinking the Public Sphere," 13, 14. Her main example of such a subaltern counterpublic is late-twentieth-century American feminism.

8. I use the terms *postmodern* and *postmodernism* in the literary sense to refer to strategies writers employ, such as the parodic exploitation of literary traditions and conventions, the emphasis on the text's artifice to destroy the illusion of the work's representational reality, the intrusion of the author/narrator into the text, and the use of multiple plot developments and endings.

Toni Morrison's transformation of the simple Dick and Jane stories into a frantic account in *The Bluest Eye* to convey the suffering of the abused black girl is an example of a postmodern parodying of tradition. The narrator in Doctorow's *The Book of Daniel* challenges the reader by saying, "I suppose you think I can't do the execution. . . . YOU: I will show you that I can do the execution" in an instance both of the stress on artifice and of the narrator's intrusion. For an expanded definition of postmodernism in relation to religion see Robert Detweiler, "Postmodernism" in *The Blackwell Encyclopedia of Modern Christian Thought,* ed. Alister McGrath (Oxford: Basil Blackwell, 1993), 456–61.

9. See Toni Morrison, "Memory, Creation, and Writing," *Thought* 59 (1984): 387.

10. Harold Bloom, *The American Religion: The Emergence of the Post-Christian Nation* (New York: Simon and Schuster, 1992).

11. *Survivance* is a term I borrow from Gerald Vizenor and use in the third section of this volume.

12. David E. Stannard, *American Holocaust: Columbus and the Conquest of the New World* (New York: Oxford University Press, 1993).

PART 1

The Body Politic

1

Communism:
The Public Enemy

McCarthy's carnival-like four-year spree of accusations, charges, and threats touched something deep in the American body politic, something that lasted long after his own recklessness, carelessness, and boozing ended his career in shame. . . . He set out to do the unthinkable, and it turned out to be surprisingly thinkable.

—David Halberstam, *The Fifties*

Considering the national and international furor provoked by the "atom spy" trial and execution of Julius and Ethel Rosenberg during the early fifties, one is surprised that these dramatic and traumatic events have not inspired more literary artistry than they have. But a prominent playwright, Arthur Miller, did write *The Crucible* at least in part as a response to the rabid McCarthyism of that era, and two highly regarded novelists in a later decade composed ambitious novels drawing directly on the Rosenberg affair: E. L. Doctorow in *The Book of Daniel* (1971) and Robert Coover in *The Public Burning* (1977).[1]

The many negative and sometimes outright hostile reviews and analyses of these works indicate that they struck a nerve—or a network of nerves—in the American corpus. Both the substance and form of the play and the novels have overt and covert (a loaded term for the McCarthy era) religious dimensions that critics have explored relatively little, so one can readily identify the task of explicating those aspects. My interpretations, however, are not intended to provide resolution to the story of the Rosenbergs and their fictional representations. To the contrary, the religious aspects of these fictions, interacting with the religious elements of the historical events that inspired them, when thoroughly examined unsettle and complicate the relationships among literature, religion, and American public life as expressed in this frenzied moment of midcentury.

In the course of charting these complications I undertake four things. First, I review briefly the clash of political ideologies in post-World

War I America—among them socialism, communism, fascism, and capitalism—that included a strong theological dimension identifying capitalism as "right" and godly and the other isms as atheistic, satanic, and evil; second, I sketch how the Rosenberg case focused the political antagonisms, by midcentury narrowed to communism versus capitalism, and intensified its theological-hermeneutical significance; third, through a close reading of the fiction I demonstrate how the excesses of ideological conflict encouraged an excessiveness of style and form that dramatized the conflict, an excessiveness meant both to convey the extremes of the struggle and to discipline them; and, finally, I suggest how the play and the two novels stress a dynamic of confession provoked by accusation, the creation of an exhibitionistic-voyeuristic public space that constitutes one pathological expression of a public realm, and a reflection on the nature of evil as human agency masquerading as superhuman force.

The Supreme Evil of Our Age

Although most Americans over, say, twenty will have had some personal experience of the "communist threat" as the "home front" angst of the cold war that lasted until the razing of the Berlin Wall in 1989, a quick summary of communist and other "seditions" at work in the United States during and since the twenties will serve as a reminder of how the "Red Scare" became a national obsession culminating in McCarthyism. Well before the Bolshevik Revolution of 1917, Allan Pinkerton (founder of the prominent detective agency), reporting on the "great strike" of 1877, wrote that when "that great class of railroad employees . . . began their strike, nearly every other class caught the infection, and by these dangerous communistic leaders were made to believe that the proper time for action had come."[2] But the fear of the intruding outsider is considerably older. Robert Jewett and John Shelton Lawrence see it as part of the "American monomyth," that which "always begins with a threat arising against Eden's calm." At first, of course, the danger is from the indigenous Indians, but gradually there is a "shift in the locus of evil" stemming from "the inability of the western Eden to provide immunity from economic and natural disasters toward the end of the nineteenth century."[3]

After the formation of the Soviet Union, the threat from the outside becomes acute. "Dangerous communistic leaders" transmogrified much more ominously into the persons first of Lenin and then Stalin, the perceived geniuses of evil, alien forces invading America and sapping its economic and moral strength. A letter sent to Harry Hopkins in Washington in 1933, the midst of the Great Depression, illustrates the xenophobia. Signed "A Taxpayer," it urges action against "the foreigners and jews

[who] spend as little as they can to help the country. . . . And, work as cheap as they can, and save all the money they can. And when they have enough they go back to their country. Why don't we deport them under the section of the United States Immigration Laws which relates to the paupers and those who become a public charge. The Communist Party is composed mostly by foreigners and jews."[4]

The Christian institutions were vocal in their condemnation of communism, and Roman Catholic journals such as *The Commonweal* were among the most vigorous. William Thomas Walsh, writing in a *Commonweal* issue from 1935, entitled rhetorically, "Is Communism Dangerous?" wonders why intelligent Americans are attracted to the "collectivism" of communism and avers,

> The answer, I think, is that Communism is not merely an economic and political theory, but a species of religion. . . . It is really the successor of Mohammedanism, Protestantism and agnosticism, the archheresy of our age. Like all heresies, it apes true Christianity, and like all heresies it has a tendency to dissolve Christianity. . . . It openly advocates murder and theft at the expense of the "exploiting" classes. Its more frank propagandists make no secret of the fact that Communism is the antithesis of Christianity and therefore, if it is to succeed, must destroy Christianity.[5]

A 1936 *Commonweal* editorial identifies communism as "the supreme evil of our age," while a 1937 editorial from the same journal responds to a charge from the Protestant *Christian Century* that Roman Catholicism was sympathetic to fascism with a counteraccusation that anticipates McCarthy tactics: "These charges are made principally by Left-wing groups who are trying to involve the United States in the threatened European war. We do not say that the *Christian Century* is such a group, but we do say that its reckless charges play the game of those more active Left-wing groups which are seeking to have the United States support the so-called Peoples' Front governments in Spain and France, allegedly . . . 'in defense of democracy.'" A decade later Attorney General Tom C. Clark referred to "the Black Bible of . . . [communist] faith," and a *Nation* editorial two years later, censuring the eagerness of one-time party members to confess, continued the religious imagery: "The ex-Communist coming to the Congressional stool of repentance needs only some small inside knowledge of his party and a lively imagination."[6]

James Agee, a Christian, could choose as an epigraph to *Let Us Now Praise Famous Men* (written in good part in 1936 and published in 1941) the communist challenge, "Workers of the world, unite and fight. You have nothing to lose but your chains, and a world to win," and follow it with a note: "These words are quoted here to mislead those who will be misled by them."[7] But few besides Agee could plot a reasonable course between the indigenous Christian right and the sinister, revolutionary powers on the left. Many writers veered toward the latter. As Elliott Gorn puts it, "More commonly, artists and writers turned to the left. Many believed that capitalism . . . made a few rich while it impoverished thousands, and the Great Depression certainly seemed to offer evidence. Their political and economic solutions varied widely, from New Deal reforms through socialism, communism, and anarchism. What united them, however, was their commitment to depicting common folk struggling against the system that exploited them."[8]

Typical is a piece by Meridel LeSueur, "Women on the Breadlines," published in a 1932 issue of the *New Masses*. LeSueur describes the bleak circumstances and outlook of the women in the city looking for work and the virtual hopelessness of those who do find employment at menial tasks for low pay. Yet the *New Masses* editor, speaking for the Communist Party, felt compelled to add a note to LeSueur's article, criticizing it as "defeatist in attitude" and reminding readers "that there is a place for the unemployed women, as well as the men, in the ranks of the unemployed councils and in all the branches of the organized revolutionary movement. Fight for your class, read *The Working Woman,* join the Communist Party."[9]

Apparently, the agenda of Christian socialism and the Social Gospel, striving to better the lot of the poor and suffering as preached and exemplified by Jesus, had been modified and adopted by the communists—and the call to communist discipleship here is every bit as fervent as the evangelicals' call to preach to the heathen or the fundamentalist revivalists' plea to sinners to come home to the Savior. Of course, not every religious thinker revealed himself or herself as a reactionary, just as not every artist or writer took up the communist or socialist cause. For every Clifford Odets and John Steinbeck there was a Eugene O'Neill or William Faulkner. Thus Robert Warshow exaggerates when he argues in "The Legacy of the '30s" that "in this country there was a time when virtually all intellectual activity was derived in one way or another from the Communist party. If you were not somewhere within the party's wide orbit, then you were likely to be in the opposition, which meant that much of your thought and energy had to be devoted to maintaining yourself in opposition. In either case, it was the Communist party that ultimately determined what you were to think about and in what terms."[10]

Overstated as Warshow's assessment is, it certainly attests to the vitality and ubiquity of communism in the United States, a threatening presence that prompted anxious legislators, led by Republicans, to found the House un-American Activities Committee in 1938, thus creating an instrument to investigate persons and movements deemed suspicious and potentially harmful to national interests—"a sounding board," as William E. Leuchtenburg states it, "for the imputation that the New Deal had taken a long step on the road to Moscow."[11] HUAC from its side of Congress helped to provide the context in which Joseph McCarthy, a Republican senator from Wisconsin first elected in 1946, practiced his reckless and relentless communist hunting in the fifties through the Senate Investigating Committee—an exercise/exorcism that exhibited its own religious coloration.

Not long after the end of World War II the cold war commenced, and with it the further polarization of communism and capitalism (soon to be labeled "Americanism") in the United States, accompanied by a rhetoric expressing the struggle on both sides in hyperbolic, sometimes apocalyptic, language. Words uttered by Dwight Eisenhower at his inauguration as president of Columbia University in 1948 are characteristic: "Ignorance of Communism, fascism, or any other police-state philosophy is far more dangerous than ignorance of the most virulent disease."[12] Since fascism had been crushed three years earlier and no other "police-state" philosophies were threatening, Eisenhower's analogy had to be grasped mainly in terms of communism, and communism came to be imaged as a disease (recall Pinkerton's use of the term *infection*)—cancer, for example, its cells multiplying out of control and metastasizing throughout the body politic. Major surgery seemed justified, and the Rosenbergs would be the victims of the most radical operation.

The Plot of the Rosenbergs

If the Rosenbergs were a cancerous growth demanding excision, the process left a wound that still festers. In literary and historical terms, the plot has as yet no conclusion; in psychological terms, the nation has not achieved closure. Although the Rosenberg affair—arrest, trial, conviction, drawn-out series of appeals, and executions—was covered extensively by the media, and although scores of books and thousands of articles have been written on the subject, it is still helpful to sketch the sequence of events as a backdrop for treating the three literary works.

In early February 1950, Klaus Fuchs, a German-born nuclear physicist doing research in England, confessed to having provided atomic information to the Soviets. In late May, Harry Gold, a Philadelphia chemist, admitted that he had been Fuch's courier in 1944–45, and David Greenglass, younger brother of Ethel Rosenberg, confessed that in 1945 he had been Gold's accomplice. In mid-July, Julius Rosenberg, a thirty-two-year-old owner of a machine shop in New York and a member of the Communist Party, was arrested and charged with having recruited Greenglass as a Soviet spy in 1944. In August, Julius's wife Ethel Rosenberg, almost thirty-five, was arrested and charged with aiding her husband, Greenglass, and Gold in their espionage. Soon after that Morton Sobell, a former classmate of Julius Rosenberg at City College of New York, was arrested by the FBI (actually kidnapped from his Mexico City apartment and charged with being part of the same Soviet spy ring). By the end of the year Gold had been convicted and sentenced to thirty years in prison.

The trial of the Rosenbergs and Sobell was held in New York City in March 1951 before Judge Irving Kaufman and a jury. All three were convicted; Sobell was given thirty years in prison, and the Rosenbergs were given the death sentence. The Rosenbergs were transferred to Sing Sing penitentiary to the respective death houses for men and women, and the Rosenberg children were sent to live with a series of relatives and family friends. The nation, as much of the world, remained divided on whether the Rosenbergs were actually guilty or were the victims of a witch-hunt against communists—and on whether, if they were indeed guilty, they deserved the unprecedented penalty of death for such a crime. Appeals were filed throughout 1952, reaching as far as the Supreme Court, and were denied. Judge Kaufman set the execution date for January 12, 1953. Various motions for reduction of sentence were presented and denied; the execution was stayed three times, the last time on June 17 through the action of Supreme Court Judge William Douglas; newly elected President Eisenhower refused clemency twice. On June 19, 1953, first Julius and then Ethel Rosenberg was executed via the electric chair in Sing Sing prison.

The deaths of the convicted couple by no means ended the Rosenberg affair. The debate continued on whether the Rosenbergs had a fair trial and on whether they were guilty or had been made the victims of American paranoia about a communist conspiracy to gain control of the world. In 1975 the publication of the first edition of the autobiography by the Rosenberg brothers, now young men who had taken the name of their adoptive parents, Meeropol, caused the controversy to flare anew. By the mid-seventies, the FBI had been forced at last, via the Freedom of Information Act, to release some two hundred thousand pages of hitherto secret material on the case, and on the basis of that information new attempts were made to exonerate the couple or confirm their guilt. For example, the fourth American edition of Walter and Miriam Schneir's *Invitation to an Inquest* appeared in 1983 and used the newly available documents to reinforce their judgment that the Rosenbergs were the victims of a federal resolve to find them guilty. In that same year, two other writers, Ronald Radosh and Joyce Milton (the Rosenbergs seem to attract other pairs), employed the FBI material to argue in *The Rosenberg File* that the Rosenbergs were indeed guilty and appeared to convince a large number of persons, but in 1986 the two Meeropol brothers used an enlarged version of their autobiography to refute the arguments made by Radosh and Milton. In 1988, Ilena Philipson published a lengthy, sympathetic biography of Ethel Rosenberg that incorporated considerable FBI information.[13]

Not all of these new and revised accounts are reliable. For example, the British novelist Rebecca West in her 1964 expanded version of *The Meaning of Treason* (1947), now called *The New Meaning of Treason*, claims, with no documentation (she did not have access to the FBI files), that a couple named Morris and Lona Cohen (Morris, like the Rosenbergs an American-born child of European immigrant parents) "were recruited into the Rosenberg spy ring" after the end of World War II and that "in 1950, after Harry Gold had been arrested and had led the FBI to Greenglass, the Rosenbergs gave the Cohens the signal to leave." The Cohens fled the United States, eventually resurfaced in London as antique dealers using the names Peter and Helen Kroger, and in 1964 were tried and convicted of espionage in connection with the British "Naval Secrets" trial focusing on Gordon Lonsdale. But contrary to West's implication, no relationship between the Rosenbergs and Cohens has ever been established and probably will not until the FBI releases its files pertaining to them.[14]

The Rosenberg case has not only refused to go away, but it has also become of late the subject of interpretations aligned to the newer fashions of literary-cultural theory. Tom LeClair's stimulating *The Art of Excess: Mastery in Contemporary American Fiction* devotes a chapter to a reading of *The Public Burning* from a systems analysis and cultural anthropology perspective, which leads him to assert (it is not clear whether it is Coover's and/or LeClair's judgment) that "historically unjust, the burning of the Rosenbergs may have been culturally necessary."[15] Predictably, a deconstructive interpretation has appeared, focusing on ellipsis, in a chapter on *The Book of Daniel* in *Models of Misrepresentation: On the Fiction of E. L. Doctorow* by Christopher Morris. Two books have adopted cultural studies approaches: Andrew Ross's *No Respect: Intellectuals and Popular Culture,* with an initial chapter on "Reading the Rosenberg Letters," and Virginia Carmichael's *Framing History: The Rosenberg Story and the Cold War.*[16]

The (to date) "undecidability" of the Rosenberg plot appeals to the deconstructionists, the minor details that may yet produce resolution attract the New Historians, and the ritual aspects intrigue the Geertzianstyle anthropologists; yet in the search for new grids to lay on the Rosenberg matter only Andrew Ross in *No Respect* has paid more than passing attention to its religious aspects. In his reflections on Leslie Fiedler's "Christian humanist" (Fiedler would be stunned) analysis of the Rosenbergs, Ross borrows the language of guilt, sin, confession, and grace. I intend to develop, among others, the line that Ross has initiated, and I will begin by addressing Arthur Miller's *The Crucible.*[17]

Notes

1. I have used the following editions: Arthur Miller, *The Crucible,* ed. Harold Clurman (New York: Viking, 1971), 135–284 (*The Crucible* was first performed on January 22, 1953, in the Martin Beck Theater, New York); E. L. Doctorow, *The Book of Daniel* (New York: New American Library, 1972); and Robert Coover, *The Public Burning* (New York: Bantam, 1978). I also considered interpreting Joyce Carol Oates's novel *You Must Remember This* (1987), which attends to, among other things, American political turmoil from 1953 to 1956, but decided that it did not focus sufficiently on American communism for my purposes.

2. Allan Pinkerton, *Strikers, Communists, Tramps, and Detectives* (New York: G. W. Carleton, 1878), 21. I have used an excerpt of this text printed in *Constructing the American Past: A Source Book of a People's History,* ed. Elliott J. Gorn, Randy Roberts, and Terry D. Bilhartz (New York: HarperCollins, 1991), 2:47–49.

3. Robert Jewett and John Shelton Lawrence, *The American Monomyth* (Garden City: Anchor Press/Doubleday, 1977), 174, 176.

4. Gorn, Roberts, and Bilhartz, *Constructing the American Past,* 288.

5. William Thomas Walsh, "Is Communism Dangerous?" *The Commonweal,* February 8, 1935, 421.

6. Unsigned editorial, "The Crusade against Communism," *The Commonweal,* October 30, 1936, 2; unsigned editorial, "Catholicism and Communism," *The Commonweal,* January 1, 1937, 258; *Newsweek,* July 8, 1946, 22; *The Nation,* August 14, 1948, 173.

7. James Agee and Walker Evans, *Let Us Now Praise Famous Men* (New York: Ballantine, 1966), xvi.

8. Gorn, Roberts, and Bilhartz, *Constructing the American Past,* 283–84.

9. Meridel LeSueur, "Women on the Breadlines," in *Ripening: Selected Work, 1927–1980,* ed. Elaine Hedges (Old Westbury: Feminist Press, 1982). I have used an excerpt from the text in Gorn, Roberts, and Bilhartz, *Reconstructing the American Past,* 299–301.

10. Robert Warshow, *The Immediate Experience: Movies, Comics, Theatre and Other Aspects of Popular Culture* (Garden City: Doubleday, 1962), 33.

11. William E. Leuchtenburg, *A Troubled Feast: American Society since 1945* (Boston: Little, Brown, 1983), 29.

12. Quoted by Andrew Ross, *No Respect: Intellectuals and Popular Culture* (New York: Routledge, 1989), 42. The infection trope appears again in Richard Pipes, *Russia under the Bolshevik Regime* (New York: Alfred A. Knopf, 1994), 501:

"Russian nationalists depict Communism as alien to Russian culture and tradition, as a kind of plague imported from the West. The notion of Communism as a virus cannot withstand the slightest examination." Jean Baudrillard also plays with the imagery of virulence in America, referring to electronic viruses in both a literal and metaphoric sense with paranoid overtones; see *Baudrillard Live: Selected Interviews*, ed. Mike Gann (London: Routledge, 1993), 158, 175ff.

13. Robert and Michael Meeropol, *We Are Your Sons: The Legacy of Ethel and Julius Rosenberg* (Urbana: University of Illinois Press, 1975, second edition, 1986); Walter and Miriam Schneir, *Invitation to an Inquest* (New York: Pantheon, 1965, fourth edition, 1983); Ronald Radosh and Joyce Milton, *The Rosenberg File: A Search for the Truth* (New York: Holt, Rinehart and Winston, 1983); Ilene Philipson, *Ethel Rosenberg: Beyond the Myths* (New York: Franklin Watts, 1988).

14. Rebecca West, *The New Meaning of Treason* (New York: Viking, 1964), 281. Radosh and Milton summarize the speculation regarding a Rosenberg-Cohen relationship, report that the FBI refused them access to the Cohen-Kroger file, and conclude, "If there is material pertaining to the alleged Rosenberg-Cohen link, it is undoubtedly among the Rosenberg case FBI files that still have not been released," see *The Rosenberg File*, 571. The publication of Pavel Sudoplatov's *Special Tasks: The Memoirs of an Unwanted Witness—A Soviet Spymaster* (Boston: Little, Brown, 1994) brought the Rosenbergs to public attention once again. Sudoplatov was, until mid-1953, a high-level KGB operator who directed efforts of Soviet espionage agents to penetrate the Manhattan Project. He recalls the Rosenbergs as "a naive couple, overeager to cooperate, who worked for us because of their ideological motivations. Their contribution to atomic espionage was minor" (quoted in "Special Tasks," *Time*, April 25, 1994, 70). *Special Tasks* is co-written by Anatoli Sudoplatov (Pavel's son), with Jerrold L. and Leona P. Schechter. A reviewer of the book gives it little credence: "What distinguishes the account of atomic espionage presented in *Special Tasks* is its complete lack of the establishing and supporting details that are the signature of genuine espionage cases." See Thomas Powers, "Were the Atomic Scientists Spies?" *New York Review of Books*, June 9, 1994, 12.

15. Tom LeClair, *The Art of Excess: Mastery in Contemporary American Fiction* (Urbana: University of Illinois Press, 1989), 112.

16. Christopher D. Morris, *Models of Misrepresentation: On the Fiction of E. L. Doctorow* (Jackson: University of Mississippi Press, 1991); Virginia Carmichael, *Framing History: The Rosenberg Story and the Cold War* (Minneapolis: University of Minnesota Press, 1993).

17. For a provocative commentary on a "new McCarthyism," see Daniel L. Zins, "'I Want My Grandchildren to Read Blake': Teaching the Humanities after the Cold War," *Nuclear Texts and Contexts* (Spring 1994): 17–18. Zins is editor of the newsletter *Nuclear Texts and Contexts* at the Atlanta College of Art.

2

The Crucible:
The Theocratic Town
and Public Evil

That there are Devils and Witches, the Scripture asserts, and mankind confirms. That they are common enemies of Mankind, and set upon mischief, is not to be doubted.

—Cotton Mather, *The Wonders of the Invisible World*

Our difficulty in believing the—for want of a better word—political inspiration of the Devil is due in great part to the fact that he is called up and damned not only by our social antagonists but by our own side, whatever it may be.

—Arthur Miller, *The Crucible*

When I turned to the chapter on "The Meaning of McCarthyism" by Earl Latham in John H. Ferres's *Twentieth Century Interpretations of The Crucible* (borrowed from my university library), I discovered that the pages of the essay had been torn out of that 1972 volume.[1] Was this the work of some unregenerate McCarthyite wishing to suppress material critical of his or her hero? Most likely it was merely the thoughtless act of a student or colleague too lazy to check out the book or copy the relevant pages, but the very fact that the suspicion passed through my mind witnesses to the tenacious hold that the paranoia of the McCarthy witch-hunt still has on us.

Arthur Miller was not the first to appropriate the term *witch-hunt* to characterize the persecution of suspected communists in the late forties and fifties. In fact, Miller protested, rather mildly, "It was not only the rise of 'McCarthyism' that moved me, but something much more weird and mysterious," that "something" being "a new religiosity," "an official piety" on the right that sought to impose on others standards of belief and behavior that had hitherto been private matters.[2] Rather than denying that his play centrally concerns McCarthyism, Miller means to place it in the broad context of the strong strain of American orthodoxy and intolerance that has been present since the founding of the colonies. Miller added in 1967, "I thought then that in terms of this process the witch-hunts [in late-seventeenth-century Salem] had something to say to the anti-Communist hysteria."[3]

Miller's mild equivocation about the "message" of *The Crucible* has encouraged some critics to charge that he botched both the Salem and fifties' materials. Robert Warshow, for example, commenting on the play soon after its opening in early 1953, states that "Mr. Miller has nothing to say about the Salem trials. . . . *The Crucible* was written to say something about Alger Hiss and Owen Lattimore, Julius and Ethel Rosenberg, Senator McCarthy, the actors who have lost their jobs on radio and television . . . and yet not to say anything about that either, but only to suggest that a great deal might be said . . . if it were not that the 'present atmosphere' itself makes such plain speaking impossible."[4]

This evaluation, which I find wrongheaded, is followed by a convoluted argument on how communists consider themselves fundamentally innocent of all charges against them because they know that their cause is just. "All lies and inconsistences disappear in the enveloping cloud of the unspoken 'essential' truth: the Rosenbergs are innocent *because* they are accused; they are innocent, one might say, by definition."[5] Thus in Warshow's reasoning it is the communists, including the fated Rosenbergs, who are most like the Salem Calvinists who had convinced themselves of the reality of evil witchcraft and, acting on that conviction, put hundreds of their neighbors and relatives to death. "Apart from all belief and all action, these people [the communists] are 'right' in themselves, and no longer need to prove themselves in the world of experience; the Revolution—or 'liberalism,'' or 'dissent'—has entered into them as the grace of God was once conceived to have entered into the 'elect,' and, like the grace of God, it is given irrevocably."[6]

After determining, then, that Miller has nothing to say in *The Crucible,* Warshow makes him mean something after all—what he surely and above all did not wish to mean. It is a strategy egregious on two counts. First, it destroys the subtlety of Miller's drama, negates the balance in the play between the weaknesses of the victimizers and the victims in order to resolve the acute tensions in the play and in society during the fifties. Second, it misappropriates theological language to make a point by analogy: The communists come to represent "a kind of extreme Calvinism" marked by its apodictic stance, whereby right makes right.[7] I would think that just the opposite is true. A central dramatic theme of *The Crucible,* and of the "drama" of the Rosenbergs on trial and their accusers, is the *uncertainty* of convictions. It is because they doubt things—their perceptions, feelings, principles, the motives of others, and the nature of reality—that they behave as they do. Their actions *create* what they believe as often as they reflect that belief.

John Ferres says that in *The Crucible* "Miller is depicting a society in moral crisis, and through character, situation, and mood he unmistakably evokes contemporary parallels."[8] It is easy to accept this judgment of Salem puritanism, but to apply it to the McCarthy era is still unsettling. Did the McCarthy years, including the Rosenberg affair, truly show a society in moral crisis? Theodore White, after all, writes that "in the 1950s, under Eisenhower, it . . . was a more humane, open, liberal society than the one that had preceded it in the 1920s."[9] The McCarthy era did, of course, precipitate and display a moral crisis; it is just harder to see it at such proximity. That crisis played itself out as a religious crisis: In making moral choices, the persons involved learned and confirmed what they believed. This is every bit as true of the Rosenbergs in mid-twentieth century as of the puritans at the end of the seventeenth. By interpreting Miller's, Doctorow's, and Coover's fictional refractions of the case, I hope to show why and how that was so.

Crying Out in Salem

The Crucible is set in Salem, Massachusetts, in 1692. In act one the widowed local pastor, Reverend Parris, in the presence of a quarrelsome and superstitious (excessive even for Salem) couple, the Putnams, learns that the comatose condition of his ten-year-old daughter Betty has something to do with the dancing (spied on by Parris) of village girls in the forest the night before with Tituba, Parris's slave from Barbados. The teenage Abigail Williams (in Cotton Mather's historical account only twelve), leader of the girls, claims at first that the dancing was only sport and that no witchcraft was involved. But when the girls are alone we learn that Abigail drank a potion from Tituba intended to harm Elizabeth Proctor, who had dismissed her as a house servant seven months earlier. In a scene alone with John Proctor, a local farmer, Abigail tries to rekindle the old affair with him that led to Goody Proctor dismissing her, but Proctor rebuffs the girl. Amid the comings and goings of various citizens who quarrel about religious and economic matters, the Reverend John Hale, witchcraft "specialist" summoned from neighboring Beverly, arrives and through his interrogation Tituba "confesses" that the devil showed her two Salem wives who belonged to him. Then Abigail, admitting that she "danced for the Devil," names others, and a revived Betty identifies still more.

In act two the Proctors one night learn from Mary Warren, their servant girl who has been at court, that Elizabeth herself has been mentioned as a possible witch by Abigail, who has hopes of becoming the new Goody Proctor with Elizabeth out of the way. Soon Hale and others appear with a warrant for Elizabeth's arrest, and she is taken off over the protests of her husband—mainly on the evidence of a "poppet," a doll in her possession found pierced with a needle, that ostensibly is an effigy of Abigail intended to harm her. Proctor tries to force Mary to promise to tell the truth in court: that she, observed by Abigail, made the doll and simply stuck the needle in it for safekeeping.

In the courtroom in act three the trials are in full sway, and various Salemites are charged and convicted of witchcraft. In the midst of all this Proctor appears with Mary Warren, who confesses to Judge Hathorne and Deputy Governor Danforth out of chambers that the girls' "crying out" the accused (identifying their guilt through hysterical, "possessed" behavior) was at first only a pretense. Proctor also has a deposition signed by ninety-one citizens who say that they never saw evidence of the devil's activity in Salem. Danforth and Hathorne, now worried about the legal basis of the trial, bring in Abigail and the other accusing girls, and Proctor reveals his adultery with Abigail to show the judge and deputy governor that she is not innocent. At this point Elizabeth is brought in from her prison cell to confirm or deny her husband's admission, and she denies it, lying to save his reputation. This seems to exonerate Abigail, but Reverend Hale, suffering a bad conscience, takes Proctor's part and against this threat Abigail leads the other girls into their act—claiming to spot a little bird up in the rafters that is Mary Warren transformed and sent there by Mary's evil powers. Mary at last succumbs to the pressure, joins the other girls in mad screaming, and identifies Proctor as "the Devil's man." He is arrested.

Act four takes place in the Salem jail. Twelve citizens have already been executed as witches, and seven more, including Proctor, are scheduled to hang on this morning. Meanwhile, Abigail has vanished with money stolen from Parris, neighboring Andover has condemned the witch trials, and doubt has spread through Salem. Proctor is permitted to see his wife, who will be spared because she is pregnant, and for her sake and their future together he agrees to confess. But when he does so, he refuses to implicate others and to sign the document of confession. Then he does sign it but refuses to hand it over. When he learns that Danforth intends to make the document public, Proctor tears it up. Defiant and with his good name intact he goes to the gallows.

A key—if there is such a thing—to comprehending the action of the play and its hermeneutical import for the Rosenberg event in the context of American public life is Miller's assertion in the commentary to act one (not part of the staged version) that "these people had no ritual for the washing away of sins. It is another trait we inherited from them, and it has helped to discipline us as well as to breed hypocrisy among us."[10] The statement is historically incorrect. Many such rituals for the cleansing of sins have existed, including a thoroughly worked-out ritual of execution in the New England colonies. They still do exist: the confession and penance of Roman Catholicism in a sacramental context; the salvation experience, adult baptism, and periodic revivalistic rededication of one's life to Christ of evangelicalism; the private forgiveness through prayer of all varieties of Christians; and the Yom Kippur (Day of Atonement) of Judaism. American art and literature are also replete with representations of these rituals.[11]

Yet Miller is also right in a way. Theocratic puritan New England did weaken the ritual aspects of cleansing in favor of encouraging the upright, sanctified life, and that shift led to a radical transformation of the understanding and practice of confession, a transformation pivotal to the play's action.

One could view the situation thus: In the Christian theocracy, where church and state merge and urge individual conformity by coercive persuasion, confession assumes a different, "cleansing" function. It is used to identify the unorthodox and force them to obedience under the threat of this-worldly and eternal punishment. It becomes a part of the judicial as well as the ecclesial system. The vehicle for producing confession is accusation so that accusation and confession, punishment and reward, become the dynamic of theocratic purification, with power and subjection as the political bases. If these are the dynamic, innocence and guilt are the moral conditions, with integrity and deception as their local expressions. Evil and goodness are the ontological conditions, with Satan and Christ, sin and forgiveness, as their theological expressions and faith and doubt (or unbelief), love and rejection, as the existential responses. Finally, the sociopathology of the situation is constituted by exhibitionism and voyeurism as the vehicles of public exposure.

Accusation and Confession

One is struck first in reading *The Crucible* by the stress on accusation and confession. This is not surprising, given the temper of the historical witch trials, but I am interested especially in how the accusations not only usually presume guilt on the part of the one accused but also themselves bring about the community's belief in that guilt. In other words, accusation virtually equals the existence of guilt, and the one charged has the generally impossible task of proving himself or herself innocent.

How does this atmosphere come about? In the Calvinist theocracy (Miller develops this line implicitly), Christians realize that they are guilty via original sin—sinful—because part of an evil world makes them vulnerable to all charges of guilt. They are predisposed to believe—or at least to fear—that they are guilty of both vaguely defined and specific crimes because they see themselves as fundamentally guilty. Thus, for example, when the stalwart Proctor, quizzed by Hale in act two, cannot recite all ten commandments (he forgets, ironically, the one forbidding adultery), he feels himself on the defensive as a possible lover of the devil, even though the test is absurd.

That sense of guilt remains strong in the modern world, even where it has lost its theological foundation and found instead psychological, existential, and historical-economical explanations. What is confession intended to consist of in this atmosphere of guiltiness? It is supposed to name names, and that is in a certain way not so astonishing. We know from the study of ancient religions, for instance, that to "confess" the name of a divinity was to acknowledge the authority of that being above other gods, and it was the habit of the divinities to "name" themselves to their people; hence, the frequent "I am the Lord your God" from the Hebrew Bible—YHWH's assertive self-confession.

In the New England framework of history and drama the naming is not confessional but accusatory. Confession turns into accusation; the dynamic becomes self-perpetuating and, eventually, self-annihilating rather than salvific—and that is one of its ironies. Tituba (late in act one) is coerced into naming two local women as witches; Abigail, seeking to deflect suspicion, confesses that "I wrote in his [the devil's] book" (181), then implicates those two and four more; Betty, coming to her senses but not to sense, names a man and four other women she saw with the devil. In act three, Proctor in court names Abigail as a whore, but she in retaliation, and the other "possessed" girls, tricks the hysterical Mary Warren into naming Proctor as "the Devil's man." Finally, when Proctor in act four refuses to name names as the substance of his confession and then refuses to give over the signed document in order to save his own name, he brings on himself the proper punishment of the theocratic court: death. The penalty for saving his name is losing his life.

Proctor, a man of integrity (although with flaws that he recognizes and confesses), is done in by the deceptions of his guilty accuser Abigail, who in effect ex post facto "confesses" her guilt by fleeing Salem with stolen money. In these turns of plot the interactions of guilt and innocence, evil and goodness are personalized in these two characters, but those moral and ontological conditions also invite a broader reflection.

Channels of Evil

It appears in the play that evil presents itself through hysteria. The teen-age girls in court "crying out" their victims—those Salem citizens they thus identify as witches—act as if they are possessed, their minds and bodies taken over by still others who have become channels of the dev-il's power. The free-floating experience of hysteria, of being out of emo-tional control, specifically becomes the experience of possession: If one is possessed, one is possessed by someone or something.

Yet another irony of *The Crucible*—in a way its causal irony—is that the girls at first only play at being possessed ("that were pretense," Mary Warren admits in act three [237]), but that play in this charged atmo-sphere of devil and witch phobia quickly turns to hysteria, and the pre-tense becomes reality. Most of the girls come to believe that they truly are possessed. We gather that Abigail is play-acting the whole time, but the others are far more labile, lose control, and surrender to the fiction of possession, allowing it to become a felt actuality. Mary Warren, of course, is the prime exhibit. She loses her rationality under the pressure of hysteria and is persuaded to believe that Satan is at work, above all in Proctor.

One might think at first that little connection obtains between pos-session and deception, but this is not so. Satan, after all, in Western lore has been known as the great deceiver. As Wendy Farley notes, "Decep-tion may be the most ubiquitous feature of sin. In the myth of the Fall, it is by way of a lie that evil finds its way into the happy Garden of Eden. . . . Deception is the mask evil wears to disguise its true nature and to make itself palatable to people who would be disturbed by concrete suffering."[12] Similarly, the trickster, who figures in many cultures in part a malevolent creature, is a shapeshifter who inhabits—possesses—other creatures and is a master of deception.

Much of *The Crucible*'s dramatic action consists of a strange, intricate interplay of possession and deception. Characters use deception to learn who is "possessed" and manipulate possession to discover who is deceit-ful. For example, the girls before the authorities crying out their victims do so in a state of "possession," and in this hysterical condition accuse cer-tain of the townspeople of witchcraft, of being among those who deceive others into the loss of their souls and sometimes their lives. In fact, it seems to be a situation of "it takes one to know one." The girls can identify the Salem witches, in this logic, because the evil and deceptive spirits who tem-porarily inhabit the girls recognize their own kind in others.

Yet Abigail, who only pretends to be possessed—and thus deceives—is behind much of the fiction of possession. She employs hysterical possession as a deception to condemn other citizens as owned by the devil, and this is part of a grander deception whereby she hopes to replace Elizabeth (upon her execution for witchcraft) as Proctor's wife.

The muddle is instructive, for it hints at the play's portrayal of the nature of evil. Evil in *The Crucible* is not an objective force, even though the Salemites (and some critics of the play) believe it to be just that. It is rather in the action of deception. Herbert Blau is wrong when he argues, regarding the play, "If you want absolute evil, you've got to think more about witches."[13] Blau means, I think, that the puritan theology about the existence of evil as a supernatural force should be taken seriously. That this is the source and nature of evil is indeed the theology *inside* the play, but it is neither Miller's nor the play's theology. Evil in *The Crucible* exists in and through human behavior and as such is always already in the world, but it is not incarnate in extrahuman form. This evil is also not merely what appears as a void. It is not just the absence of goodness, as the New England transcendentalist tradition (in reaction to the puritan objectification of it as satanic) insisted, but a terrifying human presence. Further, the play shows how the displacement of evil into the figure of the devil—the ancient and enduring mythologizing of evil whose name, *Satan,* in Hebrew means "adversary" or "accuser"—is itself one of the deceptive strategies of persons perpetrating evil. The whole action of the drama demonstrates the refusal of persons to come to terms with the reality of their fundamental evil behavior by ascribing it to a force beyond human control. And, finally, it shows how that refusal produces the very evil, and the responsibility for it, that it wishes to escape.

When Proctor at the end of act two, identified as the devil's man by the hysterical Mary Warren and challenged to confess by Danforth, blurts, "I say—I say—God is dead!" he is not only declaring his disbelief in a deity who could permit such injustice to happen to him (another instance of a "theodicy-reaction") but also announcing his disbelief in the counterforce that the authorities suppose controls him. He recognizes that this force is really human: "I hear the boot of Lucifer. I see his filthy face! And it is my face, and yours, Danforth" (251)! Miller comments, "Like Reverend Hale and the others on this stage, we conceive the Devil as a necessary part of a respectable view of cosmology. . . . When we see the steady and methodical inculcation into humanity of the idea of man's worthlessness—until redeemed—the necessity of the Devil may become evident as a weapon, a weapon designed and used time and time again in every age to whip men into surrender to a particular church or churchstate" (166–67). Indeed. One more irony of the play is that it is precisely the Christian community that practices, and thus recreates, an astonishing evil in its effort to identify and destroy it.

I make much of this exposition of the nature of evil in Miller's drama because I see a similar situation in what we have taken to be the secularized framework of the Rosenberg trial and its fictional treatments, a similarity I will discuss later.

The Prurient Gaze

One can begin reflection on the connection between deceit, evil, and public exposure with the Garden of Eden story. There Satan, as evil already mythologized, has tricked the first couple into disobedience (through a sinful act that does not strike us as evil per se). That disobedience leads to human deception (hiding from God; lying to Him) and public exposure: Adam and Eve discover their nakedness, are ashamed of it, and fashion provisional clothing to hide their genitals. One way of reading this story is to understand the exposure itself as the "original" sin and the preceding serpent-and-forbidden-fruit narrative as its displaced rationale. In other words, it is the gaze of the authoritative community (God) that causes self-consciousness and guilt. This is not to say that God or the community is evil, but it is through their initiatory actions that evil arises. God wishes to save Adam and Eve from evil and keep them innocent but in so doing sets the conditions that cause them to sin and know evil. Satan as trickster, shapeshifter, here the talking snake, personifies evil but does not constitute an explanation of what it is. He is, in fact, already spokesperson (spokesserpent?) for a community distinct from God. He is able to project what life is like beyond innocence, in the reasoning community, and in the potential of that community is the potential for evil. As Farley states it, "Suffering and sinfulness, even the most hideous, is rooted in history prior to any individual action. . . . Not only mortality but susceptibility to *radical* evil are built into the human condition prior to any individual's act or choice, prior to any possibility of guilt."[14]

The couple's felt need to cover their genitals from God's view conveys an awareness of self, a separateness, accompanied by shame. This sounds quite Augustinian, for Augustine argued that "a man by his very nature is ashamed of sexual desire."[15] We could also interpret the Genesis myth's connection of shame and exposure of the genitals as evidence that sexual desire itself is not inherently sinful. Rather, the genitals abruptly become the cause for shame because they represent what the self-aware self cannot control and thus what, in its lack of control, threatens the reasoning community. Evil lies in (not *is*, but *lies in*) the inability of the individual and the community to control themselves and each other.

Here is a basis for the neurotic—or sinful—relationship between the individual and the group, and it is also an explanation for the dynamic of public exposure. The individual wishes both to assert independence, *self*-control, and place in the community, a dependence on it, whereas the group wishes to grant the individual both uniqueness and communal place, but these relationships always go wrong. The group is a group of individuals who cannot behave reasonably as a group, not least because they cannot always—if even usually—behave reasonably as individuals. Hence the individual subjecting himself or herself to the group's gaze wants to be assured of being acceptable when both reasonable and out of control. The group, however, cannot give this assurance because it, too, is composed of individuals fearful of their identities as perceived and shaped by the group. As a result, both the individual and the group become manipulative and deceitful. The individual says, "See me as I am," yet is hiding shame and does not present himself or herself authentically. At the same time, the community watching says either, "Show us less," fearful of having their shame aroused, or "Show us more," hoping to have their shame lessened by a greater display of shame in someone else.

Either way, the fear of a loss of control threatens and arouses—arouses through the fascination with what was once beyond innocence and is now beyond reason. James W. Fowler proposes a "practical theological hermeneutics of shame" that should be developed to "unmask and equip individuals and groups to deal with the unacknowledged yet pervasive power of shame as a source of distorted relations and aborted communication."[16] Texts such as *The Crucible* contain the dramatic materials that can be shaped into such a hermeneutics.

This complicated interplay of acts of public exposure is—with a twist—easy to illustrate in *The Crucible*. The normal neurotic interactions of public life are exacerbated in the puritan town so that persons either put themselves or are put on display and are watched more acutely. Abigail and the other girls dance (some of them perhaps naked) in the forest at night, secretly displaying themselves, and are discovered by Reverend Parris (why is he out there?), the hyperjudgmental spiritual leader of Salem. Proctor publicly confesses his adultery with Abigail, which he has already disclosed in shame to Elizabeth, to a shocked and titillated audience that both fears and wishes to believe him.

But it is mainly Abigail's performance in the general court anteroom, her identity and reputation at stake, that draws together the exhibitionistic and voyeuristic aspects of public exposure and clarifies its relation to evil. Her duplicity has been found out by Proctor and confirmed by Mary Warren; if the officers of the court believe them, Abigail is finished. In this crisis she intensifies her role-playing, addresses an imaginary bird in the rafters as if it were Mary Warren adopting this shape through witchcraft, and diverts guilt from herself to Mary. It is a stunning performance that generates the hysterical support of the other girls and at last provokes Mary's breakdown, impelling her to betray Proctor.

Abigail's act is also thoroughly evil. Through it she destroys Proctor and Mary Warren and heightens the community's belief in the reality of witches just when that phobia is waning elsewhere. She knows how to focus public attention on herself, the deceptive exhibitionist ("see me as I really am"), and then send that prurient gaze, itself guilt-ridden, against her victims ("see them as they really are"). She exploits the already neurotic relationships between individual and group, plays them against each other, and for a moment controls the community's fortunes through the evocation of chaos. She controls through uncontrol in a seemingly real demonstration of the devil's power.

We learn soon that Abigail's control is short-lived. She is exposed as a thief and disappears from Salem, but her malevolent work has been done. One observation remains to be made about how she did it. Mary Warren's collapse is precipitated not just by the illusory sighting of the evil spirit-bird (supposed to be herself) but also by subjection to a cruel language game. The girls, led by Abigail, repeat everything that Mary utters (as if they were in her demonic sway and echoing her), and in doing so frustrate her ability to communicate. It is a mischievous children's sport that, as any parent knows, can quickly get out of hand and turn nonsensical and obsessive. The game does a variety of things. It focuses attention on Mary, terrifies her, and makes her an unwilling exhibitionist. It stimulates an extreme self-consciousness in her that becomes an unbearable shame and transforms her neurosis into a psychotic moment that destroys Proctor and, we imagine, Mary herself. Beyond that, it illustrates the "demonic" nature of language, the tendency of language itself, to slip out of control and slide from (childish) innocence to (evil) complicitness and use up its users.

Miller himself, and many critics of *The Crucible,* points out that the analogy between the destructive force of witchcraft and that of twentieth-century communism is flawed, for communism is real whereas witchcraft is not. Thus, the reasoning goes, to see the ordeal of the Rosenbergs as a witch-hunt, drawing on parallels to the Salem trials as articulated in Miller's play and elsewhere, is fallacious. Although the Salemites, condemned and executed, were not witches, the Rosenbergs *were* communists and represented a genuine threat to the nation and to civilization. In the often-quoted words of Judge Kaufman at the Rosenbergs' sentencing, "Who knows but what that millions more innocent people may pay the price of your treason. Indeed, by your betrayal, you undoubtedly have altered the course of history to the disadvantage of our country." Giving the secrets of the atom bomb to the Soviets was not "worse than murder."[17] It also amounted to mass murder and assumed global if not cosmic dimensions.

Kaufman's ideological hyperbole, verging on the apocalyptic, is an example of how the real, historical aspects of the Rosenberg affair were transformed into a public religious discourse in which the reality of communism is of little matter after all. The Rosenbergs, their accusers and defenders, and the larger American community then and since have engaged in a ritual of accusation and confession that both mimics and replaces a weakened formal religious ritual; Americans, in spite of their secularity, have attempted to explain the threat of communism in terms of the mythologizing of evil; and the trial not only took on substance as one of the most momentous acts of public exposure in the nation's history but also established new conditions for the engineers of such exposure in uncovering and punishing evil.[18]

Notes

1. Earl Latham, "The Meaning of McCarthyism," in *Twentieth Century Interpretations of* The Crucible, ed. John H. Ferres (Englewood Cliffs: Prentice Hall, 1972).

2. Arthur Miller, Introduction to *Arthur Miller's Collected Plays* (New York: Viking, 1957), 39–40.

3. Arthur Miller, "It Could Happen Here and Did," *New York Times,* April 30, 1967, 2:17, cited in *Twentieth Century Interpretations of* The Crucible, ed. Ferres, 6.

4. Robert Warshow, *The Immediate Experience: Movies, Comics, Theatre and Other Aspects of Popular Culture* (Garden City: Doubleday, 1962,), 196.

5. Warshow, *The Immediate Experience,* 202.

6. Ibid., 203.

7. Ibid., 203.

8. Ferres, "Introduction," *Twentieth Century Interpretations of* The Crucible, 19.

9. Theodore H. White, *America in Search of Itself: The Making of the President 1956–1980* (New York: Warner, 1982), 37.

10. Arthur Miller, *The Crucible* (New York: Penguin Books, 1981), 154. Numbers in parentheses following citations in this chapter and the following ones refer to page numbers in the respective texts.

11. See David D. Hall, *Worlds of Wonder, Days of Judgment: Popular Religious Belief in Early New England* (Cambridge: Harvard University Press, 1990), for a fascinating account of execution rituals in puritan New England in the fifteenth and sixteenth centuries. He writes, for example, "Where all these threads of meaning converged was in the ceremony of public execution. The procedures of this ceremony dramatized the cleansing of the land, the righteousness of law, and the healing powers of the gospel" (178). Hall also makes much of public confession

in relation to witch-hunting: "Not only were confessions the best evidence of witchcraft; they also were a means of reconciling with the covenanted community, of reenacting (or restoring) someone's passage out of bondage into grace. The men and women who confessed to being witches were acknowledging the power of a rite that promised them redemption if they brought all hidden sins to light" (192).

12. Wendy Farley, *Tragic Vision and Divine Compassion: A Contemporary Theodicy* (Louisville: Westminster, 1990), 44. Farley writes further, "Deception is the mask evil wears to disguise its true nature and to make itself palatable to people who would be disturbed by concrete suffering" (44). See also Kenneth Surin, *Theology and the Problem of Evil* (Oxford: Basil Blackwell, 1986).

13. Herbert Blau, "No Play Is Deeper Than Its Witches," in *Twentieth Century Interpretations of* The Crucible, ed. Ferres, 66.

14. Farley, *Tragic Vision and Divine Compassion*, 64.

15. Elaine Pagels, *Adam, Eve, and the Serpent* (New York: Vintage, 1988), 112, quotes this from Augustine, *De Civitate Dei*, 14, 17. Pagels also offers a valuable anti-Augustinian reading on shame and sexual desire (112ff). Bernard Williams, in *Shame and Necessity* (Berkeley: University of California Press, 1993), 78, provides a classical Greek perspective: "The basic experience with shame is that of being seen, inappropriately, by the wrong people, in the wrong condition. It is straightforwardly connected with nakedness, particularly in sexual connections. The word *aidoia*, a derivative of *aidos*, 'shame,' is a standard Greek word for the genitals, and similar terms are found in other languages. The reaction is to cover oneself or to hide, and people naturally take steps to avoid the situations that call for it."

16. James W. Fowler, "Shame: Toward a Practical Theological Understanding," *Christian Century*, August 25–September 1, 1993, 819.

17. Judge Kaufman quoted by Ronald Radosh and Joyce Milton, *The Rosenberg File: A Search for the Truth* (New York: Holt, Rinehart and Winston, 1983), 284.

18. Pagels, however, in *Adam, Eve, and the Serpent* reminds readers that the involvement of the state in punishing mythologized evil has a long history: "Augustine draws so drastic a picture of the effects of Adam's sin that he embraces human government, even when tyrannical, as the indispensable defense against the forces sin has unleashed in human nature" (113). And because these unleashed forces consist in good part of sexual desire, they must be exposed and dealt with publicly.

3

The Book of Daniel:
The Fatally Exposed Family

Literature can turn language, for a moment, at least,
against the sentence of death.

—Richard Poirier, "Pragmatism and
the Sentence of Death"

Joyce Carol Oates in 1988 borrowed "the medical term pathography" to
label "life stories that 'mercilessly expose their subjects' and 'relentlessly
catalog their most private, vulnerable, and least illuminating moments.'"[1]
Pathography means, literally, writing about disease, but Oates's transposed
definition, applied mainly to so-called celebrity biography, also describes
to a degree what goes on in fictional narratives about well-known historical figures. One thinks, for example, of the fictionalizing of Freud in
D. M. Thomas's *The White Hotel,* of Howard Johnson in Max Apple's "The
Oranging of America," of President Buchanan in John Updike's play
Buchanan Dying, of Mao Tse-tung in Frederic Tuten's *Mao on the Long
March,* of Lee Harvey Oswald in Don DeLillo's *Libra,* and of Roy Cohn
and others in Tony Kushner's *Angels in America.* The difference between
these and the exploitation of private lives in sensationalist biographies is
that in the fictions the historical subject is generally protected by a caveat: the reader's awareness that the subject is actually an imagined variation of the historical person. In this sense the fiction is not "about" the
historical subject but about the author's invented projection of the subject. Literary fictions, to be sure, are always voyeuristic insofar as they
explore and expose the private lives of their characters, but because these
characters, even those based on actual persons, are not real, no significant invasion of privacy occurs.

This does not mean that the authors of these narratives have no interest in the historical subjects they fictionalize. Obviously, if they didn't,
they would not bother with them at all. The strategy of turning a historical subject into a fictive one is to create a symbol, to make the figure stand
for something other than what she or he was, yet not forget that figure's

historical identity (which would be impossible anyhow). The tension created between the historical figure and its symbolic status as fiction generates an irony—a distance between what the figure was and what the author imagines for the figure—that makes us recognize, paradoxically, the historical figure's humanity. Such figures, by virtue of being in the public eye, have already attained symbolic status. As Leslie Fiedler says of the Rosenbergs, they "became, despite themselves and their official defenders, symbols of the conflict between the human and the political, the individual and the state, justice and mercy."[2]

The fictionalizing of the historical figures as a literary-symbolic undertaking undercuts the public political symbolizing and allows the reader to glimpse an individuality behind both symbols. It is, in Hegelian terms, a sublation, an *Aufhebung*, whereby the political symbol is both canceled and fulfilled in the literary one and the historical figure as literary character liberated to be thought not just as typical (of something) but as unique. In this strategy the creation of "offensive" works such as *The Book of Daniel* and *The Public Burning* has its justification.

Julius and Ethel Rosenberg are at two more removes in *The Book of Daniel*, for there E. L. Doctorow not only transparently disguises them as a couple named Paul and Rochelle Isaacson but also has their story told in complex "postmodern" fashion through another narrator, their son Daniel, in 1967, fourteen years after their execution in 1953. Doctorow has remarked that the novel is not about the Rosenbergs but the *idea* of the Rosenbergs; it is not just about the idea of the Rosenbergs reflected on by the narrator as their offspring but about the radical—in every sense—changes in American politics between the McCarthyism of the fifties and the civil rights-counterculture activism of the sixties and seventies.[3] Daniel is, after all, a hippie in a doctoral program in history at Columbia University, one of the epicenters of student revolt, and seeks to comprehend not merely the mood that turned his parents into scapegoats but the more recent charged atmosphere that has caused his beloved brilliant sister, already institutionalized, to kill herself in despair (we think) over America's inability actually to abandon its hypocritical and destructive ways.

Doctorow was well aware of the great potential of the Rosenberg story as a vehicle for a two-generational cultural-critical reflection. He has described to Paul Levine how, "terribly bored" with the first 150 pages of a draft of the novel written chronologically and in the third person, he threw out that version. In despair over his failure to respond to this vital subject, he "became reckless enough to find the voice of the book, which was Daniel, . . . started to write with a certain freedom and irresponsibility, and it turned out to be Daniel who was talking, and he was sitting in the library at Columbia, and I had my book."[4]

The voice of Daniel, the radicalized son of the fifties' radicals who died for their cause, carries the double articulation—although it is not a consistent expression because scenes occur that are not narrated by Daniel but observe him and others "objectively." For example, the novel begins with "Daniel Lewin thumbed his way from New York to Worcester, Mass., in just under five hours" (13); the "I" form does not appear until four pages later.

The merging of history and fiction, and the confusion of subjective and pseudo-objective perspectives, are matched by the formal division of the text into four books named for commemorative days. Books one, two, and four are titled "Memorial Day," "Halloween," and "Christmas," while book three, "Starfish," depicts among other things a 1967 march on the Pentagon to protest the Vietnam war. The word *starfish* evokes the five sides of the Washington war center and also refers to a rigid position that the insane Susan assumes on her hospital bed and to an ancient sign of the Zodiac. Yet the chapters do not in any consistent sense celebrate the national and religious holidays, but use them as the spatio-temporal settings for the development of many interrelated—even entangled—strands of the plot that are finally at once tied up and left unresolved.

These plot strands are: the fate of the Isaacsons as reconstructed by their narrator-son via memory, letters, conversations, and conjecture; Daniel's attempt as an adult to learn whether his parents were guilty or innocent of the crime for which they were executed; the fate of the Isaacson children Daniel and Susan as they are adopted and reared by the Lewins (recalling the Meeropols adopting Michael and Robert, the Rosenberg sons); the deep and desperate love of Susan and Daniel for each other; the marriage of Daniel and Phyllis; and the attempt of Daniel and the implied author to write a dissertation and novel as the same text.

The Isaacsons are executed, of course, but the very fact of their deaths leaves their plot without closure, just as Daniel can never learn with any certainty whether his parents committed the treasonous acts for which they were condemned. Susan's suicide, apart from leaving Daniel in a state of unresolved grief, leaves open the question of why she took her life. The unsettling sadomasochistic relationship between Daniel and his wife remains unexplained, and the conclusion of the novel leaves many other things undone (Daniel's dissertation above all) and its readers perplexed.

Daniel's Confessions

The interplay of accusation and confession that operates in *The Crucible* occupies a central place in *The Book of Daniel*, mediated by Daniel as the dominant narrative voice. Unlike the situation of Miller's drama, however, confession in this secularized environment has little to do overtly with religion. Rather, it is aligned to matters of Daniel's private life and to those of his parents' very public trial and conviction, matters that ultimately assume a deep religious coloration.

Daniel's confession, which focuses on Phyllis, his twenty-year-old "flower child" wife and on his sister, is not cast as such in any formal way, but it is still a confession. The capacity of his "child bride" to suffer humiliation and pain on his behalf excites his perversity, and this unnerving motivation may be the precarious basis of their relationship. That, at least, is what Daniel confesses. Four pages into the novel he describes how using drugs (this is 1967) brings out rather than submerges Phyllis's inhibitions: "She smokes dope on principle, and that's where I have her. All her instinctive unprincipled beliefs rise to the surface and her knees lock together. She becomes a sex martyr. I think that's why I married her" (16).

This is hardly the basis for a sound union, and it signals early on the price that Daniel (and his sister) have come to pay as the children of the Isaacsons. The parents were martyrs in the eyes of many, dying unjustly for a good cause or at least to appease a system ravenous for victims to punish for the successes of the communist conspiracy in America. Phyllis as "sex martyr" in this tortured marriage is the object on whom Daniel exercises his rage and frustration over his parents' execution.

She is also a surrogate for a deeper obsession that Daniel reveals: his projected incestuous love for his sister. When he visits Susan in the Massachusetts mental hospital after the breakdown that leads to her suicide and peers voyeuristically through her window, he finds her taking the "starfish position." "Slowly her legs spread, her feet slide over the sides of the mattress and her toes hook into the crevice between the mattress and the spring. Her arms move outward; her hands curl over the edge of the mattress and find the same ledge. She holds her bed in her hands and by her ankles. . . . She writhes gently on her back, swaying like something underwater. . . . Today Susan is a starfish" (223). It is a scene so painfully intimate that one cringes upon reading it, but it leads Daniel, having climbed in through the window and contemplating his mad sister's exposed pudendum, to reflect on their complex past. "More than once I have asked myself if I'd like to screw my sister" (224). Against this self-accusation he argues defensively that it was and is not so, yet soon after he holds her in close embrace. "I felt her backbone against my arm, the bones of her thighs across my arms. . . . *Susan,* in her ear, *Susan,* whispering, *Susan* hugging her dry weightlessness, *Susan* kissing her eyes" (226).

Earlier, when Daniel leaves his sister after a visit to the hospital, she tells him, "They're still fucking us" (19), and this phrase becomes a refrain throughout the novel. Susan means, probably, that she and her brother were orphaned by the injustice of the American government and also exploited, during and after the trial and execution, by the leftists who paraded them at political gatherings. But she also, in her sixties' countercultural mode and in her growing paranoia, means the continuing, if not increasing, repressiveness of American life.

It is even possible that she means that their long-dead parents are "still fucking us," and that twist brings home, literally, the sexual-sadistic confusion of this family romance. Susan has behaved seductively and aggressively toward Daniel in their shared past, as their parents flaunted their nakedness and "made the whole house rock. They really went at it; they balled all the time" (53). Thus, among the many things the children have had to face is their erotic relationship to the parents—whose deaths foreclosed closure—and to each other. It is one of the problems that Susan resolves by suicide. It is a problem that Daniel "works out" by abusing his wife and child.

Part of Daniel's narration, then, is this rhythm of self-accusation and confession, and this aspect of his tale, like many other elements, has a religious dimension. It begins, Daniel recalls, when Susan is eight and Daniel is thirteen. In the midst of a Yankees and Red Sox night game telecast, "Susan told me there was a God. 'He'll get them all,' she whispered. 'He'll get every one of them'" (20). That memory leads Daniel into a meditation on the biblical Daniel.

More obvious and public than Daniel's struggle with his family guilt is the public ritual of accusation and coercion toward confession that his parents the Isaacsons endure at their trial. Doctorow does very little with the trial itself, although his trial scenes are effective. Rochelle, ever astute, sees the trial as a ritual. "In her mind it is a ritual defense, a ceremony. . . . She had no doubt about the outcome of the trial" (216). It reminds her of a Greek play she once saw in which "girls in togas" danced a symbolic dance to ward off fate. The implication is that she views herself as a central figure in a classical tragedy, assigned by the capricious gods to her unhappy destiny.

The Rosenberg trial evoked such imagery, and it focused on Ethel. Codefendant Morton Sobell, describing her harrowing cross-examination in late March of 1951, called it "the crucifixion of Ethel" and went on to say, "The cross-examination of Ethel in that courtroom was the most dramatic episode I had ever seen—on stage or off . . . rather like a modern Greek tragedy."[5] Whether or not Doctorow borrowed such commentary for his novel, he does depict Rochelle in the ways that Ethel Rosenberg comported herself: composed and courageous in a hostile setting. It is not surprising, then, that the Isaacsons, like the Rosenbergs, confess very little. Rochelle sees the trial for the sham that it is, whereas Paul is naive and idealistic enough to hope that they will be declared innocent. Rochelle "worries about him. . . . Dear God, does he really look for justice?" (206).

The Isaacsons' Non-Confession

In this ritual of accusation and confession, where the couple refuses to confess, Rochelle is particularly defiant. Daniel quotes his mother as writing, "Everyone is waiting for us to confess. . . . Suppose I confess that I love my husband, and confess as to how I fell for him on our first 'date'— a Loyalist rally on Convent Avenue" (208). This would be just the sort of confession that the prosecuting officials do not wish to hear: a witness to domestic ordinariness and devotion, even in the midst of radical politics, that undercuts the effort to portray the accused couple as singularly monstrous and alien.

Even though the Isaacsons will not play their assigned role, the ritual moves forward inexorably. It is not a matter of determining guilt or innocence. With "Judge Hirsch and Prosecutor working together like a team" (213), as did Judge Kaufman and District Attorney Saypol at the Rosenberg trial, guilt has been decided in advance. But even beyond that, the guilt or innocence of the Isaacsons is not really the issue. The government—as was the case with the Rosenbergs—wants the Isaacsons to confess other, more important names in what it suspects is a grand communist subversion. Robert Lewin, Daniel's stepfather and a lawyer, tells him in 1967, "'The idea of a confession was not to make your parents penitent, or to exonerate American justice. It was to make them name other people. So you see the death sentence itself was used as an investigative procedure'" (239).

The attempted coercion, according to Lewin, was intense. "'Even after her [Rochelle's] arrest, if your parents had named other people they would have become prosecution witnesses like Mindish. . . . Even after their trial and sentence, the government let them know that if they confessed the sentences would not be carried out'" (239). Thus the Isaacsons break the ritual pattern in another way. Like Proctor in *The Crucible,* they refuse to name names, to betray anyone (if indeed they have anyone to betray) and thereby frustrate the government's design. They take the blame for something they may not have done (or not done alone) and expiate for others. Small wonder that Sobell saw in the ordeal of Ethel Rosenberg, Rochelle's historical counterpart, a "crucifixion."

As in *The Crucible,* the refusal to respond to accusation with confession, the refusal to name names, provides characters a degree of integrity based on a willingness to sacrifice themselves. Not only that: Because the government (for all of its show of a public trial and thus the assumption of a public realm) actually subverts the public dimension in order to uncover a conspiracy secretly, the Isaacsons' refusal to confess also defeats and eventually exposes the political exploitation of the public sphere.

Someone implicated in the atom spy trial does confess in *The Book of Daniel*. It is the dentist Selig Mindish, a long-standing friend of the Isaacsons who betrays them, saves himself from the death sentence, and becomes the object of the adult Daniel's obsession. Doctorow creates Mindish to replace Ethel Rosenberg's younger brother David Greenglass. We recall that Greenglass had admitted in 1950 that back in 1945 he had been an accomplice of Harry Gold, the chemist who had confessed earlier his role as courier to Klaus Fuchs, the physicist in England who gave atom bomb information to the Soviets. Greenglass, a machinist working in a Los Alamos nuclear research laboratory, had been under FBI surveillance since stealing a small quantity of uranium from the lab as a souvenir. He asserted that Julius Rosenberg had involved him twice in espionage activities that led to Julius's arrest. Greenglass's dramatic testimony at the Rosenbergs' trial played a key part in the conviction of his sister and brother-in-law. Because of his role as a government witness, Greenglass was given a relatively light fifteen-year sentence by Judge Kaufman, although his lawyer had expected that he would receive considerably less.[6]

In the plot of the novel, the adult Daniel flies to Los Angeles during the Christmas season, where the aged Mindish, his prison sentence long completed, and his wife live under another name with their daughter Linda. Daniel wishes to quiz the old man about his betrayal of the Isaacsons during the 1950 trial. In the midst of this action Doctorow introduces a flashback of the trial itself and Mindish's confession observed in part from Rochelle's perspective. It is a scene that resembles the Rosenberg trial. There Ethel is clearly distraught by her brother's words against her (uttered while insisting that he loves her), and there too Ethel stares steadily at Greenglass while he refuses to return the gaze.

In the novel, "It was at this moment [Mindish's testimony] in the trial that she [Rochelle] nearly lost her composure" (295), and Doctorow emphasizes her fixed gaze upon the old family friend. Above all, at a critical point in his performance "Selig Mindish actually began to smile" (296)—like Greenglass's seemingly reflexive strange smiling during his damning testimony. In seeking to interpret that smile, Rochelle discovers, stunned, that Mindish believes not only in the complicity of her husband Paul in the alleged theft of nuclear secrets for the Soviets but also in Paul's sacrifice of himself and Rochelle—without telling her—in order to spare the mysterious other couple. Thus Mindish's confession is, in a way, ironically justified; he has done it for the good of the cause.

This is the theory that Daniel relates to Linda and her lawyer-fiancé in California without old Selig himself present. Linda rejects it vehemently, reciting instead the "family line": "Papa didn't tell the half of it. . . . Your parents were the head of a whole network. They ran the show. . . . Another couple. My God, that's pathetic" (298). In this manner the formal accusation-confession involving Mindish and the Isaacsons is replicated, the curse of the parents is visited on the children, and an Old Testament, sadistic ferocity marks the mutual accusation. Accusation and counteraccusation take place rather than any sort of confession. Daniel in his rage for revelation only incites Linda, his childhood persecutor, to outrage in return.

Morris and Helen Cohen, the other couple somehow involved in the Rosenberg affair, eventually resurfaced in London and were tried and convicted of espionage there. In *The Book of Daniel* the "mystery couple" (295), also with two children and living in New York, disappears soon after the Isaacsons are arrested, undergo various tribulations abroad, "and were last reported living in Leningrad" (295). But even Daniel is anything but sure that his theory of the other couple is plausible or that the desire to protect them caused Mindish to betray the Isaacsons. They are a red herring dragged across Doctorow's and Daniel's plots that leads mainly to Daniel meeting at last with Selig Mindish.[7]

The encounter takes place in Disneyland, and in that pseudo-public realm, a pop-mythologized and technologized place of innocence, Selig (the name, spelled *seelig* in German, means "blissful" or "holy") Mindish's non-confession is ironically and dramatically apt. Old Mindish is senile. He recognizes Daniel and is pleased to see him, but he seems to have no sense of guilt or memory of his betrayal. His response instead is a gesture of inadvertent reconciliation. "For one moment of recognition he was restored to life. In wonder he raised his large, clumsy hand and touched the side of my face. He found the back of my neck and pulled me forward and leaned toward me and touched the top of my head with his palsied lips" (309). A cognate of "selig" is "silly," which used to mean "blessed" or "innocent," and Selig disarms Daniel with his silly, innocent gesture. Instead of confession, Daniel gets confusion. The old man, presumably culpable in the Isaacsons' death, has forgotten it all and gives the son ("Isaac's son") a patriarchal blessing.

The powerful moment has an elongated past. Selig, as his daughter maintains, has surely suffered much as a result of his involvement with the Isaacsons, and if he cannot expatiate for Daniel at least his senile act offers a reflex of reconciliation. Daniel has come to Disneyland in Anaheim, "a town somewhere between Buchenwald and Belsen" (301), and finds the family betrayer in Tomorrowland ("That's what he likes best"

[306]). Doctorow's evocation of two notorious World War II death camps juxtaposed to the commodified kitsch and mass pleasure of the amusement park is intended to shock, and it does. One possible implication is that for Mindish the suffering in his ethnic heritage has been devalued and lost in a sanitized, technologized environment where sensation replaces thinking. This is fitting for Mindish, who has largely lost the capacity for thinking anyhow.

It is much harder for Daniel. In his mock-learned (dissertation) analysis of Disneyland he sketches one of its problems: the hordes of visitors that destroy the illusion of authenticity. "There is a constant feedback of human multiplicity, one's own efforts of vicarious participation constantly thwarted by the mirror of others' lives" (302). That dilemma is also the one that Daniel discovers in his pursuit of Mindish. Mindish in this constructed, bogus public realm of the amusement park is incapable of giving Daniel his vicarious satisfaction. His senility frustrates it, and what Daniel gets instead is the short-circuited jolt of recognition (an ironic *anagnorisis*) and reconciliation that does him no good. The patriarchal kiss is also a Judas kiss, the kiss of the betrayer.

Daniel, however, is a suffering servant to his dead parents—and eventually to his dead sister—in terms of Scripture. That other Book of Daniel from the Hebrew Bible's Old Testament provides Doctorow with the first of his epigraphs (Daniel 3:4), and the conclusion of the novel is also the conclusion of the prophetic text (Daniel 12:1–4, 9). Doctorow is interested in the biblical text as analytical and metaphorical material. The epigraph concerns a strand of the Daniel narrative in which Daniel's brothers (with the Babylonian names of Shadrach, Meshach, and Abednego) are condemned to die in the fiery furnace because they will not practice King Nebuchanezzar's religious rituals, but they emerge unscathed from their crucible thanks to the intervention of the Hebrew God. Because the passage describes the festive occasion when "all the people, the nation" otherwise worship the king's golden image, it is easy to read the idolatrous royal religion as American capitalism and the fiery furnace for the dissenting, disloyal trio as the electric chair that awaits the Rosenberg/Isaacson couple. The novel's apocalyptic concluding passage hints at the catastrophic things to happen at the end of time, an apt context for what many feared would result from the cold war confrontation of the nuclear-armed superpowers as well as for the hysteria that spawned grotesqueries such as the Rosenberg affair.

But the passage also refers to Daniel as prophet and explainer of dreams, and Doctorow doubtless wishes his narrator to be, like his biblical prototype, an interpreter of bizarre political-religious visions and riddles directly affecting him, his family, and his heritage. Like the biblical

Daniel, who not only has to interpret Nebuchadnezzar's dream but also renarrate it with no help from the king (Daniel 2), Doctorow's narrator must invent much of his account as well as seek to understand and explain it.

Given the biblical texts literally surrounding the novel, it is not surprising to find it loaded with religious references and reflections—aspects that no critics have dealt with in detail. One finds, for example, contemplation on the Old Testament Daniel, a midrash on the nature of God according to the Bible, references to YHWH by Daniel's fairly crazy grandmother, information on Christian martyrdom in Japan, an interpretation of the Isaacsons' execution as Daniel's bar mitzvah, and speculation on the trial and crucifixion of Christ.

Why should Doctorow, not known as a religious writer, and his narrator, a secular intellectual leftist, wish to give the narration a religious cast? Perhaps they use religion as a vehicle for depicting the effects of public exposure. As in *The Crucible,* public exposure is here closely connected to the dehumanizing gaze of the voyeur and to shame. Daniel reports that the Isaacsons' lawyer Ascher (like the Rosenberg's defender Emanuel Bloch, well-meaning but overmatched), who "was said to have worked for years on a still-unfinished book demonstrating the contribution of the Old Testament to American law," also believed that "witchhunting was paganism" (133). He was further convinced—no doubt correctly—that Senator Joe McCarthy, the most tenacious witch-hunter of the twentieth century, saw Jews as atheistic and thus on the side of evil.

Cosmic Voyeurism

With such merciless focus on the exposure of the Isaacsons, reminiscent of the persecution of suspected witches in puritan New England, the Jewish pair has no chance at maintaining innocence; for Rochelle, at least, the trial becomes an effort to save her self-respect and dignity in the face of the maneuvers to shame her and her husband. Daniel is alert to this dimension of his parents' agony because he has felt, since their arrest during his childhood, that he is being watched—that the world is being watched: "I know exactly what is happening. A giant eye machine . . . is turning its planetary beam in our direction. . . . And when it reaches us, like the prison searchlight in the Nazi concentration camp, it will stop. And we will be pinned, like the lady jammed through the schoolyard fence with her blood mixed with the milk and broken bottles" (122).[8]

Daniel feels himself the focus of a cosmic voyeurism, his version of God studying the world. It is the result of the intense scrutiny he and his sister endured in the public eye as the children of the notorious spy couple—an ordeal suffered in real life and documented by the Rosenberg sons Robert and Michael Meeropol in *We Are Your Sons*. Susan's instinctive response is, in her madness, to play the exhibitionist, to expose herself. In psychoanalytical terms, the public focus on her in her childhood, traumatic though it is, feeds a narcissism that, in her adulthood, increases rather than matures into concern for others. Daniel in the starfish episode plays the voyeur and watches Susan, complicit with her in acting out the dynamic of shame—a dynamic that Daniel refines (if that is the proper term) in the torture of his wife.

Daniel as an adult, struggling with the shame of his parents' public humiliation (suffering the contempt and judgment of much of the world), depicts their means of dealing with it during the years of their trial and appeals and in doing so seeks to come to terms with his own shame. As he reports it, Paul and Rochelle mainly refuse to act shamed, and in the process they, especially Rochelle, become actors—exhibitionists. How could they do otherwise, since they have been exhibited, put on display for the world to see?[9]

Andrew Ross in his analysis of the letters that Julius and Ethel Rosenberg wrote in prison stresses their sense of living under the public gaze.[10] Because even their intimate communications were read by others, their writing assumed an artificial style, one that in its awkward way prepared the letters for publication (because the Rosenbergs were notorious, one wants to eavesdrop, especially on their private behavior) and acknowledged the couple's feeling of exposure.

That artificiality extends to the Rosenbergs' demeanor in the courtroom. Philipson and others describe the theatricality of Ethel's behavior—not a performance of great anguish that might have generated some public sentiment in her favour but rather an expression of stoic composure that led some to believe it was she and not Julius who was the main culprit. Philipson also recounts how Ethel in her cell, having read Shaw's *Saint Joan,* upon hearing Judge Kaufman's denial of an appeal for clemency wrote a letter to Bloch their lawyer, quoting from the play and comparing "herself directly to the martyred Maid of Orleans."[11]

Doctorow portrays Rochelle as likewise aware of the public significance of her letters, also as formally and self-consciously composed at her trial in spite of her inner turmoil, as in the scene contained in the section titled "The Theory of the Other Couple" (294ff). He even provides a reference to Joan of Arc ("We understand that when St. Joan led them into battle, none of the soldiers watched the way her ass moved" [226]), but it is a comment Daniel offers immediately following his sister's "starfish" behavior and involving his own shameful reaction.

Where is the religious dimension of such shame? Bruno Snell has a

somewhat surprising conjecture: "*Aidos,* the feeling of shame . . . origi-
nates as the reaction which the holy excites in a man." As Carl Schneider
expands on that notion, "The sense of reverence involved in *aidos* is
roughly akin to respect for the intrinsic worth of others. Its connotations
transcend the moral realm; there is a sense of awe before the mysterious
and powerful."[12]

If this is so, the shame that Paul and Rochelle Isaacson are supposed
to feel but reject should be produced by their government as awe-inspiring, as the representation of what is mysterious and powerful. Yet the government that prosecutes and persecutes them is secretive but not mysterious, and it is only blatantly and crudely powerful. It is transparent in
its attempts to command awe but succeeds only, for the Isaacsons, in evoking contempt. In trying to compel shame, it shames itself (a theme developed still more vigorously in *The Public Burning*). And because the
Isaacsons will not accept such shame from an institution that cannot force
reverence, the government (like Nebuchadnezzar) turns to its final resort:
condemnation to death and public execution. The powerful institution
that is not worthy of representing God nevertheless plays God by controlling life and death.

Schneider remarks on the creation of shameful deaths in war: "The
concentration camp of Nazi Germany perfected such shaming experiences, deliberately tying death to humiliation as families were forced to strip
naked in front of one another before entering the gas chambers."[13] The
American government in the stress of the cold war (one recalls Judge
Kaufman's hyperbole) sees fit to humiliate the Rosenberg family, and the
Isaacsons in *The Book of Daniel* receive similar treatment.

Daniel as narrator descends to the occasion. He challenges the reader,
"I suppose you think I can't do the execution. . . . YOU: I will show you
that I can do the execution" (312). He then proceeds to do so, depicting
in grisly detail first his father's and then his mother's death. It is an ultimate voyeuristic scene: the condemned pair as unwilling exhibitionists
before "the warden, the executioner, three guards, the rabbi, two doctors,
and three reporters" (312), these last as professional eyewitnesses to pass
on the sensation pruriently to a curious public. Daniel in his recounting
is, of course, both exhibitionist and voyeur, showing (and showing off to)
his reading public that he "can do the execution" and also providing the
titillating detail—although in this he is actually no more graphic than
Radosh and Milton portraying the historic Rosenberg electrocutions. They
specify, for example, how after Julius was killed "a guard stepped forward
to mop up the urine that had collected on the seat and underneath the
electric chair, using a strong ammoniac solution that also mercifully
masked the stench of burnt flesh."[14] Daniel writes, "A hideous smell com-

pounded of burning flesh, excrement and urine filled the death chamber. . . . A pool of urine collected on the cement floor under the chair" (314).

That last image is not merely a death house particular. It reminds the reader of Daniel's earlier depiction of his mad sister's incontinence as a child. Even as Daniel stages this voyeuristic public scene featuring his parents scrutinized in the intimacy of their death throes, he includes this most private detail of his sister's loss of control. It is as if he needs to have the family back together again, at their moments of utter helplessness, to share their shame and make it his own in the telling and relieve them. Daniel's story becomes an expiation, perhaps the assumption of an expiation he could not get from Mindish or could get only through Mindish's loss of guilty memory and of shame.

A Criminal of Perception?

In the biblical Book of Daniel, King Nebuchadnezzar is "preoccupied with public perception," as Danna Fewell puts it, and needs the three Hebrew youths, Daniel's brothers, to be sacrificed as a burnt offering because they will not worship him.[15] They survive by divine intervention, and the king is shamed into an acknowledgment of the one true God. In Doctorow's novel two family members are sacrificed, also as burnt offerings, to appease a nation intent on forcing loyalty, and a third kills herself years later in delayed outrage and humiliation. It is no wonder that the son and brother agonizes with the burden to tell and understand and in the process to act out his own survivor's shame—that he has not died with the others (a dynamic I will treat in my reading of Philip Caputo's *Indian Country* in chapter 11). In this sense, Daniel's shame is religious: He feels awe in the mystery and power of his parents' and sister's integrity beyond their deaths. That he concludes his tale with the narration of their funerals, before the formal closing of his book in the Columbia University library, is the proper ritual ending.

But Daniel's sadistic personality also requires further probing. Virtually all of the novel's interpreters note Daniel's cruelty. Carol Harter and James Thompson label "the character and behavior of the adult Daniel" as "often repulsive," while John Parks, commenting on the similarity between Daniel and Hamlet, says that, "unable to direct their aggression to the real object of their rage—the regime—they abuse the women they love." Robert Forrey understands Daniel's disorganized structure of narration as evidence of his disintegrating ego and thinks as some narrators do of Edgar Allan Poe (whom Daniel cites) that he may be crazy.[16]

To a query about whether he thought of casting Daniel as sympathetic "rather than giving him sadistic, at times almost monstrous, qualities" Doctorow replied, "But I see his 'sadism,' as you call it, in a slightly different way. I see the scene where he abuses his wife, for instance, as the same kind of scene where he throws his son up in the air. The act has existential dimensions. Daniel is over-tuned to the world. He doesn't miss a thing. He's a hero—or a criminal—of perception . . . [who survives] by however cold and frightening embrace with the truth."[17] This is perhaps disingenuous, for it is clear that Doctorow organizes the tropes of the novel to stress throughout an anality that, in psychoanalytic theory, is related to sadism.[18] In Doctorow's reference, in the interview, to wife abuse, he has in mind the scene in which Daniel, speeding on the freeway during a rain storm, bullies Phyllis into removing her jeans and underpants so that he can burn her buttocks or anus with the car cigarette lighter (169–73). In another scene he remembers being caught as a boy while spying on his Aunt Frieda on the toilet: "Her head was tilted back and her teeth were bared as she sat on the pot with her bloomers around her knees arching her back in an ecstasy of defecation" (175). Susan's suicide attempt that takes Daniel away from his research occurs in a Howard Johnson's toilet stall along a freeway. Daniel, recalling a nasty argument with Susan in the company of Phyllis and the Lewins, reports that she called him "a piece of shit" and told him, "You no longer exist," which leads him later to refer to "a disappearance of Daniel into his own asshole" (94).

In the midst of a scene of Daniel and Susan as children running away from their guardians and seeking to return to their old home in the Bronx, Daniel reflects on American traitors, above all "the archetypal traitor, the master subversive Poe, who wrote a hole into the parchment [of the Constitution] and let the darkness pour through. . . . He added some raven droppings. A small powerful odor arose from the Constitution; there was a wisp of smoke which exploded and quickly turned mustard yellow in color. When Poe blew this away through the resulting aperture in the parchment the darkness of the depths rose, and rises still from that small hole all these years incessantly pouring its dark hellish gasses . . . over . . . the Rights of Man" (193–94). Following this fantasy on federal flatulence Daniel returns to the childhood city scene and depicts Susan at the locked door of the Bronx house, urinating "in the middle of the porch, a darkening stain spreading under her foot" (194).

The psychoanalytic textbook connections between anal fixation and sadism are manifest. Children in the anal-sadistic stage (generally from one to three) are extremely aggressive, retentive, in need of gaining and keeping control, and fascinated with their feces and with body-eliminative functions in general. They are full of contradictions, both belligerent and submissive, withholding and forthcoming. Daniel demonstrates all of these, obviously as a result of his youthful trauma of losing his parents, their and his public shame, and his repressed anger over the years. His adult sadism—practiced, significantly, on his family, including his infant son, whom he throws recklessly into the air against his wife's protests (149)—expresses his desire to control his destructive life and to vent his sense of guilt and outrage.

Evil and the Sacred

More interesting is the relating of Daniel's sadistic behavior to his meditations on evil and to the role of evil in the novel. Daniel conjoins voyeurism, the sadistic infliction of pain, anality, and a sense of the holy, in a paragraph from the passage where he burns his wife. Typically combative, he challenges the reader: "Do you want to know the effect of three concentric circles of heating element . . . upon the tender white girlflesh of my wife's ass? Who are you anyway? Who told you you could read this? Is nothing sacred" (72)? The final sentence is not a throwaway line or cliché. To ask that question at the end of a blatantly pornographic evocation is to implicate the reader in the assault on Daniel's wife's privacy that he has just elaborated, to attempt to make the reader complicit in the taboo that Daniel has broken. One might list at least three taboos: that against sexual violation (which this action is); that against harming the spouse whom he has promised to nurture and protect; and that "strong taboo on the anal region" as Schneider puts it.[19]

Both acts, the doing and the telling, seem perverse and evil. But what precisely makes them evil? It is the transgression beyond the sacrosanct, the demonstration that nothing *is* sacred. In his anal-retentive compulsion to control, Daniel shows how horribly he and his world are out of control. He makes the political and social implications of this intimate exercise in evil more explicit a few paragraphs further on. Recalling the verbal abuse he and his sister received from their parents, he writes, "In our house there could be a laying on of words like lightning: Dispensed outrage, the smell of burning in the mouths of our mother and father" (73). The trajectory is from the fury of the parents to their sadistic violation by their government to the son's victimizing of his wife, all held together in this olfactory imagery of scorched flesh—and always in the background the memory of burning bodies in the furnaces of the Holocaust. Evil here is personal and relational, generated by and among individuals, magnified and refined by institutions, and embedded in the next generations.

Daniel knows this (he is a "criminal of perception") and embellishes it in his fantasy of Poe's witches' brew that corrodes American justice as a hole eaten in the Constitution: consisting of whisky, blood from Poe's consumptive child-wife, a "tooth of the dead Ligeia . . . some raven droppings" (193). What combusts and spreads its "hellish gasses" over the land is that embedded evil, a human force, "that darkness of the depths . . . across the smiling face of America" (193–94).

This nightmare modulates into a meditation toward the end of the novel when Daniel encounters Linda Mindish after many years, his fellow "criminal of perception," and has a flash of revelation about the nature of evil as he has felt it. "For one moment I experienced the truth of the situation as an equitability of evil. This is what happens to us, to the children of trials; our hearts run to cunning, our minds are sharp as claws. Such shrewdness has to be burned into the eyes' soul, it is only formed in fire. There is no way in the world either of us of us would not be willing to use in our sad lives; no betrayal impossible of our pain; no use too cheap of our patrimony" (291). It is a recognition of total depravity as intense as that of any Calvinist. Daniel exempts the mad and "innocent" Susan from it but finds a damned soul-sister in Linda Mindish and that makes him lustful and sadistic. "I imagined her in bed. . . ; it would not be without blood, an incest of blood and death and jism and egg more corrupt than any I could have with my real sister. There was enough hard corruption in Linda Mindish and me, flawless forged criminals of perception, to exhaust the fires of the sun" (291).

There are no references here from the son of communists, abandoned by them, to communism's "evil empire" and only an oblique reference to the perversions of the legal witch-hunt that took his parents and twisted his mind and emotions. It is a moment of deep theological insight: Evil is the capacity for self-betrayal, the exercise of it violates others and causes the corrosion of whatever good persists in institutions of family, education, government. And in the midst of this insight a terrifying possibility appears: There is no neutral public realm; it exists only as good or evil, and when it is not one it is the other.

Danna Fewell observes, regarding the biblical Book of Daniel, "The ultimate irony . . . is that the kingdom as Daniel envisions it . . . never manifests itself. . . . In the end of Daniel, there is no end."[20] But if, as Harter and Thompson maintain, Doctorow's novel "raises more questions than for which it even implies answers," that is good.[21] Like its Old Testament forebear, it is a cautionary tale of what happens when one challenges the state religion (formal or otherwise) and simultaneously a prophetic-apocalyptic warning about the personal and civic consequences of not challenging that religion.

As Daniel says early on, "The drama in the Bible is always in the conflict of those who have learned and those who have not learned. Or in the testing of those who seem that they might be able to learn" (20). Carmichael, commenting on those lines, remarks, "The implication is that in a secular age, justice is the work of human beings, and it is political work . . . the work of attempting to know and analyze real social conditions and to envision workable alternatives, in order to disrupt and intervene in unjust practices in everyday life—asking again and again what it is you can do this time." This is the part that Doctorow himself plays as the prophetic purveyor of a heuristic fiction. As Carmichael puts it in a fine concluding paragraph, "Working to analyze and develop self-awareness toward these national states of mind not apparent to ourselves—the unified free liberal subject, U.S. objectivity and moral superiority, the evasions of an elite aestheticism, and an ignorance of history—is the accomplishment of *The Book of Daniel*."[22]

Notes

1. Paul Gray, "Biography or Soap Opera?" *Time*, July 12, 1993, 57.

2. Leslie A. Fiedler, "Afterthoughts on the Rosenbergs," in *The Collected Essays of Leslie Fiedler* (New York: Stein and Day, 1971), 1:33.

3. Many critics have remarked on this. See Virginia Carmichael, *Framing History: The Rosenberg Story and the Cold War* (Minneapolis: University of Minnesota Press, 1993), 131, for example: *The Book of Daniel* is "not about the Rosenbergs but about the idea of the Rosenbergs." It is curious that neither Doctorow nor Coover introduces the figure of Roy Cohn into their plots because he was prominent as one of the team prosecuting the Rosenbergs. Cohn does play a prominent role in both of Kushner's *Angels in America* plays, *Millenium Approaches* and *Perestroika,* where he is dying of AIDS and endures Ethel Rosenberg's terrifying visits. For a sensationalist "autobiography" of Cohn, see Sidney Zion, *The Autobiography of Roy Cohn* (Secaucus: Lyle Stuart, 1988). As Zion explains it, the book is "organized by my hand but in his voice" (11).

4. Doctorow interview with Paul Levine, in *E. L. Doctorow, Essays and Conversations,* ed. Richard Trenner (Princeton: Ontario Review Press, 1983), 62. Doctorow also collaborated with Sidney Lumet to produce, in 1987, a film version of *The Book of Daniel* called *Daniel.* Parenthetical citations that follow are from *The Book of Daniel* (New York: Random House, 1971).

5. Quoted by Ilene Philipson, *Ethel Rosenberg: Beyond the Myths* (New York: Franklin Watts, 1988), 294.

6. My information on Greenglass comes largely from Philipson, *Ethel Rosenberg,* passim, especially 279–81.

7. Philipson, *Ethel Rosenberg,* 223, offers evidence that the Rosenbergs were planning "an extended trip" in June 1950.

8. The scene with the lady jammed through the fence is one from Doctorow's youthful memory and described also in his novel *World's Fair* (New York: Vintage International, 1992), 152.

9. Yet the Meeropol brothers appear to be remarkably normal persons leading relatively normal lives

10. Andrew Ross, *No Respect: Intellectuals and Popular Culture* (New York: Routledge, 1989), 27.

11. Philipson, *Ethel Rosenberg,* 294, 344.

12. Bruno Snell, *The Discovery of the Mind,* trans. T. G. Rosenmeyer (Oxford: Blackwell, 1953), 167, cited by Carl D. Schneider, *Shame, Exposure, and Privacy* (New York: W. W. Norton, 1977), 110.

13. Schneider, *Shame, Exposure, and Privacy,* 82.

14. Ronald Radosh and Joyce Milton, *The Rosenberg File: A Search for the Truth* (New York: Holt, Rinehart and Winston, 1983), 418. An editorial in *The Nation,* June 27, 1953, 534, praises the Rosenbergs in their final moments: "Guilty or not, [they] went to their deaths with a composure and dignity that won praise even from hostile newspapers."

15. Danna Nolan Fewell, *Circle of Sovereignty: A Story of Stories in Daniel 1–6* (Sheffield: Almond, 1988), 65.

16. Carol C. Harter and James R. Thompson, *E. L. Doctorow* (Boston: G. K. Hall, 1990), 41; John G. Parks, *E. L. Doctorow* (New York: Continuum, 1991), 43; Robert Forrey, "Doctorow's *The Book of Daniel:* All in the Family," *Studies in American Jewish Literature* 2 (1982): 173.

17. Trenner, ed., *E. L. Doctorow, Essays and Conversations,* 46–47.

18. Carmichael, *Framing History,* 187–90, has a helpful discussion on "anal logic" in *The Book of Daniel* and in *The Public Burning.*

19. Schneider, *Shame, Exposure, and Privacy,* 71.

20. Fewell, *Circle of Sovereignty,* 161–62.

21. Harter and Thompson, *E. L. Doctorow,* 47.

22. Carmichael, *Framing History,* 153, 155.

4

The Public Burning: Carnival, Circus, and Public Execution

Is America a liberal zoo, or is it a conservative jungle?
—John Chancellor, *Peril and Promise*

Paul Levine praised *The Book of Daniel* as "the best and most important American novel of the 1970's," and Robert Coover's *The Public Burning* earned similar accolades from Tom LeClair, who in 1989 called it "the master political novel of the last two decades."[1] That assessment has not been, however, the general critical reaction to Coover's novel. Norman Podhoretz in an indignant piece (and an embarrassing misreading) for *Saturday Review* in 1979 concluded, "Should such a book be called a novel? . . . I think it should be called a lie. And because it hides behind the immunities of artistic freedom to protect itself from being held to the normal standards of truthful discourse . . . it should also be called a cowardly lie."[2] Tom Paulin in *Encounter* thought it was "a colossally mistaken attempt to understand the disturbing politics of America," while Paul Gray writing for *Time* labeled it "an overwritten bore" and "a protracted sneer"—a not unexpected verdict because *The Public Burning* lampoons *Time* throughout as "the National Poet Laureate," a pretentious and self-righteous influence on American affairs.[3]

Coover had long been intrigued by the Rosenberg materials and read extensively in them, not least the documents in the FBI files released in 1975. At first he reworked the plot elements in the form of a play but abandoned that and began to develop them as prose fiction to accompany "The Cat in the Hat for President" (a satire on American political party conventions), but that grew too large and unwieldy.[4] Although it is far from simple, Coover remarked that *The Public Burning* "is a simple outgrowth of that Jesus thing I did at the beginning," referring to his first novel, *The Origin of the Brunists*, which plays with messianic cults.[5]

Completed at last and in time for publication during the bicentennial year of 1976, *The Public Burning* was rejected by Knopf, under pressure from Random House, publisher of Knopf books, as "immoral." It was turned down by other publishers fearful of libel suits but eventually published by Viking Press as a Richard Seaver book in 1977. No one sued, and the prepublication notoriety no doubt helped the novel gain bestseller status, but when it did Viking stopped promoting it. A Bantam paperback edition published in late 1978 did not sell well and soon went out of print.[6]

"That Jesus thing" still on Coover's creative mind, and his "predilection for theology" (a "shortcoming" Walter Clemons noted in a 1977 *Newsweek* review), combine to make religion a dominant element of *The Public Burning,* an element that functions primarily as an extravagant satire on (and indictment of) what Coover has called "the American civil religion."[7] He also says, "I wondered where the roots of it were, of this heresy of Western Christianity, why it developed, and why we don't recognize it or talk about it. Durkheim's constructs gave me valuable insights and led me to other reading about primitive societies in which festivals were set up in order to return us to dream time."[8]

The terms "primitive societies" and "festivals" are significant for interpreting the setting and action of the novel. LeClair borrows from Clifford Geertz's study of the "theater state" of nineteenth-century Balinese culture to argue that Coover creates something similar in fictional form. He writes:

> Coover reenacts the Rosenberg executions of 1953 in a negara-like [like the theater-state] novelistic context in order to demonstrate two essential points about American culture: 1).while believing in rational progress and politics as governance, America unwittingly reenacts 'primitive' cultural and religious forms; and 2) what is reenacted—power as semiotic display—becomes the essence of contemporary and, Coover implies, future politics in electronic Mediamerica. In Coover's version of the 1950s, the hysteria of McCarthyism was not an aberration but a logical outgrowth of American and European history.[9]

Jackson Cope refers to "the great carnival in Times Square . . . that must find its moment of propitiation to strange and savage gods."[10]

Coover refers to the circus element of *The Public Burning:* "Originally, it was the circus aspect that interested me most." By combining the concepts of circus, carnival, festival, and religious ritual one has a sense of the novel's social-cultural dimensions.[11] As an evocation of circus, it describes a public spectacle meant to divert and entertain through its display of energy and variety, its sheer exuberant busyness. LeClair thinks that the novel is structured as a three-ring circus, with Nixon, the Rosenbergs, and Uncle Sam providing the focus for each of the rings.[12] Continuing the circus imagery, one could say that Nixon is the clown, the slapstick figure, at least somewhat sympathetic, who leads the nation in the enjoyment of the superficial absurd, and Uncle Sam is the ringmaster who keeps the whole show moving.[13]

In its incarnation of carnival *The Public Burning* calls attention to the fleshly excesses of communal behavior, the perceived need to indulge periodically in antisocial acts, to get it out of the "system," literally, and return more or less relieved to quotidian existence. The excessive, antisocial behavior of carnival is sanctioned for a set, relatively brief period by the authoritative body—the church or the state—so that for a time that behavior becomes "social." Seen this way, the mass orgy of the huge crowd in Times Square excited by the exposure and impending execution of the Rosenbergs forms the climax of the pervasive carnival spirit in the novel.

Because Mikhail Bakhtin's criticism in English translation has reached American academic readers, his work on the evolution of the novel genre as "dialogic," as a "heteroglossia" of voices competing with each other, has become popular and certainly is an apt way for characterizing the brawling interactive voices of *The Public Burning*.[14] Bakhtin evokes Rabelais as a "carnivalesque" novelist who deals in comic excess and comic conflict on a grand and boisterous scale, and the author of *Gargantua and Pantagruel* is surely in the background of Coover's exorbitant and immoderate creation.

As denoted by its Latin roots, carnival, meaning to "remove the flesh," was and is a religious festival, that time (as much as three months) of revelry and indulgence of appetite for Roman Catholics before the fasting and discipline of Lent that prepares believers for Easter. *The Public Burning* is "festive" in that particular sense, and the title's punning suggests how: The public, that is, the crowd "burning" with lust, becomes part of a civic-religious ritual, which is the public burning via electrocution of the two sacrificial victims.

The novel's critical turn, its transition from an embodiment of carnival-festival to one of religious ritual, becomes apparent by studying it in the terms I used for *The Crucible* and *The Book of Daniel*: the dynamic of accusation and confession, the ontological conditions of evil and goodness, and the pathology of public exposure. It is tempting to attach each of these to the major characters of the novel respectively: the Rosenbergs caught up in accusation and confession, Nixon as the incarnation of evil, and Uncle Sam as orchestrating the public exposure. But *The Public Burning* does not work that way. Rather, all of the characters participate in all of these phenomena.

Nixon's Confessions

A primary working irony of Coover's text concerns accusation and confession in the framework of the broad ideological conflict that is the
novel's social setting. American freedom and democracy accuse communist totalitarianism of seeking to subvert and pervert America's
sound (Christian) values and practices, and, because communism will
not confess its nefarious ways, it is up to Americans to expose them. In
the simplified dramatic terms that Coover fashions, the evil Phantom,
the threatening incarnation of communism, is pitted against Uncle Sam,
the inspirational incorporation of a tremendously vital and healthy
Americanism. The Phantom never comes to voice, but Uncle Sam does,
in wild excess, and preaches, extols, pleads, and *confesses* the American
way, as do his mouthpieces Dwight Eisenhower, J. Edgar Hoover, Joe
McCarthy, and Billy Graham.

A critical part of their confession of Americanism is the accusation
against and condemnation of communism as thoroughly depraved. The
unnamed narrator who alternates chapters with Nixon tells how Eisenhower, in chastising Christians "soft" on communism (and in what must
be an actual quotation), "had long insisted that 'the church, with its testimony of the existence of an Almighty God is the last thing, that it seems
to me, would be preaching, teaching, or tolerating Communism.' . . . The
Chief has turned over to Edgar Hoover's G-men the names of 2300 cler-
gymen, who signed a 'special plea for clemency for the Rosenbergs,' as
well as the list of 104 signatories to a follow-up letter, taken to be the hard-
core Comsymp preachers" (208). Once again the accusation-confession
activity involves naming names; here the fictive and historic president,
following his confession of Christian faith, seeks to learn who the truly
guilty are and feeds the notorious paranoia of the FBI director.

In the chapter following, Nixon as narrator describing Eisenhower's
"conversion" makes a convoluted comparison between the president's
Americanism and the New Testament disciples' confession of Jesus' redemptive act: "The conversion of Dwight David Eisenhower was as great a
proof of the immanence and immutability of Uncle Sam as the renewed
preaching of the Disciples after their Good Friday dismay and dispersion;
of the Resurrection of Christ" (229). In such grossly overblown passages
Coover plumbs the theology of civil religion. In its American variant, Eisenhower, the revered leader (the savior figure of World War II) by announcing his devotion to the Christian God becomes semi-deific and provides
the ideology of the state a religious permeation. It is by no means an original strategy, but rather one employed by absolute (and not so absolute)
monarchs for centuries. The irony is that here it dominates a democracy.

If only the Rosenbergs would confess their crimes of betraying America and aiding the evil enemy, the Christian state and citizenry would feel their righteousness confirmed. Even more, if the Rosenbergs confessed, the state would demonstrate its magnanimity—its version of Christian grace—and commute the death sentences. But the recalcitrant Jewish couple will not cooperate.

If the Rosenbergs will not confess, Nixon will. Much of the novel, the chapters that the vice president narrates, consists of his confession, a recounting of his fears, hopes, embarrassments, secret sins, and the nature of his spiritual life—some of it making him seem an oddly endearing, vulnerable person. Like Eisenhower, Nixon has had a religious conversion, although considerably earlier in life: "that night I gave myself to Jesus in Los Angeles" (448). He continues the disclosure in a profane manner reminiscent of the historical President Nixon of the Watergate tapes: "I had to get up off my ass and move, I had to walk down that aisle" (448).

More significant than the revelation of Nixon being born again in this passage is his account of his present crisis of faith, the context of which has him musing on a train to Ossining (Sing Sing) while an orgy takes place around him and a woman is brutally raped. It is the moment when Coover accords his protagonist, portrayed otherwise as a buffoon, true insight. "This, then, was my crisis: to accept what I already knew. That there was no author, no director, and the audience had no memories—they got reinvented every day! I'd thought: perhaps there is not even a War between the Sons of Light [America] and the Sons of Darkness [the Soviet Union]! Perhaps we are all pretending" (448). He does not follow through on this conviction, but rather—and aided by digestive relief ("farting liberally" [449])—he ponders his way toward accommodation. The woman's rape foreshadows Nixon's own by Uncle Sam in the epilogue—the ritual that confirms his eventual destiny as incarnation of American civil religion.

Nixon also confesses his obsession with Ethel Rosenberg, his jejune fantasies about the naked young Ethel pulling on her panties (180, 220), then of trying to protect her from the firehoses (Freudian phallic images) during a riot (392), and, finally, his masturbatory vision of the aftermath of that rescue, when a grateful Ethel strokes him, speaking loving words cribbed from the historical Rosenberg prison letters (394). Inspired by these reveries, he determines to visit Ethel in her death cell and persuade her to confess—an undertaking eerily like that of actual efforts expended in the New England colonies to get condemned persons to confess and repent before their executions.[15] Through that act, Ethel offering up her deepest secrets to him, he will save her life (Julius is out of the picture) and resolve the state's dilemma of needing to execute someone it would rather compromise and corrupt.

Anal Obsessions

Nixon's obsession with Ethel Rosenberg focuses on her backside, which compulsive regard is just one aspect of the novel's pervasive anality that renders the pathology of public exposure stronger here even than in *The Book of Daniel.* Nixon recalls how during his vice-presidential campaign the *Time* labeling of him as the "Fighting Quaker" was changed in an anonymous parody to the "Farting Quacker," and that in turn reminds him of a leading role he had in a high school play based on *The Aeneid:* He played Aeneas but was soon called "Anus" by his classmates. In chapter 15, narrated by Nixon and entitled "Iron Butt Gets Smeared Again," the vice president relates how on the way to the White House he steps in horse dung, and two chapters later one is given a minute description of Nixon in a White House washroom cleaning his soiled shoe (360).

The imagery turns still more mischievous when Nixon and Ethel embrace in Sing Sing prison. There, in a fog of Oedipal passion ("I smelled Mom's hot pies, felt my fingers moving brilliantly on the organ keys, playing 'My Rosary'" [542]), Nixon fondles Ethel's buttocks and feels "a peace and warmth and brotherhood" (543). As the action escalates ("We patted each other's bottoms" [547]), Ethel pulls him around on his bare backside, trying to remove his tangled trousers, then "seemed to be rubbing something on my behind" (551). "'Your bottom's all filthy,' she explained breathlessly. 'I'm just cleaning it off'" (551). This is the occasion when she writes "I AM A SCAMP" in lipstick on his buttocks for the Times Square crowd to read—an act reminiscent of the time when the teenage Ethel and other girls dragged a truck driver from his cab as he attempted to drive through a picket line, "stripped him bare, and lipsticked his butt with I AM A SCAB" (377). It inspires a proleptic sensation in Nixon: "My own butt tingled with the thought of it" (377).

Uncle Sam is just as obsessed. Early on, when the Soviets set off their first atom bomb, he shouts *"I been hit by a pooper"* (17) and later during a preexecution diatribe at Times Square he indulges in folksy anal-scatological humor. At the climactic moment, when Nixon appears sans trousers onstage and inspires the raucous crowd to take off their pants, Sam appears and very deliberately drops his own trousers.[16] "There was a blinding flash of light, a simultaneous crack of ear-splitting thunder, and then—BLACKOUT!! (601). It is at once a play on atomic bomb detonation and an explosion of pent-up federal flatulence transformed into divine afflatus, and either way it provokes the crowd's mass orgy that precedes the double execution.

Nixon and Sam together generate anal moments. A portentous one occurs when Sam, in the midst of a harangue, takes a cigar from Nixon's office refrigerator, lights it, and has it explode in his face (419). Sam is furious at being made the butt, as it were, of this displaced flatulation, and Nixon fears that he may have blown his chance at the presidency. Yet it is precisely an anal act that ordains him for that office: In the epilogue Sam sodomizes Nixon, rapes him anally, and Nixon recognizes painfully the ritual by which aspirers have been propelled into the highest office as "incarnation" of Uncle Sam.

Carmichael argues, fairly ponderously, that "the book-long fascination with buttocks . . . prepares for the book's resolution of the sexual and gendered ambiguities and oppositions . . . emphasizing . . . the inextricable implications of sex, gender, and politics."[17] One can do better than that, I believe, by recalling Coover's interest in making *The Public Burning* a circus novel composed by the citizenry: "I was striving for a text that would seem to have been written by the whole nation through all its history. . . . I wanted thousands of echoes, all the sounds of a nation."[18] If many of the nation's sounds turn out to be breaking wind, that is to be expected because Nixon himself, the "Farting Quacker," is deployed as a clown.[19] This multivocal, boisterous, circuslike book is a fitting example of the dialogic, Rabelaisian novel that Bakhtin describes in which public exposure, often connected to anal and scatological humor, is prominent.

The real circus is a place of spectacle where clowns are public figures exposed to ridicule, usually through the extremes of low humor, for the amusement of the spectators. During the time of the historical Rosenberg affair the nation watched the "circus" of the trial and its aftermath, absorbed (and often scandalized) by the humiliation of the doomed couple. In *The Public Burning* the tables are partially turned. Here the nation itself fills the rings of the circus, led by its public figures as buffoons—not only Nixon himself caught with his pants down in front of thousands (an image that anticipates the historical President Nixon's exposure in the Watergate affair) but also the dignified Supreme Court justices slipping and sliding in (Republican) elephant dung (572). It is "the whole nation . . . falling on its ass" (449); the huge crowd in Times Square, along with the vice president, drops its pants "FOR GOD AND COUNTRY" and "FOR JESUS CHRIST" (597–98), and it is that vast mob that, after Sam's explosion douses the lights, engages in a superorgy. During this time the Rosenbergs awaiting their execution are relegated to the role of bystander.

In Coover's fantastic vision the nation not only speaks and writes the novel but also acts out the shameful ritual that its politicians and justice system forced on the historical Rosenbergs. But who is affected by this excess of imagination? The vice president and president, the Supreme Court justices, and many other figures belittled in the novel's anal-scatological orgy of public exposure are not really the historical figures; if they were, Nixon and others might well have sued. But they—and we—are free to ignore it all, to leave it as the fiction it is.

Coover's Transgressions

The fact that *The Public Burning* exists, that it was reviewed and continues to be written on (even though it is long out of print), indicates how it has become a part of and helps to constitute the public realm. Like the Times Square crowd, readers can comprehend themselves as both voyeur and exhibitionist. Insofar as we buy into Coover's fiction that the nation has composed the novel, we are those showing off in it as well as those showed off. Insofar as we reject that fiction (as would Podhoretz and a host of others), we still are implicated in its challenge to convention and morality. In crossing the line, in transgressing standards of decency and good taste, and in breaking taboos, the novel invites condemnation, disgust, outrage, and rejection. It also invites reflection on why one of America's best novelists would devote many years to composing a text bound to incite such reactions. The reasons are moral and (Coover's "weakness") theological. Nixon and the Rosenbergs as historical personages finally do not matter, but what they have been made to mean as events for the country matters very much indeed.

In bringing together Nixon and the Rosenbergs, *The Public Burning* offers an interpretation of American public life that is ultimately moral and theological or in a broad sense religious. The hermeneutical problem is laid out in an intentional historical inaccuracy: Nixon and the Rosenbergs had, in real life, little to do with each other. If this is so, why does Coover make them crucially interact, especially Nixon and Ethel Rosenberg? The reason is that both become unwitting incarnations of evil.

Coover's theological bent exercises itself in his play with incarnation. Perhaps in a fiction of carnival (ultimately denying the flesh), the counterpart of incarnation (enfleshment, embodiment) is also to be anticipated. The context of incarnation is actually broader than that in the novel. On a mythic-folkloric level, where the text functions as a morality fiction, Uncle Sam as incarnation of Western Christian values embodies goodness, whereas the Phantom (who appears only once—perhaps—as the diabolical taxi driver with Nixon in the cab) as incarnation of Eastern atheist values incorporates evil. These simplistic identifications are, of course, played off against each other in the international struggle of freedom-democracy-Christianity versus enslavement-communism-atheism or, in the language of pop ideology, Americanism versus communism.

The anonymous narrator as well as Nixon in the chapters he relates understands the American presidents as "Incarnations" of Uncle Sam, although Sam himself is also on hand to guide things in the crises, and it is mainly Sam who rants about Armageddon to provoke Nixon into imagining the future in apocalyptic terms. In this view the Rosenbergs are the instruments of a cataclysmic evil, "the very trigger . . . for the ultimate holocaust" (417). Yet the novel's plot works ironically against that view and demonstrates how American goodness turns evil and victimizes helpless (if not innocent) persons in order to maintain the old mythic dichotomy. Nixon the bumbling clown is also introspective. He suspects that the Rosenbergs are being framed yet succumbs to ambition and is coopted by Uncle Sam, making his projected incarnation as future president simultaneously a descent into evil.

The path from Nixon's "innocence" to his being raped by Sam to mark his future incarnation, along with the events taking place concurrently that result in the couple's executions, is developed as a ritual with religious, even sacramental, trappings. Yet it is a ritual that does not bring forth the blessings or presence of a benevolent deity but rather an explosion of wickedness. Carmichael thinks that "Coover . . . reads the immediate postwar period as an extreme example of the theological, mythological, ritualistic, and violent scapegoating (projective) nature of political order keeping in history" and calls attention to a "relative absence of female voices" in this "outrageous parody of the hegemonic American Manifest Destiny Man's World in the formative stages of the cold war."[20] Cope likewise stresses "this world of masculine energy without women. . . . As Nixon becomes the Incarnation, he has to reembrace the American Myth of continuities, of fathers and sons who, because they are Doppelgängers, need no mothers."[21] He has "forgotten all the things my Mom taught me: Don't make a fool of yourself, Richard, don't stick your neck out . . . don't expose yourself" (584). Later, after the orgy but before his initiatory sodomizing, Nixon thinks, "Maybe . . . this is what hell will be like for me: endless self-exposure" (652). He finds himself Jonah-like inside the huge maw of a whale, a Disney exhibit, and in this both womblike and threatening enclosure he longs for his mother but encounters his stern Quaker grandmother Milhaus instead, who acts—too late—as his superego (652–53).

Precisely because the women in these traditional roles are ineffective in this ritualized world of male violence, Ethel Rosenberg emerges as the female victim (Julius is effaced in the process). Her sacrifice by no means saves the country from itself but it does become a counterincarnation, an ephemeral embodiment of what the nation should be, its alternate self, its other. "Her body, sizzling and popping like firecrackers, lights up with the force of the current, casting a flickering radiance on all those around her, and so she burns—and burns—and burns—as though held aloft by her own incandescent will and haloed about by all the gleaming great of the nation" (640–41).

Ethel's death, the surreal scene of which concludes the novel proper (followed by the epilogue), illuminates the evil of the nation that has conspired to kill her and her husband. As Uncle Sam confesses (while raping Nixon), it was necessary to execute them in order to hold the community together (657); yet the nation confirms its own evil by casting the Rosenbergs as the incarnation of evil. During the mass orgy Nixon finds himself briefly sitting on the electric chair that has just killed the Rosenbergs, still slick from their excretions, and it is an apt site for suggesting the punishment that he deserves. In his complicity he loses his identity as "singled out, touched by a special kind of grace, a unique destiny. I was God's undercover agent in a secular world" (631). He becomes instead Nick's son, brood of the devil.

The rape that confirms his election to wickedness is foreshadowed by the vicious gang rape that occurs on the train with Nixon as passenger. He sees it but does not intervene, so absorbed in working out his own plans that the violence barely registers. Had he been alert and compassionate he might have projected and hence avoided his own violation. But by then that violation is what he desires. On his hands and knees and buggered by the system that has taken him over—that is his "theological position."[22]

In his *New York Times* review of *The Public Burning* Thomas Edwards comprehends Sam's strategy of killing the Rosenbergs: "The public figures . . . [and] the scared populace . . . so badly want to be reunified through ritual bloodshed."[23] Edwards sees too that the novel finally, even though written from the vantage point of Nixon's post-presidency, has little to do with the historical Nixon or the Rosenbergs. They are a point of reference and departure. "Coover brilliantly reconstructs a historical figure into a fictional one in order, I judge, to comment on too simply 'personal' an idea of history. The evident villains of the part . . . aren't the sources of evil but its agents, dupes, or victims; the evil is us, the aimless determination of a people to be up and doing something—anything—to assert our being and its power, rather than to have to know too clearly what we are, and why."[24] That assessment, written in 1977, is even more telling near the end of the century. As Edwards concludes, *The Public Burning* for all its excesses is "an extraordinary act of moral passion."[25] It is that above all because, taking the path of excess, it exposes the foundational excess of civil religion. Coover's "weakness" for theology asserts itself as his prophetic gift.

Notes

1. Richard Trenner, ed., *E. L. Doctorow, Essays and Conversations* (Princeton: Ontario Review Press, 1983), 183; Tom LeClair, *The Art of Excess: Mastery in Contemporary American Fiction* (Urbana: University of Illinois Press, 1989), 106.

2. Norman Podhoretz, "Uncle Sam and the Phantom," *Saturday Review,* September 17, 1977, 34.

3. Tom Paulin, "Fantastic Eschatologies," *Encounter* 39 (September 1978): 78; Paul Gray, "Uncle Sam Takes on the Phantom," *Time,* August 8, 1977, 70–71. An example of the heated rhetoric that Coover spoofs appears in *Time,* April 16, 1951, 23: "It was a sickening and, to Americans, almost incredible history of men [Fuchs, Gold, Greenglass, et al.] so fanatical that they would betray their own countries and colleagues to serve a treacherous Utopia. The . . . FBI had reported no successful atomic spying since mid-1946. Considering the damage already done, the nation could only hope the FBI was right."

4. See Richard Andersen, *Robert Coover* (Boston: G. K. Hall, 1981), 117, for an account of how *The Public Burning* grew out of "The Cat in the Hat for President."

5. Frank Gado, *First Person: Conversations with Writers and Writing* (New York: Union College, 1973), 154.

6. See Virginia Carmichael, *Framing History: The Rosenberg Story and the Cold War* (Minneapolis: University of Minnesota Press, 1993), 157–58, for an account of the publishing history of *The Public Burning.*

7. Walter Clemons, "Shock Treatment," *Newsweek,* August 8, 1977, 75.

8. Jackson I. Cope, *Robert Coover's Fictions* (Baltimore: Johns Hopkins University Press, 1986), 69. The citation from Coover was communicated directly to Cope, who (70–71) treats *The Public Burning* in terms of Robert N. Bellah's writing on civil religion in *Beyond Belief: Essays on Religion in a Post-Traditional World* (New York: Harper and Row, 1970).

9. LeClair, *The Art of Excess,* 109.

10. Cope, *Robert Coover's Fictions,* 76.

11. Gado, *First Person,* 154.

12. LeClair, *The Art of Excess,* 114.

13. See Cope, *Robert Coover's Fictions,* 68, for the development of the circus imagery.

14. Ibid., 72, treats *The Public Burning* in Bakhtinian terms, citing Mikhail Bakhtin, *Rabelais and His World,* trans. H. Iswolsky (Cambridge: MIT Press, 1968). For sound interpretation of Bakhtin see also Walter L. Reed, *Dialogues of the World: The Bible as Literature According to Bakhtin* (New York: Oxford University Press, 1993).

15. David D. Hall reports on such efforts to secure confession and repentance from condemned persons in the New England colonies in *Worlds of Wonder, Days of Judgment: Popular Religious Belief in Early New England* (Cambridge: Harvard University Press, 1990). For example, "The crucial moment in the [execution] ceremony was the scaffold speech in which the prisoner confessed to his crime and begged for mercy" (7).

16. Uncle Sam exposing himself so spectacularly is not unlike the drama of YHWH appearing to Moses in Exodus 33:18–23.

17. Carmichael, *Framing History,* 184.

18. Robert Coover and Larry McCaffrey, "Robert Coover on His Own and Other Fictions," in *Novel vs. Fiction: The Contemporary Reformation,* ed. Jackson I. Cope and Geoffrey Green (Norman: University of Oklahoma Press, 1981), 59. Such "thousands of echoes" were heard at public executions in colonial New England. In *Worlds of Wonder, Days of Judgment* Hall reports on one such event as related by Samuel Sewall in Boston (the numbers in parentheses refer to page numbers in *The Diary of Samuel Sewall*): "Beforehand, people jammed into a meetinghouse to view the condemned as they listened to their final sermon (1:99). Going to the Common once when pirates he had helped to apprehend were being executed, Sewall was astonished by the crowd: 'the River was cover'd with People' packed aboard at least a hundred boats. The sound effects were equally remarkable: 'When the Scaffold was let sink, there was such a Screech of the Women that my wife heard it sitting in our Entry next the Orchard' on the other side of town (1:509)" (215–16).

19. LeClair, *The Art of Excess,* 117. Coover has said, "My interest in Nixon— or my story about him—grew out of my concept of the book as a series of circus acts, bringing the show back down to the ground. You have a thrilling high-wire number, and then the clown comes on, shoots off a cannon, takes a pratfall, drops his pants and exits. And then you can throw another high-wire act at them. So naturally I looked for the clownish aspects of my narrator, and you can't have an unsympathetic clown." Quoted in Geoffrey Wolff, "An American Epic," *New Times,* August 19, 1977, 54.

20. Carmichael, *Framing History,* 161, 160.

21. Cope, *Robert Coover's Fictions,* 112.

22. In Coover's collection of plays, *A Theological Position* (New York: E. P. Dutton, 1972), the title play features a priest, a man, and his wife who, the couple claim, will bring forth the second virgin birth in human history. The priest states the impossibility of this event as the church's "theological position." Eventually, the priest copulates with the woman (who also possesses a talking *vagina dentata*), accuses her of witchcraft, and finally murders her.

23. Thomas R. Edwards, "People, Mythic History," *New York Times Book Review,* August 14, 1977, 9.

24. Edwards, "People, Mythic History," 26.

25. Ibid.

PART 2

The Body Erotic

5

Erotic Bodies
as Sites of Faith

A great sexual sermon—which has had its subtle theologians
and its popular voices—has swept through our societies over
the last decades.

—Michel Foucault, *The History of Sexuality*

It might be better to treat a problem in a family as a poem than
to deal with it as a psychological disorder.

—Thomas Moore, *Soul Mates*

The ordeal of the Rosenbergs provoked a literary response from three
prominent writers, each of whose texts invites commentary from a religious perspective that critics of the event and of the literature it inspired
have largely ignored. The structure and content of Miller's play and the
novels by Doctorow and Coover can be read as disclosures of a dynamic
of accusation and confession and a dramatized reflection on the nature
of evil as well as on a sociopathology of public exposure. Three charac-
teristics of a politicized public realm, permeated by a reflexive religiosity
and a governmental exploitation of that religious reflex, are, first, a need
by those in power to designate victims (met by a certain willingness of
persons to be victimized); second, a desire by those in control to locate
evil in and as the other, usually some foreign or alien entity (countered
by the other's ascription of evil to the accuser himself); and third, an often prurient drive by those governing to put the victims on display, humiliate them, and thus render them nonthreatening (aided by exhibitionistic impulses by those publicly exposed). This public sphere is constituted
as an arena of neurotic and psychotic, often violent, social interaction
through which a society survives: practicing periodic rituals, however unjustly ordered and executed, of excessive behavior and "cleansing."

In the following four chapters I have no single event such as the Rosenberg affair to offer as a focal point. Although certain events with national resonance come to mind, such as the suicide of Marilyn Monroe in 1964

and the Branch Davidian cataclysm of Waco in 1993, none carries the momentousness of the Rosenberg case, and none has—as yet—been taken up in equally profound ways by fiction writers, at least in ways that seriously engage the religious imagination.

This does not mean that the sexual dimensions of the public realm have been less instrumental in the national consciousness and behavior than the specifically political aspects. They imbricate the political, for instance as represented by the fictional Richard Nixon's lust for Ethel Rosenberg in Coover's fantasy—a lust that stands for the erotic qualities of the dangerous and threatening other. In the chapters that follow I want to enable the full force of the sexualized public realm to emerge and to connect the "body politic" to the "body erotic." One could write a history of this latter body, a history of American sexuality that describes the interaction of normally (or at least traditionally) private and personal sexual activity and its public expressions, including everything from attempts to regulate and legislate such activity to the use and exploitation of it in education, entertainment, and merchandising. Versions of such a history have been composed, for example, the competent *Intimate Matters: A History of Sexuality in America* by John D'Emilio and Estelle Freedman.[1]

What I have in mind is less encompassing and more incidental. I comment on six texts—five novels and a play—that illustrate what I mean by the "sexual body" or the body erotic or "embodied sexuality" and that show how that body, at once a private and public affair, holds intercourse with the institutions of family, church and convent, school, commerce, health and welfare organizations, and the judicial system. Although previous chapters concerned an actual incident of alleged treason—a couple accused of providing information on nuclear weaponry to the enemy—these texts are representative incidents of love relationships (courtship, marriage, betrayal, and family dynamics), procreation (pregnancy, giving birth, and abortion), and bodily harm (one way or another sexualized in rape, infanticide, mate abuse, and mutilation). They are representative in other ways, too: Four of the six are by women, the two by men are about women, and all but one were published during the last two decades. The single exception is a rediscovery of a 1928 novella that was republished in 1986. I have excluded major works on the American sexual body: No Henry Miller, no Faulkner's *As I Lay Dying*, no Mary McCarthy, and no John Updike. I have also excluded such sexual fetishists as William Burroughs and Kathy Acker and do next to nothing with fiction that incorporates the significant issues of homosexuality, AIDS, the pornography industry, and censorship.

The major novelists of three-quarters of this century, most of them men, have remarkably little to say about the sexual body as I define it (although plenty to say about male-oriented sex). In any case, before the sixties the "morality" of publishing fiction permitted little explicit description of sexual behavior, and such writing as was published "underground" did not exert a strong influence on the private or public sexual realms. A lack of texts that have a religious motif prevents me from discussing such issues as homosexual relationships and the impact of AIDS as these inhabit our literature. Recent drama, such as Tony Kushner's *Angels in America* and Terrence McNally's *A Perfect Ganesh,* however, suggests that this emphasis is gathering strength among playwrights.[2]

The six texts I will interpret are John Pielmeier's play *Agnes of God* (1979), Ron Hansen's *Mariette in Ecstasy* (1991), Mary Gordon's *The Company of Women* (1980), Toni Morrison's *Beloved* (1987), which I will discuss in conjunction with Nella Larsen's *Quicksand* (1928, 1986), and Elizabeth Dewberry Vaughn's *Many Things Have Happened since He Died* (1990). These range from a "lost" novel (Larsen's) to a first novel by Vaughn to fiction by the celebrated artists Morrison and Gordon. Why these texts? All of them treat embodied sexuality in ways that depict the American reluctance to acknowledge the body, especially its sexual nature, and the concomitant—and growing—insistence on the centrality of the body.

The concept of embodied sexuality is redundant insofar as sexual experience takes place in and through bodies. Yet the attempts throughout the course of Western history to isolate "sinful" sex by denigrating the body and subjugating it to the "higher" authority of the mind have succeeded in presenting sex as curiously *dis*embodied, consisting mainly of the genitals and their copulation or as articulated in languages of desire. Ironically, visual pornography of the late twentieth century, rather than returning sex to the body, aids in its disembodiment by focusing on what become fetishized body parts—breasts, vaginas, penises, and recta—and thus contributes to the felt fragmentation of persons and groups. The six texts of embodied sexuality explore the ways in which sex and the body attempt to unite and reunite, ways in which the eroticized or reeroticized body expresses itself against the opposition of the puritan and consumerist champions of disembodiment.

This conflict between the expression and suppression of the sexual body occurs in and even constitutes a public realm in these fictions; the public sphere becomes sexualized, often against the wishes of those inhabiting it. In many of the plots some revelation concerning the sexual body seems to be at hand that excites and threatens the whole community and reflects the historical anxiety-ridden attraction-repulsion that has unsettled the American experience with sex. That sense of impending revelation and the ambivalence about it are always frustrated by mystery and by writing that resists decisive interpretation and closure. The mystery in these plots is both religious and sexual, often conflating the two, and the authors abet the mystery by denying the reader clues to a conclusive, unambiguous close reading. In this manner, through fashioning "difficult" texts—"saying the unsayable" as Ron Hansen puts it—the writers dramatize our bafflement in coming to terms, individually and communally, with the sexual body and its religious reflexes.[3]

Is the bafflement as profound as the fiction suggests? The last issue of *The Christian Century* of 1993 listed its "top ten religion stories" of the year. The first three were "sexual abuse in the church," "apocalypse in Waco," and "conflict on sexual ethics." The first of these refers to sexual abuse practiced on adolescents by Catholic clergy; the second to the disaster of the Branch Davidian sect, whose leader David Koresh tragically confused sexual and religious behavior; and the third to "sharp divisions over sexual ethics, and especially over the understanding of homosexuality."[4] Among the other top stories were number four, "the Religious Right acts locally," which among other things involved "conservative evangelicals" advocating "teaching sexual abstinence rather than the use of condoms to prevent AIDS"; number five, "medicine at the poles of life," having to do with "the first laboratory replication of human embryos— an experiment that presented a formidable ethical challenge"; number seven on "the Religious Freedom Restoration Act" passed in the fall of 1993 by Congress after having languished for two years "because of opposition from the Roman Catholic bishops, who were concerned that the bill might be used to claim a religious right to abortion"; and number nine, on "women in the church," which focused on the controversy over the ordination of women as clergy. Whether or not all would agree with *The Christian Century* that these are among the most important news stories in religion for that year, certainly they figured prominently and indicate how aspects of embodied sexuality permeate American secular and religious politics—which are themselves, in spite of the constitutional church-state separation, in fateful embrace.

The next chapter concerns three works set in a Roman Catholic context and portraying eroticized bodies in tension with traditional Catholic suppression of sexual activity apart from procreative purposes: Pielmeier's *Agnes of God,* Hansen's *Mariette in Ecstasy,* and Gordon's *The Company of Women.* The following chapter treats two works that depict the sexual body in African American communities, for the most part reacting to a heritage of enslavement and continuing oppression: Larsen's *Quicksand* and Morrison's *Beloved.* The final chapter of this section concerns a novel that explores the life, especially the marriage, of a fundamentalist young woman much at odds with her body as well as with the conflicting demands of her church and her secular society: Vaughn's *Many Things Have Happened since He Died.*

Although five of these texts are recent, "postmodern" compositions, three are set in an older era: Morrison's occurs during the early postbellum period, mostly in the 1870s; Hansen's is set in 1906; and Larsen's work is contemporaneous with the time of its creation, the 1920s. Thus the six works span some twelve decades of American life, from the 1870s (actually the 1850s, which are part of *Beloved*'s setting) to the 1980s, yet from the vantage point of the late twentieth century. They offer the advantage of a virtual double perspective: the imaginatively recreated American past seen through the eyes of the present.

Seduced, Abused, Abandoned

My emphasis on recent fiction does not alter the fact that its agenda, in terms of sexual embodiment, was already announced by two American novels of the mid-nineteenth century, one of them world famous and one barely known: Nathaniel Hawthorne's *The Scarlet Letter* and Harriet Wilson's *Our Nig*. Hawthorne's classic, published in 1850, comprises the archetypal narrative in simplest terms: of a woman seduced and abandoned. Wilson's *Our Nig*, published in 1859 but virtually unknown until its rediscovery in 1982 by Henry Louis Gates, Jr., is the archetypal story of the abused or abandoned child. These two entwined form the substance of these six modern and postmodern fictions, which, in turn, bring into focus a remarkable number and variety of sexual embodiment and sexualized public realm plots in American writing.

The Scarlet Letter, once required reading in high school and college English courses, in naked summary is soap-operatic—not surprising when one considers the traditions of the sentimental novel, romance, and religious allegory that inform it. In the Puritan community of Salem (the same one of *The Crucible*), the young woman Hester Prynne, having borne a daughter out of wedlock and refusing to name the father, is punished and publicly humiliated by being required to wear a scarlet letter *A* for adultery on her breast. The child's father, the guilt-tormented Reverend Dimmesdale, does not confess his role until, goaded into it by Hester's cold and calculating husband Roger Chillingworth (unbeknown as Hester's spouse to the townspeople), mounts a scaffold in the town square, confesses dramatically (tearing open his shirt to reveal—perhaps—a scarlet *A* branded on his chest), and dies.

Our Nig, rescued from oblivion by Gates, is an autobiographical novel in the sentimental fiction tradition by an African American woman who lived in Massachusetts and was one of the first two black women to publish a novel in any language.[5] That woman, Harriet E. Wilson, endured misfortunes perhaps as grim as those she describes for her protagonist Frado, a mulatto who is abandoned by her white mother and sent to toil as an indentured servant in the white Bellmont household, where she is abused by the racist Mrs. Bellmont and her equally bigoted daughter over the objections of the other family members. Wilson in her disarming preface reveals that she wrote the novel to earn some money to support herself and her ailing young son, deserted by the husband and father. At the end of the narrative (against the happy ending convention of the sentimental novel), Frado, abandoned again, this time by her husband, seeks to survive with *her* son by making and trying to sell an unnamed "useful article." *Our Nig* is, along with its sentimentality, an exposé of how blacks were treated by the supposedly less prejudiced citizenry of the North, a plot of abandonment and abuse writ large and recovered opportunely in the late twentieth century to mark, retrospectively, an early literary expression of minority social protest.

Seduction, abuse, abandonment: Are such actions at the core of these archetypal novels truly central to the politics of sexual embodiment in American private and public life? They are, and they elicit a number of affective-physical elements that the characters of the six fictions experience in various permutations: shame, pain, awe, and ecstasy. The traditional assumed norm for sexual relationships in America has been the opposite of seduction, abuse, and abandonment. It consists of the courtship that leads to marriage, the mutual nurturing of spouses and their children, and the lifelong monogamous loyalty by which conjugal couples endure and families find their foundations. Yet little of this is celebrated in serious fiction, and where it is the erotic aspects are not emphasized. The stress in American novels has been rather on "abnormal" relationships that, by virtue of their frequency, suggest another kind of paradoxical norm: dysfunctionality.

All of this has been explored in nonliterary critical texts such as the D'Emilio and Freedman volume and in literary studies such as Tony Tanner's *Adultery in the Novel* and Elizabeth Hardwick's *Seduction and Betrayal.*[6] What has not been addressed, apart from a few studies such as Ann-Janine Morey's *Religion and Sexuality in American Literature,* is the pivotal role of religion in these normative dysfunctional relationships as they are dramatized in literature.

At the heart of *Agnes of God, Mariette in Ecstasy,* and *The Company of Women* is the problem of belief. It is a problem in ways that are not in the archetypal fictions of *The Scarlet Letter* and *Our Nig.* In Hawthorne's narrative Dimmesdale and Hester Prynne, for all their passionate rebellion, remain within the confines of traditional Christian faith. It is the acceptance of the truth of Christian doctrine, and the guilt it incites in the minister, that undoes them. Frado in *Our Nig,* on the other hand, as Gates declares, "Never truly undergoes a religious transformation, merely the *appearance* of one," so that her "innocent joy signifies her ironic rejection of Christian religion."[7] But in the texts I discuss, belief is rendered problematic by and for the characters, and in two of them that problem is posed in a manner that urges a particular belief or denial from the reader. In simplest terms, the problematic question in *Agnes of God* and *Mariette in Ecstasy* is for the characters—and reader—to believe or doubt that the protagonist has been seduced and abused (and perhaps abandoned) by God himself, whereas in *The Company of Women* it is the question of whether the immensely influential priest has abused his office in his relationships to the women, believers all, who are spiritually dependent on him.

Ann-Janine Morey turns frequently to the concept of passion to connect religion and sexuality in American fiction and reminds us how erotic desire resembles—is sometimes indistinguishable from—the desire for the excitements and satisfactions of faith. I intend to enlarge the concept of passion through the quartet of elements of shame, pain, awe, and ecstasy to reveal how the sexual body plays out its dance of desire along with the desire to believe and be believed. This enlarged passion is a deeply and widely felt affection among Americans; our conflicted expressions of sexuality are profoundly moved by our struggle to learn and feel what we believe. To put it slightly differently, we have since our inception as a nation (and no doubt before that) tried to codify both sexuality and religious faith, to set the rules and formulas for them both and thus get them under rational control. Yet their very bodiness resists such governance and renders them passionate and problematic.[8]

The literature I will examine is of great value for its depictions of the entanglements of religious and sexual passion and their role in our "desire to love and to be loved" focused on the body in American culture. The prevailing sense that we know all we need to know about passion is nicely illustrated by a southern anecdote about baptism by immersion. "Do you believe in it?" a doubter asks an acquaintance. "Believe in it?" the acquaintance replies, "I've seen it done!" Seeing passion "done" (and it is now displayed publicly more than ever) does not necessarily lead to a comprehension of its complex motions; one needs to appreciate the interplay of its parts.

Notes

1. John D'Emilio and Estelle B. Freedman, *Intimate Matters: A History of Sexuality in America* (New York: Harper and Row, 1988).

2. Terrence McNally's *A Perfect Ganesh* opened off-Broadway in 1993 at the Manhattan Theater Club, and Tony Kushner's *Angels in America, Part One: Millennium Approaches* opened at the Walter Kerr Theatre in New York in the spring of 1993. *Angels in America, Part Two: Perestroika* opened at the Walter Kerr Theatre in New York in the fall of 1993. The scripts of both parts are published by the Theatre Communications Group (New York, 1993, 1994).

3. Ron Hansen, "Writing as Sacrament," *Image: A Journal of the Arts and Religion* 5 (Spring 1994): 57.

4. *Christian Century,* December 22–29, 1993, 1291–93.

5. Harriet E. Wilson, *Our Nig; or, Sketches from the Life of a Free Black,* ed. Henry Louis Gates, Jr. (New York: Vintage Books, 1993), xiii.

6. Tony Tanner, *Adultery in the Novel: Contract and Transgression* (Baltimore: Johns Hopkins University Press, 1979); Elizabeth Hardwick, *Seduction and Betrayal: Women and Literature* (New York: Random House, 1974).

7. Gates, "Introduction," in Wilson, *Our Nig,* xlix.

8. Iris Marion Young, commenting on Julia Kristeva's approach to language and its relevance to theories of communicative action, observes, "It entails that communication is not only motivated by the aim to reach consensus, a shared understanding of the world, but also and more basically by a desire to love and be loved" (107). Young's argument and evocation of Kristeva are in a chapter entitled "Impartiality and the Civic Public" in her *Throwing Like a Girl and Other Essays in Feminist Philosophy and Social Theory* (Bloomington: Indiana University Press, 1990). Here she also takes issue with Jürgen Habermas and his theory of communicative action, complaining that Habermas in his search for consensus ignores the role of the body and of affectivity. For Young, "Julia Kristeva's conception of speech provides a more embodied alternative to that proposed by Habermas" (106). Young has in mind Kristeva's by-now familiar concept of the semiotic, which "names the unconscious, bodily aspects of the utterance, such as rhythm, tone of voice, metaphor, word play, and gesture" (106).

6

Sisterhood and Sex: *Agnes of God,* *Mariette in Ecstasy,* and *The Company of Women*

> And again Continence seemed to say, "Close your ears to the
> unclean whispers of your body, so that it may be mortified. It
> tells you of things that delight you, but not such things as the
> law of the Lord your God has to tell."
>
> —Saint Augustine, *Confessions*

Agnes of God: Between Mother and Virgin

The popularity of John Pielmeier's drama *Agnes of God* indicates the willingness of the theater-going public to tolerate religious and even theological themes, at least if they are enlivened by a sex scandal, pop psychology, and infanticide.[1] Its first performance at the 1980 Festival of New American Plays in Louisville was not auspicious in the opinion of *Newsweek* reviewer Jack Kroll, who called it "the festival's one real failure," because "Pielmeier hasn't done the hard thinking and deep feeling necessary to earn validity and power for his theme."[2] Nevertheless, Norman Jewison in the introduction to the novelized version could report in 1985 that the play had been "translated into seven languages and performed in fourteen countries," and Jewison himself was sufficiently impressed to produce a Hollywood film version in 1985.[3]

The name in the title refers to Sister Agnes, a twenty-one-year-old nun in a remote convent (in the film version it is the Little Sisters of Mary Magdalene in the province of Quebec). Agnes has given birth to a child in the convent following a pregnancy known only, we learn later, to Mother Superior Miriam Ruth, who, we also discover later, is the elder sister of Agnes's dead mother and thus Agnes's aunt. The baby is found in a wastebasket in Agnes's room, strangled by its umbilical cord, and Agnes stands accused of killing it. Enter Dr. Martha Livingstone, court-appointed psychiatrist and lapsed Catholic who hates the church because her younger sister Marie, a nun, died from a burst appendix and lack of medical care in a convent.

In a series of scenes with Agnes, usually in the presence of Mother Miriam and sometimes with the young nun under hypnosis, Livingstone learns of Agnes's adolescent suffering from an abusive mother, sees her stigmata (bleeding hands), and finds out that Mother Miriam was there at the difficult delivery but not when Agnes strangled her baby daughter in order to "give her back to God." Livingstone removes herself from the case, and Agnes is "sent to a hospital . . . where she stopped singing . . . and eating . . . and died" (111).

As is generally the case, such a stark recapitulation does little to convey the art or power of the fiction. For one, the performed play depends strongly on Agnes's near-constant singing, usually Latin liturgy. The play begins and ends (except for a short final scene with Livingstone alone) with Agnes singing. Her voice is so ethereally beautiful—"the voice of an angel" (11)— that it restores the mother superior's waning faith: "One evening . . . I heard a voice and looking up I saw one of our new postulants standing in a window, singing. It was Agnes, and she was beautiful; and all my doubts about God and myself vanished in that one moment" (69).

Agnes's voice, in fact, conveys the shame, pain, awe, and ecstasy that make up the drama's passion. For example, the young woman describes to the psychiatrist a gruesome vision she had as a girl of ten when she first saw the "Lady," a Virgin Mary figure complete with stigmata, who struggles with her (now dead) mother for control over her. The Lady "uses me to sing. It's as if she's throwing a big hook through the air and it catches me under my ribs and tries to pull me up but I can't move because Mummy is holding my feet and all I can do is sing in her voice, it's the Lady's voice, God loves you" (24). Here the singing mediates the girl's suffering and pain and also carries the mystery of her role (as she feels it) as an instrument of divine music. The secular ditty—"Charlie's neat and Charlie's sweet"—that she sings at the end, signaling her breakdown and slide into silence, more than hints at the shame she feels over the pregnancy and childbirth and perhaps over yielding to a lover or a rapist whose existence she consciously denies, insisting on her virginity. Yet that very madness she manifests by singing the "Charlie" song is also her ecstatic retreat to an untouchable innocence beyond rationality.

For the most part, though, Agnes sings Latin liturgies, expressions of public worship, although as she appropriates them they seem to be private and even intimate articulations of her devotion, even if it is God or the Lady singing through her. Such tension of public and private is also the tension of the dramatic plot, just as it has been a primary trait of the relationship of sexuality to the public realm in American life. Although the play seems to be an example of the conflict of two authorities, ecclesial versus secular state, whereby each tries to assert dominion over a weak member (who is essentially a victim), a closer look shows that the dramatic tension operates just as critically within each of the three characters as they struggle to find some equilibrium.

For Agnes, it is not only that her incessant singing buffers the demands of her psychotically puritan (private) mother and the awesomely puritan (public) mother church (the one pulling her down and in and the other up and out), but it is also that a crucial element of the plot, the infanticide she commits, is her way of resolving the unbearable tension between her private sexual and public convent life.[4] In returning the baby "back to God" she tries to regain a sexual "purity," a chasteness that only becomes her complicity with a corrupt world "out there." Indeed, her insistence on her virginity in spite of the pregnancy and birth is already a denial (and perhaps a repression of a rape or an affair) of her sexuality and at the same time a desperate accommodation to it. The ecstasy she seeks madly is to be another, a second, mother of God, to be the instrument of another Incarnation, but when the messiness of the actual birth corrupts that ideal she short-circuits the process and kills the child. Only the psychiatrist's relentless pursuit of the truth makes the postulant face her guilt long enough to be shamed and retreat into her sanctuary of silence and madness.

My Christ, the Mind

Dr. Martha Livingstone the psychiatrist, rationalist though she claims to be, is as conflicted as the young nun. Reviewers have remarked on the similarity of her role to that of the psychiatrist in Peter Shaffer's *Equus.* As T. E. Kalem puts it, "Like the psychiatrist in *Equus,* who was forced to question his reasoned image of civilization vs. the boy's irrational Dionysian passion, the psychiatrist in *Agnes of God* is forced to question her reliance on scientific knowledge vs. Agnes' beatific display of faith."[5] Actually, it is more complicated than that. Livingstone has lost a sister to and through the church, and she holds the church responsible for her death. Livingstone practices and believes in psychiatry, in the power of the rational mind to heal sick minds, so that her encounter with Agnes is both a professional and personal challenge. As she muses early in the play, "I remember waiting to view Marie's body in a little convent room, and staring at those spotless walls and floors and thinking, my God, what a metaphor for their minds. And that's when I realized that *my* religion, *my* Christ, is this. The mind. Everything I do not understand in this world is contained in these few cubic inches. Within this shell of skin and bone and blood I have the secret to absolutely everything" (16). Livingstone's passion is the rational mind; mystery for her is concentrated in what goes on in the brain. She has, for all practical purposes, renounced sex, so her devotion to the mind becomes a kind of chasteness like that of the abstaining nuns—a chasteness that allows her to endure her pain and focus on her cerebral desire.

Yet Livingstone's probing of Agnes's unconscious lets loose her own "Dionysian" yearning, and although she gets at the truth of the murder, she is transformed in the process. Through her encounter with Agnes she regains (or gains for the first time) a sense of mystery that humbles her reliance on reason. She changes her behavior (she stops chain-smoking) and even undergoes a bodily change—she starts menstruating again at age forty-eight, after a three-year hiatus and after a vivid dream of bloody childbirth that leads her to contemplate what motherhood would have meant for her. The brief last act opens with Livingstone alone on stage, and now *she* is singing—not the Catholic liturgy but the "Charlie" song that Agnes has sung in the previous act as the last we hear from her. Among the words that end the play are the questions of the psychiatrist who now, her objectivity gone, tries to understand the events in terms of theodicy: "Why was a child [Agnes] molested, and a baby killed, and a mind destroyed? Was it to the simple end that not two hours ago this doubting, menstruating, non-smoking psychiatrist made her confession? What kind of God can permit such a wonder one as her to come trampling through this well-ordered existence? I don't know what I believe anymore. But I *want* to believe that she was . . . blessed" (111).

The mother superior likewise, in spite of her facade of self-control, suffers deep conflict. She is perhaps more complicit in the infanticide than Agnes herself because she tries to keep the girl's pregnancy hidden from the rest of the convent; she also lies to Livingstone, insisting, until Agnes under hypnosis tells the truth, that she was not present at the delivery. Hence she is more responsible, has more to be ashamed of, than the unstable and visionary Agnes. Mother Miriam, who—before convent life had been married and the mother of two children—fled the secular world's pain, wants to live vicariously through her niece's innocence and thus prefers to believe in the preposterous miracle of a virgin birth over the more obvious probability that the girl was seduced and impregnated. In her effort to maintain Agnes's "mystery" she abets the murder of the baby. Yet even when Agnes confesses the deed, Mother Miriam, rather than showing contrition, turns viciously (and surely not in a Christian manner) on Livingstone: "She remembered. And all the time I thought she was some unconscious innocent. Thank you, Dr. Livingstone. We need more people like you to destroy all those lies that ignorant folks like myself pretend to believe. . . . But I'll never forgive you for what you've taken away. . . . You should have died. Not your sister" (108).

Faith Is in the Blood

The question bears repeating, Why was (and is) this manipulative drama so popular, even inspiring a still more manipulative Hollywoodized film version? Pielmeier has articulated what was on his mind when he wrote the play, and his reflections speak to the doubts that still plague a secular America. "The questions I asked myself—are there saints today? miracles? . . . —paralleled, I feared, some kind of personal religious awakening. I had always been spiritually concerned, but for some years had been a member of that set of disenchanteds called lapsed Catholics. . . . I realized that the asking of the questions was enough: that our determined search for *any* solution today has eliminated from our lives the mystery and wonder of the universe around us."[6] Many among those thousands who have seen *Agnes of God*, in other words, may have come to it hoping (along with being titillated by a tabloidesque plot in which a beautiful young nun kills her baby) for straightforward answers to old religious and theological questions but depart frustrated and unnerved, like the psychiatrist and the mother superior, by a new awareness of the timeliness of the questions rather than satisfied by any solution.

They have been upset by a timeliness that has little to do with the pivotal (according to Pielmeier) question of whether a miracle such as a virgin birth is possible. Some critics complained that the play is too evenhanded in its balancing of the possibilities of the miraculous and the normal. Brendan Gill, for example, "found the lack of a possible alternative to divine parenthood disconcerting"; and Pielmeier was apparently undecided as to whether the miraculous should be played as a genuine possibility.[7] In any case he muddles the strategy in the moving scene at the end of act two, where Agnes, having confessed, now succumbs to visions "and speaks simply and sanely" (109). After describing how "for six nights He sang to me," she continues, "And on the seventh night He came to my room and opened His wings and lay on top of me. And all the while He sang."

What "he" sings is not at all ethereal but the ditty, "Charlie's neat and Charlie's sweet, / And Charlie he's a dandy, / Every time he goes to town, / He gets his girl some candy" (109). The scene and the song make it easy to imagine that the naive Agnes in this moment of ecstasy has actually been visited and charmed not by God but by an enterprising young man, and thus we are given a way around the possibility of a virgin birth after all.[8]

Nevertheless, this penultimate scene is also the one in which Agnes shows her bleeding palms, and the display recalls the powerful literal and metaphorical presence of blood throughout the drama. If the play attempts but fails to establish a heuristically disturbing possibility of a miracle for a secular (and "lapsed"?) audience, it may succeed on another level by its evocation of blood.

The literal-metaphoric interplay of the blood trope is not hard to trace. It consists of the blood that accompanies the eruption of Agnes's stigmata, of Agnes's bloodstained sheets that she burns and that hint at her loss of virginity, of the bloodied sheets from the difficult delivery of the child, and of the blood of the psychiatrist's renewed menstruation. In this orchestration of images is a connection between religion, sexual embodiment, and public expression that invites interpretation. One way of reading it is in terms of the vast and intricate symbolic complex of the properties of blood itself, a complex to which audiences surely responded and respond. Blood vivifies; purifies; causes fear, awe, and shame; prompts mystery; and inscribes pain and death. In *Agnes of God* it also signifies the triad of seduction, abuse, and abandonment and prompts a perhaps scandalous counterreading to the reflexive understanding of the girl as a saintly victim. For it is Agnes who by her singing and bloody stigmata charms—"seduces"—the mother superior and the psychiatrist into regarding her as blessed and the carrier of blessing. It is she who kills her baby, following the bloody delivery, to send it back to God and who in that act abuses motherhood as well as any common moral code. And it is she who by this act and the subsequent retreat into insanity abandons those who had drawn strength from her.

The sexual body in *Agnes of God* turns out to be the site on which shame, pain, awe, and ecstasy are reflected back to the audience. Agnes, abused by her mother, seduced, and abandoned, becomes the innocent seducer and abuser who abandons herself to madness. As a creature beyond blame and condemnation she fascinates American audiences still enamored of the myth of American innocence yet troubled by the shameful awareness of blood on our hands. In Agnes as abused and abuser-unto-death, as the one whose sainthood exists only in the attribution of others, as the one whose carnal desire can be expressed only in the "mystery" of divine impregnation, we find a character so mishandled and manipulated that she becomes an archetypal victim valorized into the one who suffers for others. She suffers for religion and science, and not least for science (here represented by psychiatry) as a belief system replacing traditional religious faith, and she does it in ways that captivate Americans: through the struggles with the repression of sexuality in religion and psychology.

She is after all *agnes,* lamb of God, a stock figure of Christian imagery connoting innocence and sacrifice. What American up to a generation ago, of Christian heritage or not, did not understand being washed in the blood of the Lamb? What is compelling about *Agnes of God* is not that it presents, with any serious plausibility, the possibility of a second virgin birth that might inspire the renewed faith of the lapsed. If that plot were to be followed through, one would have to consider that in killing her baby Agnes denies the future to a second Incarnation (and a female savior at that). Rather, the play on a more complex level demonstrates how desire (or passion) permeates institutions and how that drive involves Americans' deeply unresolved attitudes toward religious belief as a vehicle of such desire. The play's last words are the psychiatrist's: "'And I hope that she has left something, some little part of herself with me. That would be miracle enough.' (Silence) 'Wouldn't it'" (111)?

Well?

Mariette in Ecstasy: Public Agon

Whereas *Agnes of God* seeks, and ultimately fails, to dramatize convincingly the possibility of the miraculous, *Mariette in Ecstasy* succeeds. Ron Hansen's exquisite 1991 novel risks more by depending on the embodiment of the affections in lyrical language. Or to put it more sharply (and not altogether fairly to Pielmeier), whereas the play's characters talk about Incarnation, Hansen incorporates the flesh as word. But he is in any case more the postmodernist than Pielmeier, willing to undercut realism by populating his narratives with evil spirits, monsters, and borrowed dreams, as in his acclaimed *Nebraska* story collection.[9] One reviewer remarked that these events are "to remind the reader that life is full of surprises, that the extraordinary dwells next to the mundane."[10] One should not, perhaps, be surprised when *Mariette* concludes with Christ himself whispering to the protagonist, "Surprise me" (179). Pico Iyer, another reviewer, declares that the environs of the novel constitute "a world as close and equivocal as Emily Dickinson's alive with the age-old American concerns of community and wildness, of sexual and spiritual immensities, of transcendence and its discontents," and Hansen himself says that he thought of the plot as involving a nun who "would have a kind of love affair with Jesus."[11]

Much of the power of *Mariette* is in its unfamiliar ordinariness, its depiction of daily life in the upstate New York Convent of Our Lady of Sorrows (home of the Sisters of the Crucifixion) in 1906, its attention to the harsh life of the thirty-odd nuns who live and work there (up at 2 A.M., to bed at 8 P.M.), yet whose privations are lessened by such things as (in the convent's French tradition) wine with dinner, good music, and readings from the works of women mystics. Into this austere yet both serene and charged environment comes the seventeen-year-old postulant Mariette Baptiste. Beautiful, well-off (the daughter of a wealthy widowed physician), and passionate, she exhibits a total devotion to Christ, and her announced desire is to become a saint.

The theme of sainthood pervades the text.[12] Patricia Hampl remarks that Mariette "appears to be modeled in part on Thérèse of Lisieux, the saint known as the Little Flower . . . and like Thérèse, Mariette is an ecstatic."[13] At mealtime the sisters take turns reading to each other from, among other things, Dame Julian of Norwich's *Revelations of Divine Love*, which includes Julian's plea for "three gifts from God: one, to understand his passion; two, to suffer physically while still a young woman of thirty; and, finally, to have as God's gift three wounds" (25). Mariette, not even close to thirty, wants the first two of these herself, and the fragile plot turns on how—and whether—she gets them and the third, the stigmata, authentically as well.

It is clear that Mariette suffers physically—and not just the privations, with the others, of the harsh convent life, but more severe pain. We know from some passages that she scalds and lacerates herself (70, 103), and whether her Christlike wounds in hands, feet, and side are true stigmata or self-inflicted, they obviously cause her agony. It is the matter of the stigmata that provokes the greatest controversy over Mariette inside the convent, and outside as well, and that eventually brings on her dismissal. After Sister Céline, who is the prioress and Mariette's older sister (by twenty years), dies of cancer, Mariette appears to break out sporadically in bleeding. Viewed by some as singled out and blessed, she is considered a fraud by others. She claims that although she prayed to share Christ's pain she did not request his wounds, and she professes to be confused by them. When a physician, her father, inspects the sites of her wounds and finds them unaccountably vanished she is pronounced a deceiver and sent home.

Whether or not one chooses to accept the wounds as true stigmata or chicanery—and Hansen makes it thoroughly undecidable—the stress on pain leads one to inquire into the role of physical pain in private and communal religious practice. Mariette claims to welcome the pain as an intensity of feeling that brings her closer to Christ. Indeed, she defines the pain of her wounds as a gift from Christ that is an earnest of their intimacy. When her father's examination reveals no sign of the stigmata, she explains, "Christ took back the wounds" and, soon after, "Christ let me keep the pain" (173, 175). Carolyn Walker Bynum in her studies of late-medieval women mystics argues that their often spectacular obsession with physical pain and its symbolic relation to Christ's passion allowed them a heightened sense of participation in Christ's redemptive suffering, provided them a worthy role in a civilization that denigrated women, and offered them tangible experience of eros in a life otherwise devoid of it. In Bynum's words, "Both male and female saints regularly engaged in what modern people call self-torture—jumping into ovens or icy ponds, driving knives, nails or nettles into their flesh, whipping or hanging themselves in elaborate pantomimes of Christ's Crucifixion."[14] Is Mariette a throwback to those gothic aspirers to sainthood? In a way, she is. Although a good five to seven hundred years have passed since those days and those efforts, and although a great deal about Western views of the body has changed, Mariette in the early twentieth century uses self-laceration, perhaps stigmata, and certainly pain in medieval ways. She seeks to reestablish an older material-spiritual relationship to the body that in our era is considered at least troublesome, usually implausible, and often scandalous—if indeed she is not practicing a skillful deception.

Yet assuming for the moment that she is not dissembling and that her self-torture (she pierces herself with rabbit wire and plunges her hands in scalding water) is meant as honestly as that of those medieval Christians, one could argue that her actions are merely an excessive application of the convent norms: The nuns are expected to endure the discomforts of cold, little sleep, hard physical labor, and fasting as a discipline that frees their minds of worldly concern. The order stresses a life of bodily denial, if not outright mortification, as a means of purifying the sisters for the experience of Christ. Yet when Mariette attempts to intensify and accelerate the process, she is thought prideful and self-serving by some in her community. Among the Sisters of the Crucifixion, paradoxically, too much discipline must be disciplined.

Christ and the Culture of Pain

We can ask a question at this point similar to the one asked about *Agnes of God* and its reception. Why would a postmodern novelist choose to write about an early twentieth century teenage would-be saint, and why has his text been—for a serious novel about religion—so widely read? One answer has to do with the entangled roles of religion and the body in the evolution of a new "economy" of pain. David B. Morris in *The Culture of Pain* identifies one aspect of his agenda as examining the "modern denial of pain—through pills, narcotics, alcohol, pornography, televised violence, social isolation, and the endless pursuit of youth and pleasure."[15] It is such aspects of the modern denial of pain that reveal the significance of pain while disguising its religious dimensions.

Putting it like this suggests that there has been an old culture of pain in the West, and of course there has, diffuse as it has been. It has had many manifestations, most of them religiously determined: early Greek Dionysian *sparagmos;* Roman blood lust indulged in religious festivals and public spectacles; the uses of pain in medieval and Renaissance Christianity (in the orders, in the Inquisition); the civilizations based on public blood sacrifice on the American continent (and their painful eradication by the European conquerors); the harshness of theocratic colonial life in the New World; and the unspeakable cruelties inflicted on each other by Christian white invaders and Native American defenders. Should all this (and more) not have left an imprint on the American psyche? It could not be otherwise. In the secularizing twentieth century, though, we have treated ourselves to the illusion of great progress in moving beyond pain through vastly improved medical technology (not least advances in anesthetics) and the seeming rise of comfortable and often luxurious living—ignoring the increasing suffering of an underclass and the brutalizing of everyday public life.

Hansen's depictions of a precocious teenager's bodily travails in a serene and isolated convent provide a contrast to our current public (and not so public) practices of pain. Recent memory encompasses the Holocaust, the devastation of aerial bombardment in many wars, and the atrocities of Vietnam. We recognize the continuing key role of rape and torture by so-called civilized governments in their struggles for dominance. In the United States we are forced to admit the dismaying frequency of child and spouse abuse, rampant adolescent violence, the obsession of the entertainment media with portraying mayhem in its grossest forms, and—perhaps harmless, perhaps not—the growth of sadomasochism as a leisure-time diversion and the escalating popularity of scarification and body-piercing.[16]

What characterizes all of these but the last is their peculiar anomie, that they happen or are performed randomly, without reason, capriciously, or with deliberate malice and viciousness for the sake of pleasure. We hear, see, and think more about pain. Thanks to the national and global media coverage, we experience more pain in spite of our sophisticated defenses against it; yet our tolerance for it, at least in others, seems to expand even as our fascination with it does. This is the culture of pain in and as a public realm.

Mariette in Ecstasy offers a contrast: a return of pain with a purpose, or, because much pain these days is inflicted for malignant reasons, the return of pain for a benign purpose. In one of the novel's many striking passages, Mariette seeks to describe to Father Marriott, the priest who serves the convent and is her confessor, a recent vision-trance during prayer:

As I began to meditate on the crucifixion and Christ's own trials in this world I became rapt in thought and I found myself again before Jesus, who was suffering such terrible pain. He was horrible with blood and his breathing was hard and troubled, but his pain had less to do with that than with his human sense of failure, injustice, and loneliness. An unquenchable desire to join him in his agonies took hold of me then, as if I could halve his afflictions by sharing them. . . . Kneeling there below his cross, I saw that blood no longer issued from his wounds, but only flashing light as hot as fire. And all of a sudden I felt a keen hurt as those flames touched my hands and feet and heart. I have never felt such pain before, and I have never been so happy. (129)

The vision of Christ's pain that the postulant comes to share (and that has resulted in her stigmata) is symbolically redemptive, not in the sense of soul-saving but in helping her relieve the world's pain by assuming some of it herself. What Mariette experiences ecstatically, and in terms of Christ's symbolic blood sacrifice, is a sensible and practical project; moreover, it is as old as religious reflexivity itself: to share the world's suffering. But the world seems unable to share its pain in any broad redemptive sense. Its citizens seem bent more on spreading and intensifying suffering than in relieving it, and why this is so is reflected in the nature of Mariette's ecstasy that is her downfall. Very simply, Mariette, whether a fraud or on the verge of sainthood, finds compassion through passion. Some of that passion lies in her eagerness to join Christ in his agony: her vision is of the crucifixion and of those marks of the Passion per se. But it is also a passion of urgent erotic desire.

Transcendent Sexuality

This ardor offends the sisters—some of them, at least—and unnerves the old priest. Other nuns are infatuated with Mariette and display various degrees of adoration even before she becomes, as a result of her stigmata, the object of veneration. One senses the omniscient narrator himself (*Is* it a male voice? Could one imagine a woman narrating the tale?) erotically attracted to the protagonist, and some of the text's postmodern complexity consists of double teasing: Mariette teases the other characters, and her actions tease readers, causing them to wonder how sexually "innocent" she really is. Yet her explanation for her behavior is that she herself is teased by Christ.

There is, at the start, some doubt about Mariette's virginity. Although upon her arrival in the convent she is to go "to the infirmarian to prove that you're a virgin" (19), that nun in charge, Sister Aimée, only asks her (after Mariette prompts her) if she is. "Mariette says nothing, and then she says, 'yes'" (22). Later, when other sisters recount a scene of heavy petting they spied out in the fields from the bell tower, Mariette suggests that she might have been the girl involved in her preconvent life. And still later, Sister Marguerite, irritated by Mariette's demeanor, tells her, "And you, my dear sweet child, are a flirt" (70). Most disturbing, though, is the scene late in the novel when sounds of scuffling echo in the middle of the night from Mariette's cell. A sister "hears flesh smack against a wall. She hears hoarse breathing and heaves and hard, masculine effort" on the other side of the locked door (151). Soon after that Mariette is seen "kneeling there on the floor all bruised and red like he'd hit her a hundred times. And her clothes were half off her" (152). An open window in her room (in midwinter) hints at the presence of a rapist or rough lover, but it could just as well have been self-flagellation or a wild nightmare. Compellingly and mysteriously dramatized here is the intricate relationship of pain, sex, and religion, a relationship that the contemporary West grasps only dimly and that thus continues to fascinate.

In balance, however, (if balance has a place in this fiction), the novel's erotic passion is far less directed toward such violence and more toward the girl's ardor for Christ. Not long before Mariette is expelled from the convent a sister snooping in the postulant's room finds hundreds of letters under a floor plank, letters from Mariette about her devotion to Jesus and some of them outright love letters to him. Soon after that, Mariette is encouraged to describe to other nuns an encounter with Jesus in the midst of an ecstatic trance. "Christ tells me to undress," she relates. "And then he gently washes me with his hands. . . . Every word penetrates me as softly as water entering a sponge. . . . When he tells me to sleep, I do so at once, and he holds me. And I share in him as if he's inside me. And he is" (167–68). This is too much for the mother superior (Céline's successor), who has been listening in. "Mother Saint-Raphäel firmly purses her mouth and harshly slaps Mariette's face" (168). A sister's marriage to Christ apparently may not include an imagined sexual dimension.

Yet the novel essentially begins and ends with such expressions of Mariette's bodily surrender to Christ. Shocked as the mother superior is, such expression is in character for the girl. Before she enters the convent she stands naked at home before the mirror. "She esteems her full breasts as she has seen men esteem them. She haunts her milk-white skin with her hands. *Even this I give you*" (9). These sentences are repeated during a similar act near the end of the novel, when Mariette, now forty, has long been gone from the convent but maintains her chaste and erotic faithfulness to Christ.

Bynum mentions historical precedents for Mariette's behavior among medieval women visionaries. For example, "The thirteenth-century poet and mystic Hadewijch spoke of Christ penetrating her until she lost herself in the ecstasy of love." As Bynum continues, in these experiences recorded by such women, "The point is not to provide proof that one woman or a group of women received charismatic gifts so much as to communicate and share a piety in which spiritual-somatic experiences lie at the center."[17] Such piety is flaunted in the novel's most erotic scene, a playlet based on the Song of Songs and performed one evening by Mariette and two of the novices for four other sisters. Mariette is "glamorously" at its center, "her great dark mane of hair in massacre like the siren pictures of Sheba. She's taken her habit and sandals off and shockingly dressed her soft nakedness in a string necklace of white buttons that are meant to seem pearls and red taffeta robe that is like a bloodstain on linen" (82–83).

Mariette plays the role, and Hansen fashions the imagery, that conflates the Song of Song's lover longing for her suitor with the Bride of Christ, and the language she and Sister Geneviève (playing the Bridegroom) borrow is straightforwardly sensual: "Let my Beloved come into his garden, let him taste its precious fruits. . . . Open to me, my sister, my love . . . for my manly head is damp with dew. . . . My Beloved thrust his hand through the opening, and my heart pounded within me" (83–84). Yet at the conclusion Mariette "gets to her knees below Christ on the crucifix, and one by one the novices get on their knees too" (85).

The scene, a miniature public display (that also contains some very funny lines), celebrates a passion for Christ undifferentiated from human desire, and that similarity provides the scene with both its force and its scandal. It challenges the assumption, through a paradoxical innocence conveyed by the girls' daring ("We shouldn't be doing this," Sister Philomene says as she watches), that spiritual love must be "pure," free of sensuality, and asserts that spiritual love thoroughly engages the erotic body rather than rejects it. The powerful evocation of this view that the novel embodies, in good part through its lush language (an apt instance of Kristeva's "semiotic"), may be what mainly attracts its readers: the projection of transcendent sexuality, the opposite of ascetic body negation, always elusive yet the heart of deepest devotion and desire.

A Passion beyond Shame

But the convent as microcosm, although it would seem to be the ideal site for the exercise of somatic spirituality, is no more ready for it than the society surrounding it. As Mariette matures into her sensual, and painful, passion for Christ and seems to evoke his response on her body, the reflex of the convent leadership is to shame her. The new mother superior and certain other nuns stress the traditional (the convent-ional) association of shame and desire and make the postulant pay for her passionate spirituality. The shaming reaches an extreme when she is attacked in bed one night by four figures whom we assume are nuns: "She's fiercely pressed down to the pallaise and miseried by hands. . . . She can't scream or wrestle from the harsh kisses and pressures and hate and insistence. Hands haul her nightgown as high as her thighs and hoist it underneath her haunches. She prays as her knees are held wide. Horrible pictures are put in her head" (143). Although the assault stops at that point, she has, after a fashion, been raped, and it is quite clearly an effort to humiliate her, an abuse of her vibrant sexuality that threatens many in the cloistered community.

But the primary and decisive shaming takes place when Mariette's private ecstatic agony, already the focus of public veneration and opprobrium by the sisters and townspeople, is forced into the open in the examination of her stigmata conducted by her own father, no less, in the presence of Father Marriott, the mother superior, and Sister Aimée. Stripped naked, she endures Dr. Baptiste's probing and his exposure of the fact that she shows no wounds and no scars. As far as her father is concerned, Mariette is a fraud. He convinces the mother superior, and Mariette is sent away from the convent in disgrace.

But even after this shaming the mystery remains. Mariette returns home and lives in her father's house, still there at age forty-eight when the novel concludes. Back in the secular world, she continues her spiritual vocation, her devotional focus, as if she were a nun, and her life remains a combination of sorrow and pain, fulfillment and ecstasy. In the 1937 letter to Sister Philomene (now mother superior) that ends the narrative she relates how she still suffers the gazes of the curious "when I hobble by or lose the hold in my hands," and how sometimes "the Devil tells me the years since age seventeen have been a great abeyance and I have been like a troubled bride pining each night for a husband who is lost without a trace" (179).

Yet she knows the comforts of Passion as well: "Christ still sends me roses"—her stigmata. "We try to be formed and held and kept by him, but instead he offers us freedom. And now when I try to know his will, his kindness floods me, his great love overwhelms me, and I hear him whisper, Surprise me" (179). In this perfectly rendered ending one encounters the mysterious power of language conveying—perhaps creating—mystery itself. The surprise that Christ requests, mischievously, of his lifelong faithful lover, by her confession, is what the novel itself comprises. The text as a whole is an astonishing catachresis, a packed erotic trope that translates into the inexpressible, and a metaphor of mystery that, full of penetrations, at last shows forth its impenetrability.[18]

Like *Agnes of God, Mariette in Ecstasy* is a plot of seduction, abuse, and abandonment, but it is more complex than the play, for Mariette even more than Agnes is a trickster—how advertently we never know. In any case, she is the seducer, generating excessive adoration from the sisters who, for example, daub themselves with her blood (one even licks her wound). She abuses the decorum and the rules of the convent—flagrantly if she has actually duped the sisters, as her father insists. But perhaps most significantly, she is seduced, abused, and abandoned by Christ in this bodily spiritual lovers' tale. It is, though, an acute twist to the usual narrative of seduction that has influenced American fiction via such diverse tales as William Hill Brown's *The Power of Sympathy,* Stephen Crane's "Maggie: A Girl of the Streets," Edith Wharton's *The House of Mirth,* and Flannery O'Connor's "Good Country People." From Mariette's perspective, seduction-abuse-abandonment is not a destructive sequence but a rhythm of redemptive repetition. Christ "seduces" her again and again; his abuse, however pathological, she receives as a sign of their mutual commitment; even his abandoning of her is relieved by influxes of joy. His absence she transforms into his present: his gift, as she puts it, of freedom.

The Company of Women: A Pure Centered Life

Mary Gordon's *The Company of Women* offers an instructive contrast to the Catholic-oriented fictions I have just discussed.[19] Also inhabiting a Catholic sphere, Gordon's 1980 novel emphasizes religion and family and reminds one that *Agnes of God* and *Mariette in Ecstasy* portray religious orders as alternate families into which blood relatives intrude to damage the protagonist. In *The Company of Women,* however, five women without husbands, one of them with a daughter, and an aging priest make up a substitute for the traditional family that is at the same time—and like the situation of the convent novels—a small congregation of worshipers, even a miniature Catholic church. And like those two texts, this one has as its protagonist an impressionable girl who becomes entangled in the intricacies of sex and religion.

Some reviewers, in retrospect, thought *The Company of Women* (1980) inferior to Gordon's highly praised *Final Payments* (1985). Thus for Francine du Plessix Gray it is only the "obstinate refusal to capitulate to the romantic tone [that] rescues the novel from bathos," and Peter Prescott among others faulted Gordon for her seeming inability to portray plausible male characters.[20] *The Company of Women* also provoked highly colorful phrases from the reviewers themselves. For Prescott, Gordon's men are either "pillars of illegitimate authority or predatory swinishness against which women may press and scratch in an attempt to define their own female sensibilities"; Judith Thurman defines the relation of the women with the priest as "chaste polygamy"; while Gray refers to the novel's "singular and fascinating streak of monastic Amazonism."[21]

Such extravagant language mirrors Gordon's own, which she employs to redeem the narration of the day-by-day with the influx of the ineffable (like Hansen but ultimately less successfully). A number of reviewers cite the novel's first sentence, "Felicitas Maria Taylor was called after the one virgin martyr whose name contained some hope for ordinary human happiness" (3), and in a 1981 interview a choice of such a life is ascribed to Gordon herself.[22] Even more, Gordon like Hansen sees her writing as much like a religious calling: "From early childhood I knew what I was going to be, and I felt it . . . to have the same kind of purity as a religious vocation. . . . I think the image of the nun is something that every Catholic girl works against. . . . Which is very different from other religious traditions. You do have the notion of a woman, without men, living a very pure centered life which has nothing to do with the domestic."[23]

In crucial ways *The Company of Women* works out the conflicts of women's religious calling, dealing in good part with mateless women addicted to a priest who is a reactionary, "charismatic despot."[24] It also seeks a secular lay version of the pure life that has everything to do with domesticity. The novel's three parts focus on Felicitas when she is fourteen (1963), twenty (1969–70), and twenty-eight (1977). As a teenager she is precocious, an exemplary pupil, and coddled by her mother Charlotte and the other women, Charlotte's contemporaries who meet each summer for a three-week retreat with the eccentric Father Cyprian in rural upstate New York. Cyprian has been relieved by the church of normal priestly duties; to these women, the only congregation he has left, he is both priest and occasional paterfamilias.

Gordon has announced her interest in how otherwise strong women "will suddenly buckle to the authority of a male mentor, whether it is a priest or professor or a lover."[25] In the second part of *Company* Felicitas, finally rebelling against her stifling upbringing (and in the midst of America's "sexual revolution"), trades Father Cyprian's mentorship and authority for those of a young counterculture professor at Columbia University, Robert Cavendish, who becomes her lover. Trendily left-wing yet socially and personally irresponsible, Cavendish seduces Felicitas and gets her pregnant (or another sex partner arranged by Cavendish may be the impregnator). Desperate and ignored by Cavendish, Felicitas arranges to have an abortion but literally at the last minute calls it off and decides to have the baby.

In the third part we learn that when Felicitas confessed her pregnancy to her mother they agreed that the girl should deliver her child in Cyprian's town. After the child (a girl, Linda) is born, all but one of the group of women settle in near the priest. Felicitas marries a stolid local Catholic hardware dealer, and the little community quietly, anxiously lives out the ordinary, their twin focus on the baby Linda and the impending death of the old priest.

One Must Suffer Because of the Church

The seduction-abuse-abandonment sequence is classic in *Company:* The magnetic, seemingly suave professor charms the naive young student into bed but soon tires of her, and even before she learns she is pregnant he thrusts her out of his self-centered, chaotic life. But the older women in the novel also suffer a kind of seduction at the hands of the church via Father Cyprian and are certainly—although in no way physically—abused by him. Gordon has remarked that "one of the things that helped me in life is Flannery O'Connor's statement that . . . in this day and age one must suffer because of the church and not for the church."[26] The women are so obsessed with the overbearing priest because they are desperately afraid of abandonment (four of them have lost husbands one way or another). They are damaged creatures who seek security from an ineffective spiritual guide who welcomes them because the church has, in a sense, abandoned him and left him virtually to his own designs in isolation. Cyprian and the six females (seven, after Linda is born) function as a fragile family-congregation marked by a fear of being left alone. It is a situation involving little pain or ecstasy (unlike those in the other two texts) but rife with shame and mystery.

Shame flourishes in the family environment, and perhaps even more so in this peculiar company of women. One reason it does so is that desire is sublimated into a devotion that overvalues purity, so that shame takes shape as the result of one's inability totally to transcend eros. Sensual thoughts do not belong in this "holy family," that is to say, and the women (less so Cyprian) are embarrassed by their surges of feeling, even if these center more on visions of traditional domesticity than on sex.

Shame is pivotal in a key scene of the novel: in the waiting room of the abortion clinic where Felicitas becomes one of yet another company of women who form a countergroup to those at Cyprian's retreat and those drawn to Cavendish. Four other pregnant women are there, the youngest ten years older than Felicitas, and the abortion doctor serves as the dominant male who is the opposite of the priest. He even wears "his medical whites with a solemnity of a French communion child before the

First World War" (231). The women converse casually in the anteroom, waiting for the abortionist to relieve them one by one, but the conversation as Felicitas senses it covers desperation. "The others . . . made rude jokes; they carried needlepoint. No man would save them" (233). For Felicitas, beyond the desperation is shame, but it is not so much the shame of her "negligence," of allowing herself to get pregnant and seeking an abortion to avoid the disapprobation of her company, especially Cyprian, as it is her growing awareness there in the waiting room of the shame of wasted human life. This dramatized recognition, like the *anagnorisis* of Greek tragedy, is the accomplishment of the scene that Gordon orchestrates as witness against abortion, and she does it with a startling image often employed otherwise in contexts of shame: an image of blood.

The last one in the abortion clinic anteroom, Felicitas abruptly changes her mind when her predecessor returns from the operation dripping blood. Felicitas sees that "someone had made a footprint in the blood that had come from the woman's body. The print had repeated itself to the door" (235). It prompts Felicitas' revelation: "All the dead women, hacked and bled, eyes closed in a violent death because they preferred to die rather than to give birth" (235–36). She decides—on the spot, as it were—that she cannot go through with the operation and flees the clinic.

This scene, in the volatile battles over abortion rights in the nineties (even more inflammatory than the eighties) could probably be construed as both an anti-abortion and pro-choice message. Although it seems at first to speak against abortion per se, on closer reading one sees that Felicitas is actually horrified by a vision of badly performed abortions. But I am less interested in the ideological use of the scene or in its appropriateness than in the mere fact that it exists as an example of literary fiction impinging on the sexual-political public sphere. Much of this is, of course, circumstance: Gordon writing in the late seventies could hardly have projected the hostility and violence pervading the abortion issue a decade later, although it was already intense then.

What prevents this scene from functioning merely as an ideological expression then and now is its powerful use of a primal symbol and its integrity as literary art. The bloody footprint is a compelling example of what Paul Ricoeur in *The Symbolism of Evil* calls "stain, the most archaic symbol" that conveys a sense of sin and guilt.[27] But also conveyed artfully in the scene is Felicitas' anguish over whether or not to have the abortion, a dilemma that Gordon compassionately and plausibly works through, as she does the social-symbolic role of the other women in the clinic. As Judith Wilt says, "Though the women Gordon puts in the New York abortionist's office in 1970 have, every one, a history of abuses or pregnancies or poverty that makes abortion a sympathetic choice for them, abortion becomes in this novel a symbol of the refusal to sacrifice potentiality to actuality, a denial of the necessities of change."[28] Wilt offers an agonizing statement on abortion in the preface to *Abortion, Choice, and Contemporary Fiction:* "As a feminist and a Catholic, I believe a woman's freedom to abort a fetus is a monstrous, a tyrannous, but a *necessary* freedom in a fallen world. I must call, even for myself, and certainly for my countrywomen, for the necessary freedom of choice within which to make my soul, if I can, free from that necessity."[29] Wilt's book as a whole is an example of a judicious study of fiction whose plots both magnify and reflect crises of the public sphere.

The Gaze of Permanent Choosing

The essence of Felicitas' denial, as Wilt explains, is that she does not want to face motherhood, but once she decides against abortion, she becomes committed to the mother's role. In this she is aided greatly not only by her own mother, who is understanding rather than condemning, but also by others of the "company." Their embracing of her as an adult in need, following her estrangement from them through her "childish" (but no doubt necessary) rebellion also marks a transition from shame to mystery.

Her brief fellowship with the desperate company of women in the abortionist's office is actually the critical moment on her way from another company—that of Cavendish's "commune"—to this renewed one. As Wilt says, "Cyprian imagined her in the company of virgins dedicated to intellectual and spiritual achievement; Robert's [Cavendish's] imagined company, antivirgins wedded to an intellectual principle of erotic freedom, is a parody of this."[30] What gives this new situation promise is its sacramental and incarnational (small *i*) qualities.

Father Cyprian's vision of guiding a company of virgins is at best unrealistic and at worst patriarchally ludicrous, and yet, from the perspective of the church and its faithful, it has the advantage of providing the sacraments. In an era of dysfunctionality, these women without traditional families become a tiny *communitas* of believers bonded by the holy communion dispersed regularly by the frail old man. How precarious this arrangement is, though, is illustrated by Muriel, one of the aging company who comes briefly to word near the end of the novel. Mean-spirited and the least lovable of any of them, Muriel has moved years earlier to Cyprian's village, built a house next to his, and lives the frustrated life of a worshipful would-be spouse. "Apart from him, I belong to no one," she confesses (274). And yet, "Each day when I saw him in the morning at the altar, it was a miracle. I offer my mass every day now in thanksgiving that he has been spared" (274). She is a moving and even terrifying example of the passion to love and be loved that Iris Young sees in Kristeva's vision. Both looking toward death and resisting it, Muriel says, "I wait for a face to meet my face; I wait for the singular glance; the gaze of permanent choosing, the glance of absolute preferment" (275).

This is the passion of Agnes that led to madness, the passion of Mariette that took her to a life of physical pain, still the "troubled bride" whose Christ sends her "roses" but only whispers of himself. Incarnation is lacking here. Agnes finds and loses it. Mariette suffers for it in compensation. Both try to experience Christ in the body, in their bodies, with a virginal vengeance. Felicitas, named for the virgin martyr who stood for "ordinary human happiness," abandons virginity and its Catholic connotations. Her way of secular incarnation, enfleshment, in the midst of the sacraments is a choice that means something precisely because of what she has forfeited: the singular virginal life that the others projected onto her. Married to a devoted, unexciting, religious man, a part of the local community as well as of her special company, and rearing her child, she is embodied in all these ways, fulfilled in ways that Mariette is not. Yet, as Morey says, "If the question of incarnation is 'how does one give and receive love in the body,' the question is especially poignant and urgent for women who theologically and culturally speaking have never simply been in a body (which implies potential points of transcendence of physical imperative) but rather *are* the body, a condition that makes any other than biological achievement look like an oddity if not a madness."[31] Here is something of Felicitas' quandary: her desire both to fulfill and transcend that condition of being the body.

Thus, like Mariette, she waits, although unlike Mariette with a quiet defiance and a lack of submission couched in sexual terms: "If I could see the face of God as free from all necessity . . . then I would look for Him. . . . But I will not let Him into my heart. My daughter is there, my mother, Leo, Cyprian, the women whom I love. I will not open my heart to God. If He is the only God I could worship, He will value my chastity. But I will not be violated: I will not submit myself. I will wait. But I will wait for light, not love" (267). This young Catholic mother, who has traded first quasi-vocational virginity, then erotic rebellion for ordinary embodiment, refuses to be seduced or abused by God and even now senses His threatened abandonment. Once the cosseted child (rather than an abused one) who had to transcend the others' overvaluation of her, she has grown shy of the promises of transcendence and turned instead to the satisfactions of the everyday.[32] Gordon, referring both to Felicitas and the heroine of *Final Payments,* remarks that they "have been in some way damaged by male authority. And so they've been rendered unfit for ordinary life."[33] God is a part of that damaging male authority, in Felicitas' mind. Yet she remains intrigued by divine mystery, and she waits.

Notes

1. John Pielmeier, *Agnes of God* (New York: New American Library, 1985). Citations in the text refer to Pielmeier's script.

2. Jack Kroll, "Kentucky Home-Fried," *Newsweek,* March 31, 1980, 70–71.

3. Norman Jewison, "Introduction," in Leonore Fleischer, *Agnes of God* (New York: New American Library, 1985), vi. Fleischer's version, which served as the basis for the film directed by Jewison and produced by Columbia Pictures, differs considerably from Pielmeier's script, and I have used only the script for my analysis. Jewison says, regarding the film, "I was able to retain the intensity of the interaction between the three women while expanding the landscape of the play and adding a number of supporting players who lent a needed quality of realism to the story" (vi-vii). I saw the play at the Music Box Theatre in New York, with Amanda Plummer as Agnes, Elizabeth Ashley as Dr. Livingstone, and Geraldine Page as Mother Miriam Ruth.

4. Agnes's singing reminds me of Julia Kristeva's use of the term *chora,* although Kristeva's usage has nothing to do with chorus or choir. Rather, she employs it to play on Plato's *chora* as enclosed space or womb and transforms it via Jacques Lacan's psychoanalytic theory into a notion of significant flaws in symbolic language. As Toril Moi puts it, *chora* "can be perceived only as . . . contradictions, meaninglessness, disruption, silences, and absences in the symbolic language." Agnes's singing, in other words, is a sort of unconscious protest against the rational "Symbolic Order" of the church and eventually of the psychiatrist. See Toril Moi, *Sexual/Textual Politics* (London: Methuen, 1985), 162.

5. T. E. Kalem, "New Crop of Kentucky Foals," *Time,* March 31, 1980, 58.

6. Pielmeier, "Introduction," *Agnes of God,* vii.

7. Brendan Gill, "Incarcerations," *The New Yorker,* April 12, 1982, 125; Pielmeier, "Introduction," *Agnes of God,* vii-viii.

8. This is the probability developed in the novelized version; see 209ff.

9. Ron Hansen, *Mariette in Ecstasy* (New York: Harper Perennial, 1992); Ron Hansen, *Nebraska* (New York: Grove/Atlantic, 1990).

10. Michiko Kakutani, "In a Convent, Rapture and Questions of Reality," *New York Times,* November 5, 1991, B2.

11. Pico Iyer is quoted by Hansen in "Writing as Sacrament," 57; Hansen's comment on the nun appears in "Writing as Sacrament," *Image: A Journal of the Arts and Religion,* no. 5 (Spring 1994): 53–58.

12. That theme is reinforced by the cover illustration of the paperback version, a facial closeup by Honi Werner that looks like Bernini's famous sculpture of "Saint Teresa in Ecstasy" in the Santa Maria della Vittoria church in Rome.

13. Patricia Hampl, "Her Imitation of Ecstasy," *New York Times Book Review,* October 20, 1991, 12. Hansen says that he "first thought about writing *Mariette*

in Ecstasy after finishing Saint Thérèse of Lisieux's *Story of a Soul.*" See "Writing as Sacrament," 55.

14. Carolyn Walker Bynum, "The Female Body and Religious Practice in the Later Middle Ages," in *Fragments for a History of the Human Body,* part 3, ed. Michael Feher (New York: Zone Books, 1989). 163; see also Carolyn Walker Bynum, *Fragmentation and Redemption: Essays on Gender and the Human Body* (New York: Zone Books, 1993).

15. David B. Morris, *The Culture of Pain* (Berkeley: University of California Press, 1993), 48.

16. On modern torture practiced by governments see *Reading the Social Body,* ed. Catherine B. Burroughs and Jeffrey David Ehrenreich (Iowa City: University of Iowa Press, 1993). On contemporary body piercing in the United States see Vicki Glembocki, "A Ring in Her Navel," *Playboy* 10 (February 1994): 82, 118, 134, 136–38, and Dean Kuipers, "Bondage a-Go-Go," *Playboy* 10 (March 1994): 27.

17. Bynum, "The Female Body," 168–69.

18. I use "catachresis" here in the sense in which J. Hillis Miller expands on the notion in *Ariadne's Thread: Story Lines* (New Haven: Yale University Press, 1992).

19. Mary Gordon, *The Company of Women* (New York: Ballantine Books, 1981).

20. Francine du Plessix Gray, "A Religious Romance," *New York Times Book Review,* February 15, 1981, 24; Peter S. Prescott, "Honor and Humiliation," *Newsweek,* February 15, 1981, 89.

21. Prescott, "Honor and Humiliation," 89; Judith Thurman, "Sad but True," *The New Yorker,* March 12, 1990, 97; Gray, "A Religious Romance," 24.

22. Le Anne Schreiber, "A Talk with Mary Gordon," *New York Times Book Review,* February 15, 1981, 26. Felicitas in early Christian lore was the slave of the aristocratic Perpetua; both were martyred for their faith, torn apart by wild animals in 202 or 203 in Carthage. The manner of their death suggests why Gordon chose the name. Her Felicitas also faces the threat of mutilation, in her case from an abortionist.

23. Schreiber, "A Talk with Mary Gordon," 27.

24. Gray, "A Religious Romance," 25.

25. Schreiber, "A Talk with Mary Gordon," 26.

26. Ibid., 26.

27. Ricoeur discusses stain as archaic symbol at length in *The Symbolism of Evil,* trans. Emerson Buchanan (New York: Harper and Row, 1967). I have taken the citation from an essay by Ricoeur, "The Hermeneutics of Symbols and Philosophical Reflection," in *The Philosophy of Paul Ricoeur: An Anthology of His Work,* ed. Charles E. Reagan and David Stewart (Boston: Beacon Press, 1978), 39.

28. Judith Wilt, *Abortion, Choice, and Contemporary Fiction: The Armageddon of the Maternal Instinct* (Chicago: University of Chicago Press, 1990), 89.

29. Wilt, *Abortion, Choice, and Contemporary Fiction,* xii.

30. Ibid., 89.

31. Ann-Janine Morey, "Beyond Updike: Incarnated Love in the Novels of Mary Gordon," *Christian Century,* November 20, 1985, 1062.

32. Morey thinks that "Felicitas functions as a latter day Christ child, a girl of extraordinary gifts, raised to cherish the realm of intellect, who violates her status as a junior Jesus by becoming Mary at the last minute." Letter to the author, August 16, 1994.

33. Schreiber, "A Talk with Mary Gordon," 26.

7

Possessing Bodies:
Quicksand and *Beloved*

Way Down South in Dixie
(Break the heart of me)
Love is a naked shadow
On a gnarled and naked tree.

—Langston Hughes,
"Fine Clothes for the Jew"

Quicksand: The Price of Exotic

The three texts I discussed in chapter 6, works that leave women in various concluding postures of passivity, would appear to be typical female narratives. Other texts I will address in the remaining chapters of this section, all of them by women, likewise depict women protagonists in conditions of deferral, frustrated and anxious anticipation, and suspended action. But such waiting is not only women's traditional lot, determined by the often religiously endorsed machinations of men, although it is certainly that. It is also part of a larger, complicated pattern of American life that is, even in its modern secular guises, profoundly apocalyptic: a half-expectation of cataclysmic endings, a sense of doom blended with a hope of relief, a fascination with excess along with a condemnation of "unrighteous" behavior, and an obsessive watching of the self and others that has overtaken a normal (if there ever was such a thing) curiosity about the world.

Indicative of the tenor of our time is the fact that one could scarcely conceive of writing such a study as this one these days without the inclusion of ethnic perspectives—the result of a public sensitivity that was much weaker just a few years ago. The vigor of African American writing in particular is the result of struggles by earlier black authors for a voice in a cultural setting hostile or indifferent to them. That voice is now being heard, and it has modulated into a cultural force. As Toni Morrison states it, "As a metaphor of transacting the whole process of Americanization, while burying its racial ingredients, this Africanist presence may be something the United States cannot do without."[1]

My juxtaposition in this chapter of an obscure novel from the Harlem Renaissance with the best-known work of Morrison, a celebrated contemporary black novelist, is not forced. Although the milieux are markedly different, Nella Larsen's *Quicksand* and Toni Morrison's *Beloved* have a great deal in common, especially in regard to the seduction-abuse-abandonment sequence and the elements of shame, pain, awe, and ecstasy. In *Beloved* the roles of family and community represent a tension of private and public spheres in determining the characters' definition and accommodation of their sexual bodies. To put it succinctly if too simply, in *Quicksand* the lonely protagonist falls prey to a religious enthusiasm that uses, and uses up, her erotic and maternal body because she exhausts, or feels she has exhausted, the alternatives. In *Beloved,* a cast of black characters agonizes toward a sense of possessing their own bodies, and sharing them with those they choose, against a horrific history of ownership by others that defies morality and yet enjoys a religious endorsement.

Nella Larsen, born of a Danish mother and a black West Indian father, was a brief bright light on the Harlem literary scene before fading into obscurity in the early thirties following a charge that she plagiarized her only published short story. Before that, the publication of two short novels *Quicksand* (1928) and *Passing* (1929) brought her quick recognition, including a Guggenheim fellowship in 1930.[2]

Larsen's mulatto status is reflected in Helga Crane, the Danish-African American protagonist of illegitimate birth in *Quicksand* who struggles throughout her adult life to find a proper place amid the pitfalls of her ambiguous ethnic and social world. Having left her teaching post at a conservative black school in the South, the twenty-two-year-old Helga moves to New York, but the freedom of the Harlem atmosphere threatens her sexual reserve, and she leaves to visit her maternal relatives in Copenhagen. There, in northern European fashion, the Danes treat her as an exotic creature whose black heritage means that, in spite of her refinement, she must smolder with primitive erotic desire. She rejects a marriage proposal from a Danish artist (he is insulted by her refusal) and returns to the United States. Following a dramatic religious conversion experience, Helga marries a black preacher and moves south with him to begin a life of Christian service in a small Alabama town. There she becomes quickly absorbed in childbearing and childrearing and in attending to her various illnesses. At the novel's end she is sick, dispirited, full of hatred for her husband, and about to bear her fifth child. The "endless stretch of dreary years before her appalled vision" (108), which she glimpsed much earlier, has come to pass.

I will concentrate on a single scene, the one portraying Helga's unexpected conversion in a Harlem church. Trying to deal with her sexual energies after the Copenhagen sojourn, she has kissed a married man to whom she is attracted; when he comes to apologize rather than, as she had hoped, declare his love and reveals his lack of interest in her, she reflexively slaps his face. Shamed and embarrassed by her loss of control, she wanders the streets at night, gets caught in a severe rainstorm, and takes shelter in a church, where a revival meeting is in progress. Her "clinging red dress" leads the already excited congregation to mistake her for a "Jezebel," and they set about to save her soul.

Helga is at first "amused, angry, disdainful" regarding the "performance [that] took on an almost Bacchic vehemence," but gradually she gets caught up in it, feels "an echo of the weird orgy resonate in her own heart . . . possessed by the same madness," and at last "with no previous intention [she] began to yell like one insane, drowning every other clamor, while torrents of tears streamed down her face" (113). The ecstatic members of the church embrace her, and she does feel "within her a supreme aspiration toward the regaining of simple happiness . . . unburdened by the complexities of the lives she had known" (114). Soon after that she enters into a fateful marriage with the Reverend Pleasant Green, who had escorted her home that night from the church.

What has brought about this "confusion of seduction and repentance" (118)? In her admirable introduction to Larsen's two novels, Deborah E. McDowell finds a reason in the plight of the author herself. McDowell declares that against the background of slavery, where the "white slave master constructed an image of black female slaves . . . [with] wanton, insatiable desires," and with the "myths about black women's lasciviousness" persisting beyond the slavery era, "a pattern of reticence about black female sexuality dominated novels by black women . . . and Nella Larsen could only hint at the idea of black women as sexual subjects beyond the safe and protective covers of traditional narrative subjects and conventions."[3] In other words, black women were perceived in the public realm as lust-driven creatures, and as a result Larsen, inhibited in her design to portray Helga as sexually frustrated, transfers the site of passion from sex to religion.

The revival scene is described in orgiastic language and reinforces Ann-Janine Morey's claim that in American literature the emotions aroused in sex and religion are often interchangable.[4] Yet however Helga allows her sexuality to emerge transformed into religious fervor, she has not learned to know her body in any critical way. That happens only after her marriage (as some would still claim it should), and then in excruciating fashion. Less than two years into the marriage, and with three children (twin boys and a girl), she feels depleted by domesticity and experiences little of its pleasures—pleasures she had hoped would substitute for the fulfilling erotic life she had both wanted and feared.

Helga's new body awareness is burdensome. "She, who had never thought of her body save as something on which to hang lovely fabrics, now had to think of it constantly," for she is usually ill, "weak and spent" (123). She too endures a version of the threefold sequence: seduced by what seemed to be a caring religious community, abused by the "normal" travails of frequent pregnancies and births, and "abandoned" by a reverend husband who, although kind and deferential, "had rather lost any personal interest in her" other than to point out her ingratitude at being saved "from hell-fire and eternal damnation" (124).

There is, then, no mystery in Helga's life, and the ecstatic moment of her conversion was just that: a moment preceding a lifetime of greater and lesser pain. The main motivating factor in her failed struggle to mediate a strong self and healthy relationships is shame. It permeates her existence, beginning with her shame over her illegitimate birth and concluding with shame over her marriage, "this sacred thing of which parsons and other Christian folk ranted so sanctimoniously" (134). In between she suffers shame in most of her relationships with men and is driven to her fateful conversion that is the vocabulary of the revival songs ("Oh, the bitter shame and sorrow. . . . When I let the Savior's pity / Plead in vain") and relieved, briefly, by the antics of the congregation acting as shamelessly as she.

Why *is* Helga so driven by shame? It is her double heritage of race and sex. As a black woman she is expected by the white world (and some of the black) to do shameful things, and it is just that expectation that deepens her sense of shame. Her mixed heritage makes it perhaps even worse. In the public eye black sensuality clashes with white restraint, and the woman trying to overcome self-bias must almost inevitably suffer shame over the near-impossibility of finding an equilibrium. McDowell writes, "Both *Quicksand* and *Passing* are poised between the tensions and conflicts that are Western culture's stock ambivalences about female sexuality: lady/ Jezebel or virgin/whore. Larsen sees and indicts the sources of this ambivalence: the network of social institutions—education, marriage, and religion, among the most prominent—all interacting with each other to strangle and control the sexual expression of women. But, like her heroine Helga, Larsen could 'neither conform nor be happy in her nonconformity.'"[5] It is ironic that Larsen, poised at the start of what looked to be a brilliant literary career, was abruptly shamed in the public realm and sent into more than thirty years of silence (she died in 1964) by an accusation of plagiarism from which she was exonerated. It is a far happier irony that her fiction has reappeared late in the century; her quicksand has turned to firmer ground and helped to form the foundation for the powerful writing of later black women.

Beloved: Spirited Rebellion

Among those women one has emerged whose voice has caught the widest public attention in America and abroad: Toni Morrison, winner of the 1993 Nobel Prize. It is surely a fine irony that two major candidates for serving as exemplars of that mythical creature the Great American Novel are by black novelists: Ralph Ellison's *Invisible Man* and Morrison's *Beloved.* Morrison's 1987 novel (winner of the Pulitzer Prize for fiction in 1988), an epic-lyric, realistic-surreal rendering of the horrors of American slavery and its aftermath, focuses on a monstrous dimension of American history, a scrutiny that might seem to disqualify it as a role model for exemplary American writing. Yet as Paul Gray reminds in his review of *Beloved,* "Imaginative literature at its best does not reinforce received opinions but disturbs them."[6]

Beloved disturbs not by evoking grandiloquence, sentimentality (in the tradition of *Uncle Tom's Cabin*), or even moral indignation but more subtly by showing how "those who possessed and those who were possessed struggled . . . to get through their days."[7] It is an evocation, in the words of another Nobel Prize laureate, William Faulkner, of the belief "that man will not merely endure: he will prevail."[8] This novel does portray, from a minority perspective ultimately more persuasive than that of, say, the intrepid white settler questing westward, the tenacity of the American underdog against the American suppressor. The Great American Novel would need to feature this conflict; the transcendental abstractions of a *Moby-Dick* or the naturalism of *The Grapes of Wrath* will not suffice, for in these fictions it is brutal nature (the whale, the climate) more than brutal humans that sets the challenge.

Elissa Schappel calls Morrison "a master of the public novel, examining the relationships between the races and the sexes and the struggle between civilization and nature, while at the same time combining myth and the fantastic with a deep political sensitivity."[9] This is the first time I have heard that "the public novel" exists (What would be in contrast— the private novel?), but it is a provocative designation that is useful for discussing how Morrison employs her writing, and the reputation she has earned through it, to attempt to influence the public realm.

First, a sketch of the plot. The narrative begins in 1873 at the home, the notorious 124 of Bluestone Road outside Cincinnati, of Sethe and her daughter Denver. Sethe, her mother-in-law Baby Suggs, and Sethe's four small children (Denver born en route) had settled there in 1855 following their escape from slavery on the Sweet Home farm in Kentucky. 124 is notorious because of what happened there in 1855. A month after the escape to freedom by Sethe and the others, men from Sweet Home and the local sheriff arrive to take them back. Rather than allow her children to be forced into slavery, Sethe attempts to kill them on the spot but manages to murder only her other daughter, Beloved, by slitting her throat with a hacksaw (the scene is portrayed more than halfway through the novel). Sethe's former owner decides not to take back this crazy woman and her surviving children after all, and after some time in jail Sethe is set free. The spirit of the murdered child haunts the house, and eventually its maliciousness causes the two boys to flee. When Paul D, "the last of the Sweet Home men" (90), a former slave on that farm, shows up at 124, Baby Suggs has already died and only Sethe and Denver remain. Paul D gets rid of the ghost, and he and Sethe become lovers, but soon this new family is disturbed by the appearance of the beautiful young adult Beloved, who seems to be both real and ghostly and who seduces Paul and becomes Denver's constant companion. When Sethe tells Paul of killing her child back in 1855 the passion of her convictions unnerves him, and he leaves. Sethe, Denver, and Beloved are left alone.

For a time the three indulge an excessive, claustrophobic intimacy, as if mother and returned daughter were compensating for what they had missed, but soon Beloved shows herself to be a selfish infant in an adult body. She eats, sleeps, grows fat, and abuses her mother. Black women in the community, long estranged from the 124 household and moved by concern for Denver, decide to exorcise the ghost-daughter. They do so, thirty-strong, via singing, although in the tension of the process the distraught Sethe nearly stabs an innocent white man. Soon after that Paul D returns and a healing begins.

My bare-bones summary makes the novel sound like soap opera, and indeed one critic called it that.[10] This is a misperception, but the plot, which in any case does not unfold chronologically, proceeds through flashbacks to slave existence on the Kentucky farm and attempts at escape and extends to depictions of the black community on the outskirts of Cincinnati and to dramatic monologues by Sethe, Denver, and Beloved.

Beloved as a ghost story has troubled many critics, and the author does not relieve them, because she has labeled it as such and describes an Ohio childhood in which "she grew up hearing folk tales of the supernatural."[11] Composing fiction that confounds the realistic frame of mind with physically implausible occurrences is a ploy that Morrison shares with numerous minority writers, among them Native Americans such as Ray Young Bear and Louise Erdrich, Asian Americans such as Maxine Hong Kingston, and Latin Americans such as Cecile Pineda. The strategy is to upset and thereby weaken the hegemony of the dominant tradition by insisting on precisely those elements the tradition rejects, suggesting other ways of grasping and interpreting reality. One can, to be sure, try to mitigate these stylistic-generic revolts by giving them names such as "magical realism," but these actually explain little and seem to serve mainly as efforts at cultural damage control.

Morrison's particular rebellion in *Beloved* consists in the sometimes perverse twists she applies to the concept of spirit. In the other texts I have addressed thus far in this section, spirit has meant the spirit*ual,* that component of humankind that is attuned to divinity and religious worship, that is (one hopes) immortal. This fairly clear-cut distinction, derived from the Greek and Christian traditions, is blurred in Morrison's work by an evocation of African and African American spiritism, a perspective that clashes with the dominant one but that can be neatly deliteralized; for example, Beloved symbolizes (psychologically) Sethe's guilt, a broader guilt over slavery that haunts American life, and everybody's libidinal urges. I have no serious quarrel with such readings but am more interested in how Morrison contrives this spirit as emphatically *fleshly.* She is, at first, extremely desirable physically, enough to entice Paul D and make him her lover. She eats and sleeps to excess, but it is somehow her carnality, her fleshly corruption, that makes her inhuman, a tangible presence of evil. The women of the black community recognize this solid corruptability and resolve to rid themselves of it. In a conversation between two of them, one asks, "You talking about flesh?" and the other responds, "I'm talking about flesh" (255). It is clear that Beloved poses a threat because she is flesh as well as spirit.

One could say that Beloved is a species of incarnation, evil embodied in and as a person yet evil not as an animated abstraction but as human excess. She is unlimited passion, a totally consuming desire to love and be loved that literally devours her mother, who wastes away as Beloved grows enormous. She is, in Freudian terms, undifferentiated, primary narcissism, but even to put it like that offers too easy an explanation. Morrison, I believe, wants her to remain a mystery and to have the ecstasy that she brings (to Sethe, Denver, and Paul D) appear awesome because it offers fulfillment at the cost of self—not the voluntary self-abnegation of a Mariette but a forced, overwhelming annihilation of oneself as other.

Morrison teases the reader even more by hinting at a realistic way out of the ghost story. Late in the novel we learn through a conversation between Paul D and a character named Stamp Paid of the Deer Creek girl, a young black woman imprisoned at Deer Creek, perhaps since infancy, by a white man. "Found him dead last summer and the girl gone," Stamp

Paid says. "Maybe that's her" (235). Further, when the black women arrive at 124 to exorcise Beloved as a ghost they see her having "taken the shape of a pregnant woman, naked and smiling in the heat of the afternoon sun" (251). The suggestion is that this is no spirit but a real woman impregnated, perhaps during one of her trysts with Paul D. It is as if Morrison is saying, "If you need a realistic explanation, try this one."[12] Yet to follow it strains one's credibility as much as accepting the plausibility of the ghost story. Above all, to accept this "explanation" would undercut the force of the most arresting passages of the novel, Beloved's lyrical monologues that constitute two brief chapters two-thirds of the way through the text. Here Beloved comes to word as a disembodied voice (with echoes of the Song of Songs) that conflates her identity with Sethe's, here and there with Denver's, perhaps with the Deer Creek girl, and with an unnamed woman on a slave ship.

This last voice particularly invites interpretation. In less than four pages an elusive "middle passage" impression is conveyed, a poetic monologue that recalls the outrageous treatment and inconceivable suffering of Africans packed into ships over three centuries and freighted to America to be sold, many of them dying en route of disease, starvation, and mishandling.[13] The paragraphs are saturated with unspeakable pain, rendered all the more effective through their blending with Beloved's late-nineteenth-century voice, itself merging in desire with Sethe's and done in an imagistic style.

Why should this monologue, a dreamlike effusion not only of experienced suffering but also of naked longing, be inserted into the novel at this point—or anywhere? It connects the private and the public; the suffering of the Sweet Home blacks is expanded to embrace millions of Africans sold and worked as animals to facilitate an American economy and way of life. Beloved as a lost soul, whether human, spirit, or both, speaks for that vast community of the oppressed, their lives treated as valueless or valuable only for their owners' advantage.[14] Against the fact of this unbearable history, one begins to understand why a slave mother, recently escaped, would slit her baby's throat.

A Gnarled and Naked Tree

The emphasis on spirit in *Beloved*, however conceived, is more than balanced by a stress on flesh. As Gray says, "The flesh-and-blood presence of Beloved roils the novel's intense, realistic surface."[15] But even more, the other major characters are identified in deeply physical ways. Foremost of these is Sethe, marked literally by the scars on her back from a severe beating she endured at Sweet Home just before her escape in 1855.

In a flashback to that time her open wounds are described during her lucky encounter en route with a runaway white girl, Amy Denver, after whom Denver is named. Exhausted, footsore, in great pain, and about to give birth, Sethe chances on the brash Amy at an isolated spot near a river. Before Amy delivers the child she tends to Sethe's feet and mutilated back, which has been incised by the rawhide whip and is now infected and bloody. Amy describes the sight to Sethe, who never sees it, as like "a chokeberry tree. . . . You back got a whole tree on it. In bloom. What God have in mind, I wonder" (79).

Without wishing to read too much into the scene, one can discern an orchestration of Christian tropes there. Echoes of the Passion and crucifixion abound in the imagery of the tree and cross created by the lashing, while Denver, delivered half-underwater in a sinking boat at the river bank, undergoes a birth and a natural baptism. Neither is it altogether far-fetched to think of Sethe's bloody feet and back as her stigmata—if not in the sense of Agnes's and Mariette's Christ-inspired wounds then certainly according to another meaning of stigma, which *Webster's Dictionary* defines as "a distinguishing mark cut or burned into the flesh, as of a slave or criminal." If the Catholic women suffer in devoted imitation of Christ, Sethe's wounds are the result of a brutal, forced submission inflicted to destroy the spirit rather than refine it.

This whole scene, in the plot's disruptive chronology, fills out an early one in the first chapter, where Paul D arrives at 124 in 1873, eighteen years after Sethe's escape, and discovers the intricate scar-tree on her back. Here Sethe reveals to the other survivor of Sweet Home what brought on her beating. She had already sent her three children on ahead, as part of the escape plan, and was lactating copiously because she was nursing the baby Beloved. Her master's nephews trap her and suckle her, stealing her milk, and when the master, "Schoolteacher," learns that Sethe has complained to the mistress of the plantation, he has the boys flog her. Thurman calls this scene "one of the most shocking in a novel stocked with savagery of every description," and Sethe's emotional scars from it are every bit as acute as the bodily ones.[16]

Paul D, acting on instinct, attempts to heal the emotional trauma by responding to the physical manifestations. He presses his mouth to "every ridge and leaf" (18) of the scar-tree (which she cannot feel because the scar tissue receives no sensation), and by this profound lip-service he tries to transform the stigmatization, this mark of disgrace, into something of high value and regard. "The sculpture her back had become, like the decorative work of a blacksmith too passionate for display" (17) signals for Paul D an icon of erotic compassion. It arouses his pity and desire and also gives him, barely arrived at 124, the energy to rid the house of its poltergeist-baby. We know that no resolution is immediately at hand, for Sethe has not yet encountered Beloved the palpable ghost; she has not yet confronted and dealt with her overwhelming maternal obsession, her fierce need to love and be loved caused by the death of her daughter. But Paul D, who is a healer by nature, by speaking to her mortified flesh offers her a place to start.

"What God have in mind," Amy's stunned theodical question when she sees Sethe's bloody back, gets answered after a fashion in a sermon by Sethe's mother-in-law Baby Suggs in the chapter immediately following the one on Denver's birth. Having preceded Sethe to freedom in Ohio, with Sethe's three children, Baby Suggs has become a lay preacher and in summer preaches to other blacks outdoors in a clearing deep in the forest. Her sermon spoken in the novel urges the celebration of the flesh, against the denigration of black bodies by whites, in a fashion that reminds one of the radical incarnational theology of the so-called death of God theologians, particularly that of Thomas Altizer. "She told them that the only grace they could have was the grace they could imagine. That if they could not see it, they would not have it. 'Here . . . in this place, we flesh. . . . Love it. Love it hard. Yonder they [the whites] do not love your flesh'" (88).

Baby Suggs preaches the response to what Helga Crane recognized, bitterly, in *Quicksand:* "How the white man's God must laugh at the great joke he played on them! Bound them to slavery, then to poverty and insult, and made them bear it unresistingly, uncomplainingly almost, by sweet promises of mansions in the sky by and by" (133–34). Baby Suggs doesn't persuade her congregation that "they were the blessed on earth . . . or its glorybound pure" (88). If one were to translate her message into theological terms, it might stress kenosis, Christ's total self-emptying into this world and being incarnated into humans whose flesh must be loved hard. Or it might be a version of what David Cunningham calls "perichoresis: the 'divine dance' in which the three persons [of the Trinity] participate in one another, rather than one person being subordinate to another."[17] Baby Suggs's proleptic gospel of the flesh, looking ahead to the late twentieth century with its seemingly simple accent on laughing, crying, dancing, and singing, is a profound incarnational event. Her services are not just pronouncements about the word become flesh; they are its enactment.[18]

The gospel of Baby Suggs fails in its time, according to her own lights. Not long after Sethe arrives from Kentucky, her mother-in-law begins her decline, disheartened and exhausted from a lifetime of struggle against "whitefolks." The private sphere of this timid black community cannot prevail in the public realm of powerful white society, even though the context is the free North. This impotence affects another relationship: Sethe's family, before and after Baby Suggs's death, draws the animosity of the black community and isolates itself from it. In both instances the larger, more public community abuses the smaller, more private one. The larger unit seems to feel threatened by the privacy of the smaller one; it desires to know the intimacies of the smaller unit and thus bring it under control, as was the case in the Salem of *The Crucible.*

Although the reasons for such behavior are unclear, they do not have to do with sheer size. History displays many examples of powerful smaller units abusing and controlling larger, weaker ones; South Africa for generations was such an instance. Yet in all cases the powerful unit is the more public one, even if it is smaller, by virtue of being in power and needing thus to intrude into and attempt to legislate the privacies of those it governs or oppresses. In a way this powerful public, even in a democracy (and even in coercive groups such as the Ku Klux Klan), is always jealous of its "subjects," for they appear to possess some secret knowledge not accessible to those in control; they represent a contingency that those in control cannot control. The more oppressive the powerful unit—the oppressive state—is, the more threatened it feels by the subjects' secrets, and it will institute, formally and informally, forces to discover and counteract these perceived dangers. The House un-American Activities Committee that American politicians used and abused in the search for suspected communists had just such a founding. Such forces created by the state become their "intelligence" or secret police. When they are organized among a powerful citizenry that thinks itself threatened, they can take the form of vigilante groups such as the Klan.

This fairly unsophisticated discussion of social psychology can set the background for an explanation of how shame becomes a key weapon of attempted state control.[19] An irony of public-private, powerful-weak dichotomies is that the secrets threatening those in power are usually not political secrets at all but rather privacies and intimacies that people do not wish to share broadly because they are bonds of love and affection. But the oppressive state is jealous of such intimacy because it wants its subjects' loyalty and devotion to supersede their familial and communal bonds. A way to command such loyalty and to destroy intimacy is through tactics of shaming.

Reflexes of Shame

Of all the texts I address in this book, *Beloved* offers the most detailed account of shame and shaming (Louise Erdrich's *Tracks* is a close second). It was clearly a subject much on Morrison's mind when she composed the novel. In a *Time* interview she dwells at some length on restraining devices that slaves were made to wear (descriptions of some of which, for example, metal bits in the slaves' mouths, she incorporates into *Beloved*) and discusses specifically the "masks slaves wore when they cut cane . . . to keep them from eating the sugar cane. . . . These things were not restraining tools, like in the torture chamber. They were things you wore while you were doing the work." Then she makes her point: "It seemed to me that the humiliation was the key to what the experience was like."[20] Humiliation, closely aligned to shame, is accomplished as a gratuitous act of cruelty disguised (masked) as an economic measure. Not only would the masks have caused their wearers great pain (Morrison says they tore off the skin when removed) and made them feel less than human, but they would also have prevented interchange—the exchange of secrets—among the slaves.

The scene in which Sethe is suckled by the slavemaster's nephews is an example of intimacy perverted to generate shame. It is so shameful for Sethe that she tells the plantation mistress (who weeps helplessly at the news) and risks the severe beating that is inflicted on her. It is one of the first things that she reveals to Paul D eighteen years later, but he as a male, empathetic though he is, does not grasp the enormity of what has been done to her.[21] Twice she tells him, "And they took my milk" (17), but Paul D understands only the horror of the lashing. As Thurman says, Sethe's "pride has been invested in her maternity," and it this center of her pride, this vulnerability, that the whites know how to attack.[22]

Shame-instilling experiences such as this have driven Sethe to the edge (and they have driven her husband Halle back at Sweet Home mad), and they accrue to propel her toward infanticide—an ultimately shameful act in virtually all circumstances but here a desperate one to avoid having her children returned to the site of shame and grow up in the shadow of its evil.

That act revenges itself on Sethe through Beloved's return, first as a mischievous presence at 124 and then, after Paul D rids the house of it, as the ghostly but palpable young woman. One of the Beloved's main traits is her shame*less*ness. A root meaning of "shame" is concealment and cover-up. Beloved is blatant in her nakedness, her refusal to cover up, and this is how the hitherto hostile black community of women finds her when they march to Bluestone Road for the exorcism: "naked and smiling . . . thunderblack and glistening" (261). The exorcism, then, whereby Sethe and Denver are reconciled with the community, is a triumph of *healthy* shame: Beloved disappears, Sethe is prevented from a rash act that would provoke the wrath of the whites, she and Denver are offered again the normal intimacy of a family in the context of a compassionate community, and things are set for Paul D's return. Yet the last image of that chapter is of a "hill of black people falling. And above them all . . . with a whip in his hand, the man without skin, looking" (262). He is a slavemaster, "without skin" because he is white (also skeletal, standing for death), and his vocation and beliefs render him also without shame. He is looking at Beloved, the other figure in the scene without shame. He is the cause of her. They belong together.

Bernard Williams's penetrating *Shame and Necessity* provides stimulation for still another reflection on shame, particularly through its comments in the fifth chapter on shame and slavery in ancient Greek civilization.[23] Williams is not shy about drawing comparisons between the moral dilemma posed by a slave-based society in Greece and modern exploitation of humans. As Bernard Knox, reviewing Williams's book, says, "The ancient Greeks did not try to defend" slavery. Aristotle, who did try, was the prominent exception. "But they could imagine no alternative; the life of the citizens of the polis, the only form of civilized organization they know or could imagine, would have been impossible without that leisure they prized so highly."[24] This leisure was, of course, enabled by the labor of slaves.

It is depressing to think that classical civilization, Greek high culture, still held up by many as the exemplary society, was grounded on the massive enslavement of persons and maintained through their constant and persistent shaming. Beneath the highly prized honor of the Greeks was the stark necessity of shame. In fact, one of the reasons why honor was so highly valued was the awareness that through fate or bad luck one could be taken prisoner in a war with some other city-state, abruptly find the roles reversed, and become a slave oneself. Against a strong current of interpretation that sees ancient Greece as a shame culture (involving a high valuation of honor) rather than a more evolved guilt culture (involving a strong sense of personal responsibility, an internalized sense of sin) Williams also maintains that shame for the Greeks also involved a developed concept of guilt.[25] Hence, the shame felt by slaves over their dishonorable condition would have in some sense been shared by slave owners as a guilt for subjugating other humans.

Williams carries over his argument to the present day. "We have social practices in relation to which we are in a situation much like that of the Greeks with slavery. We recognize arbitrary and brutal ways in which people are handled by society, ways that are conditioned, often, by no more than exposure to luck." We recognize the injustice of these circumstances and systems, he says further, but are reluctant to act to change them "partly because we have no settled opinion on the question . . . how far the existence of a worthwhile life for some people involves the imposition of suffering on others."[26]

Beloved reinforces and fills out Williams's philosophical discourse by offering what he cannot: the perspective of those who have been shamed and have had suffering imposed on them for the convenience of others and, even more, whose suffering has been manipulated so skillfully that they, the victims, assume the guilt that their masters ought to feel. It is like an extension of the contemporary abused-spouse rationalization: If I am constantly punished and made to feel inferior, I must be inferior and deserve the punishment. Seen in this context, Sethe's murder of her baby daughter is not just an act of desperate defiance but of self-punishment, a reflex of shame and felt inferiority, just as Beloved's return as a ghostly young woman imprisons Sethe and Denver in a tenacious cycle of shame and guilt. Ella, who leads the hostile black community to cast out Beloved and free the mother and daughter of her spell, understands their entrapment: She "didn't like the idea of past errors taking possession of the present" (256). Ridding the little family of its curse, the abusive (although only moderately so) black community breaks its servitude to the abusive larger white power structure, reconciles itself thereby to its shame, and in that act absorbs the shame and transforms it into a positive force. It also responds at last, embraces its weaker unit, takes it into itself, and becomes stronger as a result of dealing with that weakness.

In a way, transforming shame is what Morrison has been doing through her writing and speaking. Her fiction as a whole, not just *Beloved*, deals substantially with shame in black communities. Often, as in *Sula* and *The Bluest Eye*, the shame (involving adultery and incest) that permeates, affects, and challenges the whole community is private. The recognition of Morrison's skill in depicting the shame of the black community has provided her a rare stature that enables her to address the shame of the dominant force, the white majority. Through her craft she has become a moral spokeswoman whose nonfictional writing and teaching, interviews, and speeches express what has only been implicit in her fiction: The dominant white society continues its tactics of shaming blacks and attempting to make them feel guilty for their history of oppression. She charges, for example, that "black people have always been used as a buffer in this country between powers to prevent class war, to prevent other kinds of real conflagrations. If there were no black people here in this country . . . the immigrants would have torn each other's throats out, as they have done everywhere else. But in becoming an American, from Europe, what one has in common with that other immigrant is contempt for *me*—it's nothing else but color."[27]

Morrison suffers little contempt these days. She is an immensely admired artist. Her work exists in the public realm, and she has also entered that realm as an individual who is invited frequently to pronounce on everything from—inevitably—race relations to women's agendas to issues of education. In a society obsessed with instant gratification and the trivialization of its celebrities—indeed, that creates trivial celebrities—it is refreshing to see Morrison respond as a scholar, another of her roles. However controversial her stances may be, they are clearly thought through and offered with reinforcing evidence. I do not think that she is a "master of the public novel." She is a master of the novel, usually novels of intensely private moments forced into the public, who has gained an authoritative public voice and exercises it responsibly. One has to go back to another black novelist, James Baldwin, to find another American artist of, in his time, similar public impact, although Baldwin's influence was probably more the result of his essays (direct expressions of his public role) than of his uneven fiction. How ironic and hopeful that Morrison modulates the cacophony of voices in America among whom are those who, even now, would wish her silent.

Notes

1. Toni Morrison, *Playing in the Dark: Whiteness and the Literary Imagination* (Cambridge: Harvard University Press, 1990), 47.

2. Nella Larsen, *Quicksand* and *Passing,* ed. Deborah E. McDowell (New Brunswick: Rutgers University Press, 1986). *Quicksand* was originally published by Knopf in 1928, and *Passing* in 1929.

3. Deborah E. McDowell, "Introduction," in *Quicksand* and *Passing,* xii, xiii. See also Deborah Gray White, *Ar'n't I a Woman? Female Slaves in the Plantation South* (New York: W. W. Norton, 1985), 38: "Whether or not slave women desired relationships with white men was immaterial, the conventional wisdom was that black women were naturally promiscuous and thus desired such connections."

4. Ann-Janine Morey, *Religion and Sexuality in American Literature* (New York: Cambridge University Press, 1992). See also Zora Neale Hurston, *The Sanctified Church* (Berkeley: Turtle Island, 1981), for a discussion of class distinctions in Northern black churches that led to the encouragement or condemnation of ecstatic worship.

5. McDowell, *Quicksand* and *Passing,* xxxi.

6. Paul Gray, "Something Terrible Happened," *Time,* September 21, 1987, 75. Although it is a relatively recent novel, *Beloved* (New York: Knopf, 1987) has been written about extensively. I refer to only a few of the many articles and reviews.

7. Gray, "Something Terrible Happened," 75.

8. William Faulkner, "Speech of Acceptance upon the Award of the Nobel Prize for Literature, Delivered in Stockholm on the Tenth of December, 1950," in *Twelve American Writers,* ed. William M. Gibson and George Arms (New York: Macmillan, 1962), 776.

9. Elissa Schappel, "Toni Morrison: The Art of Fiction," *Paris Review* 34 (Fall 1993): 83–84.

10. Judith Thurman, "A House Divided," *The New Yorker,* November 2, 1987, 180, remarks that "the novel is vulnerable to the kind of morning-after synopsis that one critic gave it when, quoting cooly from its steamier passages, he labelled it a 'soap opera.'"

11. Schappel, "Toni Morrison: The Art of Fiction," 84. See Gray, "Something Terrible Happened," 75: "Morrison's attempt to make this strange figure [Beloved] come to life strains unsuccessfully toward the rhapsodic."

12. Elizabeth House, "Toni Morrison's Ghost: The Beloved Who Is Not Beloved," *Studies in American Fiction* 18 (Spring 1990): 17–26, argues that Beloved is actually a girl who has escaped from slavery. One might also call *Beloved* realistic insofar as it has a historical occurrence as its background. In 1851 Margaret Garner, an escaped slave, under somewhat similar circumstances killed one of her three children. See Gloria Naylor, "A Conversation: Gloria Naylor and Toni Morrison," *The Southern Review* 21 (Summer 1985): 567–93.

13. For a powerful poem on the sufferings of Africans on slave ships see Robert Hayden, "Middle Passage," in *A Native Sons Reader,* ed. Edward Margolies (Philadelphia: J. B. Lippincott, 1970), 23–28; see also Charles Johnson's compelling novel *Middle Passage* (New York: Atheneum, 1990).

14. Morrison has estimated that as many as sixty million blacks died because of slavery. Bonnie Angelo, "The Pain of Being Black," *Time,* May 22, 1989, 120.

15. Gray, "Something Terrible Happened," 75.

16. Thurman, "A House Divided," 176.

17. David S. Cunningham, "Trinitarian Rhetoric in Murdoch, Morrison, and Dostoevsky," in *Literature and Theology at Century's End,* ed. Gregory Salyer and Robert Detweiler (Atlanta: Scholars Press, 1994), 201. On the use of the Bible in Baby Suggs's preaching and other passages of *Beloved* see Carolyn Mitchell, "I Love to Tell the Story: Biblical Revisions in *Beloved,*" *Religion and Literature* 23 (Autumn 1991): 27–42.

18. One might also read into this homily a tenet of liberation theology as stated, for example, by Gustavo Gutiérrez or Leonardo Boff. These would argue that minorities freeing themselves from histories of suppression and exploitation should trade a stress on eschatology for social action. Rather than continuing to tolerate oppression in return for a better life in an illusory future heaven, those subjugated communities should use their energies for effecting immediate change. Especially in environments in the developing world, where oppression has generated liberation thinking, the new accent is on the physical, the fleshly, on creating conditions of better health, improved living and working conditions, and breaking patterns of abuse of women and children. If such efforts do not appear to be overtly religious it is because religion, specifically Christianity, has preached a gospel of sin and redemption, of reward and punishment in a life after death, that by and large reinforces rather than challenges those structures that keep minorities "in their place." See Otto Maduro, "Liberation Theology," in *A New Handbook of Christian Theology,* ed. Donald W. Musser and Joseph L. Price (Nashville: Abingdon Press, 1992), 287–93.

19. See Lawrence Thornton's fine novel on the Argentinian "disappeareds,"

Imagining Argentina (New York: Doubleday, 1987) for a dramatization of the use of rape as a government-practiced shaming tactic.

20. Angelo, "The Pain of Being Black," 121.

21. Thurman, "A House Divided," 176.

22. Ibid. The shaming consists also of a voyeurism and public exposure. Sethe is held down by one of the boys while the other sucks her breast, with "their book-reading teacher watching and writing it up. . . . Add my husband to it, watching, above me in the loft . . . looking down on what I couldn't look at all" (70).

23. Bernard Williams, *Shame and Necessity* (Berkeley: University of California Press, 1993); see my reference to Williams in chapter 2, note 15.

24. Bernard Knox, "The Greek Way," *New York Review of Books,* November 18, 1993, 45. Knox's review has been helpful to me in my reading of Williams.

25. Williams, *Shame and Necessity,* especially chapter 4, "Shame and Autonomy."

26. Ibid., 125.

27. Angelo, "The Pain of Being Black," 120.

8

Subjected Wife:
Many Things Have Happened since He Died

A woman or man raised in a Christian environment and sexually abused as a child may be particularly vulnerable to an incomplete resolution of that sexual abuse. It is seldom, if ever, asked whether religious factors themselves play a role in the creation of the illnesses from which these children later suffer.

> —Sheila A. Redmond, "Christian 'Virtues' and Recovery from Child Sexual Abuse"

Marriage, like mourning, is a ritual that binds the self to the beloved, to the community, and to God.

> —Carolyn M. Jones, "*Sula* and *Beloved*"

Beloved (essentially unnamed), about two years old when her mother slits her throat, returns eighteen years later to haunt the woman who committed the ultimate child abuse. Elizabeth Dewberry Vaughn's twenty-year-old unnamed narrator in *Many Things Have Happened since He Died* has likewise suffered as a child. She has been molested by an alcoholic uncle, and that is one of the reasons why she is suicidally confused about religion, sex, marriage, and vocation—about practically everything. Like the other women characters discussed in this section, she is a victim of the seduction-abuse-abandonment pattern, although in her case the seduction is as much religious as sexual. Vaughn's emphasis is on the complex nature of the abuse, and the abandonment is not merely the final stage of the sequence but something that happens to the young woman repeatedly. The four components of the novel I will discuss in this chapter all anticipate the concerns of the third and final part of this volume: the narrator's voice, the influence of biblical language and other institutionalized religious expression, the acute fragmentation of characters' personalities, and a high incidence of violence.

The narrator of *Many Things* begins her story (spoken on tapes, written as notes, and eventually produced as a draft of an autobiographical novel) some fifteen months after her father dies on holiday in Florida. She marries the unstable Malone, a dental student at the University of Alabama in Birmingham, and works as a legal secretary to help support them. Malone's vicious temper counteracts the young couple's efforts to lead an "ideal" Christian marriage in which the husband, St. Paul-style, is the authority and the wife the helpmeet. Their arguments focus often on money, especially on what Malone and his meddling mother suspect is an insurance payout from the father's death kept by the narrator's mother for herself. The acrimony deepens, and Malone turns abusive, hitting his wife, breaking her finger, and eventually raping her and making her pregnant. His disintegration is hastened by his involvement with drugs and two unscrupulous male friends. He spends budgeted money, neglects his studies, and leaves home, only to return full of remorse and promises to change.

Things go from bad to worse. The couple learns that no insurance money exists. The young wife catches Malone with his two friends in her own bed, and a church-sponsored "Living Loving Marriage Weekend" brings only brief reconciliation. Malone dies of a drug overdose, and the young widow discovers that she is pregnant. Unable to consider an abortion, she delivers the child, a boy, but gives him away through an adoption agency. At the conclusion she has sent the manuscript of her life events, disguised as a novel, off to an agent and is "contemplating her options."[1]

The plot is like the narrator's mind: confused, erratic, moving in fits and starts, and yet always emerging from the muddle with something resolved, however naively accomplished it may have been. Although her life proceeds (one cannot say progresses) in terms of the bad luck that marks classical tragedy, she is in partial control of her plot via an immensely energetic, comic inventiveness, and her story becomes a version of a Christian comedy. Yet it is a comedy, finally, not of plot and action but of voice and perspective. These are unique because, among other reasons, the narrator is half in and half out of the tradition of evangelical, fundamentalist Protestantism, the target of considerable satire from Mark Twain and Johnson Jones Hooper (the author of Captain Suggs's comic camp meeting travails) in the nineteenth century to Sinclair Lewis, Flannery O'Connor, Peter DeVries, Frederick Buechner, and Ishmael Reed in the twentieth.

Vaughn's character has more of an insider's view, however, than most. Although the author uses her narrator's often manic monologue to poke fun at sectarian enthusiasm and pieties of doubtful conviction, the tone is warmer, more sympathetic, and more like that of Clyde Edgerton in

Raney than of Harry Crews in *The Gospel Singer.* Humor generally works through some strategy of excess that causes surprise—what Arthur Koestler has called "a collision of matrices"—and that holds true for this novel.[2] The title, which one reviewer thought "flip and silly," is excessive in its wordiness, yet it jars as a flat, laconic understatement.[3] "Many things" indeed: merely abuse, rape, death, pregnancy, and the birth and relinquishing of a son.

Running on for Jesus

Understatement typifies the narrator; her naively forthright language masks an agitated, overwrought mind that seems to be responding to too many stimuli. Pondering suicide and murder, she says, "If I had to kill myself or somebody else it would not be bloody. You can stick a nail in somebody's ear when they're asleep and they won't be able to figure out what did it if you pulled it back out. . . . If you do the nail you should probably give them sleeping pills too because if you accidentally woke them up how would you explain" (7). Here are mayhem and manners juxtaposed, a reflection on how to kill merged with a concern for decorum—a curious throwback to the tone of Jacobean drama. The narrator has little discriminatory sense, little ability to distinguish between what is important and what is not, and the lack makes her both funny and pathetic. One laughs at and with her; her insights born of dissonance are surprising because of the comedy of the unexpected. Like the workings of metaphor (which is, among other things, an exercise of metaphor), her joining of unrelated realms forces readers to make an imaginative leap. One pities her because her failure to read society's conventions is bound to land her in trouble.

Her writing style, intended to imitate oral transmission onto tape, is also a version of stream of consciousness, with its run-ons and sparse punctuation. The simple sentences go on and on to form compound declarations that one expects will end long before they do. Indeed, they keep accruing like the narrator's woes. Madison Bell thinks that the "narration [which] indiscriminately smashes together wish-fulfillment daydreams, lunatic-fringe fundamentalist dogmas and what seem to be shards of an incipient psychosis" is "like listening to someone possessed by a succession of individual demons."[4] An example is a frenetic two-and-a-half-page chapter that begins with a reflection on food and slides into one on earrings:

> I love canned soup especially Campbell's Chunky all kinds except the ones that have ham. You shouldn't eat ham because God gave it to the

Jews as a rule not to eat for a reason and that is pork is filthy. . . . You should eat beef and chicken and fish and not drink alcohol because your body is a temple and you wouldn't pour wine all over the pews in a temple would you? . . . The point is that if the Holy Spirit dwells in you then you should not drink alcohol or He will have to drink it too and you do not want God drunk. . . . He who has ears to hear let him hear. If your ear offends you cut it off and cast it into the ocean it is better to enter the kingdom of heaven without an ear than not to. Don't pierce your ears God did not make them that way. (169–70)

The passage is funny not only in its compulsive projection of bizarre images (pouring wine over pews) and in its theological chop-logic (getting two-thirds of the Trinity drunk) but also in the "anything goes" rhetoric typical of the discourse of media evangelists, call-in radio shows, and the more surreal of the stand-up comedians whose routines can be viewed on many television channels. The verbiage of the *Many Things* narrator may be a bit more excessive than these but not by much. She belongs to an overstimulated generation inundated with "bytes" of this and that, overwhelmed by details, and armed with little instruction on how to filter the worthwhile from the trash or to systematize and set priorities. MTV provides an apt model for comprehending the young narrator's mind. In the typical music television song-spectacle, a narrative flow is replaced by juxtapositions of images or ministories that provide a fragmented impression or mood, and a surprising number of them, such as some of Madonna's videos, blend traditionally sacred imagery (the cross, figures of saints, nuns, and people praying) with secular scenes in dissonant, clumsy, and naive ways that can be inadvertently comic or uncanny. Vaughn's novel is much like this. "Many things" clutter the narrator's head, and trivial bits vie with the serious for attention, her unconscious struggling to break through her strong repressions and the motions of her faith like a frantic sheepdog trying to circumscribe the unruly flock of thoughts.

In all of this, though, the young woman follows her American Protestant heritage even though her church has left the mainstream for a narrower and shallower sectarian venue. Although she is erratic, she is also, along with her clichéd fundamentalism, determinedly practical, even pragmatic. She wants life to work, and she wants to make it work through the application of Christian formulas. It is no cliché to say that the nation was colonized by people—Puritan dissenters, Anglicans, Catholics, Methodists, Presbyterians, Reformed, Quakers, and others—who understood their faith to be the foundation of their labors to transform what they perceived as a savage wilderness (its more perilous parts, at least, ruled by the devil) into a garden of the civilized and redeemed. For many of these the Bible was the book of rules, the sacred text that provided a practical guide for survival to those who knew where and how to look.

The Biblical Public Sphere

For the young secretary of *Many Things* the Bible is such a book of rules, containing not only the formula for personal salvation by being born again through Christ but also the precepts for daily, normative behavior—for attaining to the life of perfection that is her ideal. Even more, it influences her language, pervades her imagery, and provides a reflexive response in her frequent times of crisis. Much of her Bible literacy seems incongruous, for she (an electronic media child) is also a devotee of *Wheel of Fortune* and Oprah Winfrey, and she can curse impressively, yet the Bible (perhaps, but not necessarily, the King James version) and the rhetoric it has inspired are still the core of her communication. In this she mirrors millions of Americans who, in the face of a perceived growing secularism, continue to view and use the Bible as their indispensable source of truth and not only worship through it but also worship the Bible itself. Charles Strozier, after a caveat about relying too heavily on polls, provides a statistical report on those in America who believe in the Bible:

> The survey data suggest that some 40 percent of the American public believes in the Bible as the "actual word of God and is to be taken literally, word for word." That would approach 100 million people. Approximately 84 percent of Americans believe that Jesus is the son of God, and 80 percent said they were convinced they will appear before God on judgment day. The same percentage believes God works miracles, and half the population believes in angels. Nearly a third of all Americans firmly believe in the rapture. As Garry Wills puts it, "It seems careless for scholars to keep misplacing such a large body of people."[5]

The Bible constitutes the textual arena of and for a public realm in America more widespread and more enduring than any comparable phenomena—more than, say, the Constitution, which few know comprehensively and fewer still have actually read. This realm possesses, of course, popular cultural dimensions. As Allene Stuart Phy states in "The Bible and American Popular Culture,"

> For millions of southern people the Bible is an account of origins, a history, and a record of God's continuing wrestling with humanity, inerrant in its every jot and tittle. It provides all one wishes to know or needs to know about life in this world and the world to come. . . .

Though the expansion of southern attitudes has not made the entire nation students of the scriptures, southern ideas have permeated popular culture, and evangelical religion, often promoted in the media by southern evangelists, has in the last two decades gained at the expense of traditional "mainline" denominations, although there is now some indication this trend is slowly reversing.[6]

Toni Morrison (whose *Beloved* is full of biblical allusions) has called attention to biblical influence in her background: "I have a family of people who were highly religious—that was part of their language. Their sources were biblical. They expressed themselves in that fashion."[7] *Many Things* illustrates the continuing pervasion of American public life by biblical and Christian-inspirational language, and the narrator's expression of it—like America's—is comic and also reflects her social and spiritual confusion. Early on, pondering her father's death, she says, "Satan tempts me with weak and selfish thoughts but I talk myself out of them and prove how strong I am. I believe God rewards the little things he who is faithful in little. I may have added a diamond to my crown just now by overcoming that selfish thought" (4). The "he who is faithful in little" (see Luke 16:10: "He that is faithful in little things") combines with the "diamond in my crown," a slight variation on the phrase from the gospel hymn "Will There Be Any Stars in My Crown?" The sentiment is comic, among other reasons, for in the very act of declaiming her unselfishness the young woman displays her self-centeredness.

On the next page, still thinking obsessively of her father's suicide, the narrator plays with the Lord's Prayer (Matthew 6:9) in an italicized stream-of-consciousness passage: "*Your father is dead your father is dead. Your father is in heaven. Our Father who art in heaven. Our father who is dead*" (5). This is typical of the woman's morbidity. She is much preoccupied with death and its physical aspects, yet the emphasis on the body that ensues is far less erotic than in the other novels I have discussed in these chapters except, perhaps, *Quicksand*. The potential eroticism is suppressed and redirected into the quotation and imitation of biblical language, as when she, with suicide on her mind, tries to explain the "tough time" in her marriage: "I count it all joy my brothers when I experience various trials knowing that the testing of my faith produces endurance and let endurance have its perfect result that you may be perfect and complete lacking in nothing" [James 1:2]. Malone just better realize that there is a limit to God's patience. If you do something to the least of these you do it to Christ [Matthew 25:40], and He won't take much more of this" (21). This mishmash of cited fragments from a Pauline letter and Jesus' gospel utterance, culminating in the young wife's exasperated "prophetic" warning to her irascible spouse, is at once risable and impoverished—funny as a misappropriation of scripture and inadequate in its effort to have the biblical phrases somehow, formulaically, encompass and heal the couple's distress.[8]

Her biblicism, in curious ways, both undermines her love life with her husband and compensates for its lacks. Because she believes, along with many real-life Americans, that sex is sinful because it is of the flesh, she participates in sexual acts guiltily and seeks to assuage that guilt by immersing herself in biblical language, trying as literally as possible to embody that language. This sounds fatuous until one recalls that many evangelical and fundamentalist Christians attempt to live the Pauline injunction to put on the body of Christ (Romans 13:14), although this imperative is a metaphor that can be communicated only in and as language.

"I have been crucified with Christ" (Galatians 2:20) the narrator declares, and she identifies with Christ's body by borrowing Jesus' words, often at moments of corporeal crisis. Remorseful after Malone's death and after she has allowed his body to be cut up for organ donations, she says, "Oh God forgive me for I knew not what I did" (142), an ironic inversion of Jesus' words on the cross exonerating his executioners, "Father, forgive them, for they know not what they do" (Luke 23:34). Later, when she is in the hospital delivery room, about to bear the boy she will give away and breathing in the anesthesia, she thinks to herself, "It is finished I lay down my life for my baby" (242), reminiscent of Jesus' final words before he dies on the cross according to John 19:30. In the first of these, then, she assumes guilt for her husband's mutilated body, and in the second she is ready to die for her still-unborn child. If neither of these sentiments is precisely Christlike, they do suggest her reflexive desire to incorporate the gospels' salvific language.

Sometimes the narrator adopts apocalyptic-eschatological rhetoric from the Bible. Early on, during one of the hopeful moments in this doomed marriage, she asserts, "We are going to read the Bible together every night. We have been brought through fire and now we are shining and pure." The language is like that used to describe the saints who have survived the endtime tribulation according to the Book of Revelation narrative (see chapters 21–22), and, typically, the young woman renders the figuration ludicrous. A huge difference obtains between those martyred for their faith and an immature couple caught up in marital troubles. The fire that "purifies" them reminds one more of the domestic and communal betrayals in Miller's The Crucible than it does of triumphal saintly steadfastness. Nevertheless, the narrator persists in her chiliast imagery. Visions of death, immortality, and eternal bliss and punishment are prominent in her Bible Belt imagination, and she also draws on them at critical moments. After Malone's death she worries obsessively about him: "What if Malone is in Hell weeping and gnashing his teeth. What if his arm or his hair has been on fire for the past two weeks and he can't put it out" (154). The "weeping and gnashing his teeth" derives from the so-named miniature apocalypse depicted parabolically by Jesus to his disciples in Matthew 24 (see especially verse 51), and the inextinguishable fire is a standard element of eternal punishment in New Testament apocalyptic (Matthew 18:7).

Finally, in the hospital scene, the young woman in labor and half-expecting that she will die, thinks she will "go to Heaven and be together with Daddy and Malone no more sorrow no more pain live in a mansion walk the streets of gold" (242). This is more imagery from the Book of Revelation (chapter 21), a vision of bliss followed, after the boy's birth, by the narrator's musings on new life borrowed from Genesis 3:24 ("And the two shall be one flesh") and John 3:7 ("Ye must be born again"). As usual, she distorts the traditional meaning of the passages, making them refer to her new maternal condition rather than to the institution of marriage and to redemption through Christ; yet such a naive hermeneutic is by no means rare among American Protestant biblicists. If, as the feminist slogan goes, "the personal is political," in this milieu the politics of the biblical public realm are also reduced to the idiosyncratic personal: every believer for herself, with the Word of God assumed to speak directly to the immediate situation of the reader or listener, with textual context and history ignored. Here is another reason why the hapless young wife, soon to be a widow, is so confused: Her church provides no substantial spiritual guidance (although it does sponsor a ridiculous retreat for married couples), only an endorsement of personalist Bible reading and interpretation ignorant of hermeneutical principles.[9]

The irresponsible, deceptive Malone is even more damaging, for he, a true hypocrite, twists biblical and Christian-edification language to his selfish designs. He manipulates the narrator, especially with the sexist Pauline command that wives should submit to their husbands because the man is the "head" of the woman just as Christ is the head of the man (1 Corinthians 11:3). It is clear that Malone cannot function honorably as part of that spurious hierarchy, not least because he is involved in a sexual affair with two male friends. The shock of discovering him with the two in the couple's marriage bed induces a desperate and effusive prayer (89–90) by the narrator; it contains liturgical language ("please be merciful for I have sinned") and references to Jesus' words on belief and supplication ("I really believe and you said that if we believe and ask then whatever we ask you will do" [Matthew 7:7]) and concludes with the complete Doxology ("Praise God from whom all blessings flow").

Such traumatic events turn her sadder but not necessarily wiser, and she remains sexually unfulfilled in spite of her attempts to supplant human eros with spiritual love; the only rapture she knows of is the one attached to the Last Judgment. When, after Malone's death, she avers, "I will never go on *Love Connection*" (175), she reveals the superficial level of her erotic maturity. It is the same level at which she understands the Bible and her religious life.

In what sense, then, do this confused, pathetically funny protagonist and her world represent the Bible in and as an American public realm? Phy suggests an answer:

> The majority of U.S. citizens . . . claim to be devoted to the Bible, even though many actually know very little of the scriptures and would indeed be shocked to discover some of the assertions contained therein. . . . When the Bible is actually read, the reading is selective. Perhaps this has always been true. Here is the ultimate paradox. The culture echoes the Bible at every level, yet actual knowledge of the scriptures is slight and declining even in the Bible-thumping American South. The Bible itself is studied less than ever before, and it may be that it reaches Americans today, for better or worse, largely as it is filtered through the popular culture.[10]

Vaughn's thoroughly modern Birmingham secretary is also postmodern, able to believe simultaneously in Jesus and Oprah Winfrey, to be both submissive and assert her feminism ("I am woman hear me roar" [67]), to accept as literal truth the figurative biblical language and the fiction of soap opera, and to nurture an apocalyptic vision and an expectation that life may yet be materially good for her—if she doesn't decide to kill herself. This brilliantly drawn creature, so nuanced in her many confusions, resembles millions of Americans who constitute a popular religious, Bible-worshiping public realm informed by idiosyncratic readings of our central sacred text: readings that have assumed—here is another paradox—a certain superficial cohesive (if not coherent) power as fundamentalism flourishes. This public realm is above all fundamentalist in its rigid miscomprehension and abuse of the Bible, and Vaughn demonstrates how the misfortunes of her main character derive predominantly from the flaws of that coercive pseudo-community.

Family Faultlines

The world of religious fundamentalism is a pseudo-community because it is at its base extremely fragmented, just as its biblical interpretation is atomized and disjointed.[11] Fragmentation marks all aspects of the life of the *Many Things* narrator. Bell has also remarked on the woman's "strangely fractured language."[12] It is fractured, of course, because she herself is; it is a significant synecdochic moment when Malone breaks her finger, causing her to go to the hospital emergency room for treatment. One broken finger stands for her fractured psyche as well as for the couple's broken relationship. What is the cause of the fracture and fragmentation? Where are the fault lines? They run, not surprisingly, through families: the narrator's, Malone's, and the one that the young couple constitute. The narrator's father has committed suicide (as did his father and grandfather), leaving her and her mother distraught and, as they eventually discover, in debt. Malone's father does not figure in the narrative, only his busybody mother. It is understandable, then, that the two dysfunctional families have produced children who form a third one.

One relative in particular, other than the woman's parents, has contributed to her fragmentation: the alcoholic Uncle Dwight, who is mentioned infrequently but who apparently molested her when she was younger. Her aversion to sex, along with her preoccupation with it, thus seems to have a source other than her puritan suspicion that it is inherently sinful; she is reacting to abuse from within the family that dislocates her still more.[13]

The way she deals with her disintegration is as instructive as the portrayal of the parts of personality at war with each other—hermeneutical, spiritual, familial, psychological, and sexual personae all striving to assert themselves. Most obviously, she compulsively creates lists, among them things that have happened since her father's suicide (the "many things" of the title), ways not to kill herself, New Year's resolutions, and what to wear to the hospital. The novel even concludes with a projection of her list of "options." The lists are a way of asserting momentary control over the chaos of her life. Lists impose sequence and order out of many pieces and thus project a model of wholeness. They make sense out of the mishaps that dog the narrator and instruct her on the steps she should take to maintain her composure and, thereby, her precarious sanity. Yet this hermeneutic of listing also distorts. It does not truly heal her fractures, for the wholeness it suggests is illusory, a misinterpretation that does nothing to help her understand why she is so at odds with herself.

The narrator responds more thoughtfully but no more successfully to her fragmentation by addressing death. She is strikingly morbid, dwelling on her father's decomposition in the grave, on suicide and murder, on an afterlife in heaven and hell, and on body organ donations. This strategy (or compulsion) of looking death in the face might work if she carried it through to a consistent philosophy or at least perspective on death.[14] But she cannot or will not do that, apart from her lack of philo-

sophical sophistication. She is too conflicted between pop Christian scenarios of death and immortality and her impulse to end her life.

That her thoughts on death are essentially narcissistic—seeking to overcome fragmentation by making the self the annihilating center of being—
is revealed by her comment on one of those occasions when she contem-
plates suicide: "I want to look beautiful. There is something wonderful
about a beautiful young woman who is dead" (32). As Poe aficionados
know, that sentiment is not original with the *Many Things* narrator but
was voiced by that earlier morbid southerner in "The Philosophy of Composition" from 1846. There, he argues with typical Romantic extremism,
"The death, then, of a beautiful woman is, unquestionably, the most po-
etical topic in the world."[15] Poe is a more apt avatar (as he was for Daniel
in Doctorow's novel) than the philosophers of the sublime whom he tried
to adapt for his art. Like the young woman of *Many Things*, he tried to
transcend the mess of his everyday life by fantasies of death, beauty, and
the spiritual combined—a blend that has always fascinated American artists. One thinks, for example, of Emily Dickinson's verse, Wallace Stevens's
"Sunday Morning," Jack Kerouac's maudlin versions, Hansen's *Mariette
in Ecstasy,* and all manner of New Age kitsch.

Vaughn's narrator seeks to heal her dislocations not only by fantasies
of death but also by fantasizing itself. She is close to clinical delusion in
any case (to the extent of being an unreliable narrator of the most problematic sort), and her fantasy life constantly threatens her sense of reality. Its dimensions range from the projection of the four invisible friends
she once had and drowned to her grandiose view of herself as a famous
author. In a sense, the latter fantasy pays off because, as we surmise via
the text's self-reflexive twist, the recording of her tribulations becomes
the novel that she sells and that we read. Thus, she does reach public attention, but we have no evidence that the living-out of this fantasy world
makes her fractured life any more whole. If anything, the sad ends of historical authors (Ezra Pound, Sylvia Plath, Jack Kerouac, Richard Brauti-
gan, Anne Sexton, and Jerzy Kosinski, among others) suggest that professional success does not necessarily cure but may instead exacerbate the
artist's disjuncture.

More broadly, the young woman's clichéd vision of reaching fame and
fortune is a particular American fantasy—in a way, a national obsession—
fed by the celebrity cults that the news, entertainment, and evangelism
media create by lotteries and game shows. These, in turn, have evolved
from the older myth of America as the land without prohibiting class
structures, where through industry, skill, luck, nerve, and God's blessing
great fortunes can be made.

But if the narrator falls for this fantasy of the American dream, she is also taken in by a fundamentalist sect that proclaims to offer wholeness but is actually deeply fragmented. The shallowness of this church is exposed in a chapter (107–26) that is a delicious satire on religious marriage counseling. Malone, without his wife's knowledge, signs them up for a "Living Loving Marriage Weekend: Turn Your Relationship from a Tragedy into a Triumph" at their church. During the event they undergo a series of old-hat maneuvers to improve their union that mimic the evangelical Christian marriage manuals as well as *Reader's Digest*-style "so-and-so-many steps toward improving your marital/sex/love life." Predictably, the underlying principle is the Pauline hierarchic concept of women deferring to men as the ones with authority: Women are the "weaker vessel" who need protection and honor, whose duties are domestic, and who should be silent in church. It is the "philosophy" expressed, for example, by "Moral Majority" spokesman Jerry Falwell in an attack on the Equal Rights Amendment: "I believe that women deserve more than equal rights. And in families and nations where the Bible is believed, Christian women are honored above men. Only in places where the Bible is believed and practiced do women receive more than equal rights. Men and women have differing strengths. . . . Women need to know Jesus Christ as their Lord and Savior and be under His Lordship. They need a man who knows Jesus Christ as his Lord and Savior, and they need to be part of a home where their husband is a godly leader and where there is a Christian family."[16]

This attitude makes Vaughn's narrator queasy, but she goes along with it, willing to try virtually anything to make her short and troubled marriage work. She absorbs the facile solution of "The Four A's": "Accept him. . . . Admire him. . . . Adapt to him. . . . Appreciate him" (110), but the reconciliation that the weekend brings about lasts only briefly. Soon Malone, for all of his pious platitudes, is back to his usual nastiness, and the disintegration of the marriage, and of the individuals in it, accelerates.

Is this plagued narrator's failed search for coherence and wholeness plausible? Does it go with or against the American grain? Joyce Sweeny in a remarkably forthright review of *Many Things* ventures an answer:

> This character really rings true. We don't want to admit it, but we have heard this kind of thinking before, from friends and relatives and acquaintances. . . . We know people who believe their sorrows are really a mystical blessing from God and who therefore endure more than they should. . . . If we are truly honest, we know we have all been like her at one time or another. . . . We are all still in love with someone who abused us. We are all desperately gluing veneers of philosophy and self-confidence over the holes in our psyches.[17]

Dionysus in Birmingham

Madison Bell, also trying to get a perspective on this purported (according to Sweeny) American Everywoman and her elusive text, declares, "It would be easy to say this novel is a bitter satire on the way in which ostensibly Christian doctrine can be twisted into a Machiavellian weapon of injury, so it is all the more impressive that the narrator does manage to make certain lifesaving decisions within the borders of her belief."[18] He is correct in this assessment, but I want to emphasize the role of violence in the novel, the nature of the "weapon of injury" that determines the otherwise meandering plot and looks ahead to the interpretation of American violence that I will attempt in the final part of this study.

First, it is worth pointing out that the multifold fragmentation of the woman's personality has a terrifying literal dimension to it that marks a great deal of recent American and other writing. One could refer to a Dionysian tradition in American fiction, a kind of writing that, like Euripides' *The Bacchae*, features *sparagmos,* a dismemberment, often frenzied and ritualistic, of persons. Tennessee Williams's *Suddenly Last Summer* (at least according to Catharine's account) has a gang of street boys tearing apart and devouring Cousin Sebastian; Saul Maloff's *Heartland* has an obnoxious visiting poet emasculated by a group of girls at the Donner Pass College for Women; in Thomas Pynchon's *Gravity's Rainbow* Slothrop is "broken down . . . and scattered"; Thomas Sanchez's *Rabbit Boss* opens with a scene in which humans are massacred and the heart of one eaten; and in Bernard Malamud's apocalyptic *God's Grace* a group of humanized apes tears apart and feasts on other primates.[19]

Nothing this gruesome occurs in *Many Things;* a broken finger and a blackened eye are not the equivalent of body dismemberment. Yet the novel is pervaded by a sense of violence all the more shocking because it marks the personalities of these aspiring-to-middle-class characters. The narrator thinks of mutilation, as in her reflection on killing someone with a nail in the ear, and she wakes from a dream of someone trying to stab her: "Lying there thinking about murderers," she "feel[s] tied to the violence" and speculates on "how everything springs from violence" (172–73). In this context the teeth that Malone has in the house to study (as a dental student) and that his wife abhors take on a singular meaning. They are reminiscent of the flesh-tearing instruments with which humans consume each other in *sparagmos.* One is not surprised when she takes a "sparagmotic" revenge on Malone after his death by having "his heart cut out . . . his eyes poked out" (146).

In his review of *Many Things* Richard Eder observes that the woman's mind "zig-zags around the scars of abuse," but they are not merely scars, they are open wounds as well, and these betray a psychopathic nature. "I used to have four invisible friends until I got tired of them and we went to the beach and I threw them in the ocean. None of them could swim. I wish I could do that to God" (11).[20] She is in a long line of those who have wished to kill off divinity, although her mode lacks by far the subtlety of Nietzsche or Altizer.[21] What does distinguish it is its unreflective violence, in keeping with a strong trait of her personality. She not merely wishes God dead, she wishes she could drown him. Her impulse reminds one of the ancient connections between religion and violence that have reemerged so forcefully in the late twentieth century in phenomena such as ethnic-religious strife among Muslims, Christians, and Jews and the suicidal acts of apocalyptic sects such as those at Jonestown and Waco. The Dionysian tradition in American writing has its inspiration in the primitive blendings of religious and corporeal passion in American life. Such passion assumes power—inevitably destructive power—when it invades groups, and often that communal power displays a sexual thrust, as in the licentiousness of a Jim Jones and David Koresh, the charismatic leaders at Jonestown and Waco, or in the agendas of abortion protesters who employ intimidation and force, ostensibly to save fetuses in the name of the sacred but in fact to control the sexuality of women.[22]

Philip Vellacott, commenting on *The Bacchae,* says that "Dionysus . . . is himself the embodiment of excess; and while in the play no conditional way of accepting his divinity is proposed as an alternative to Pentheus' insane attempt to expel him by force, it is made clear that the attempt to ignore or banish him will render his nature not merely amoral but bestial, and hostile to the highest human values which the slow progress of man has won to distinguish him from beasts."[23] That judgment, composed during the fifties, seems dated in some ways yet is essentially valid. A society that tries to control its irrational components, such as its sexuality, by using religion as repression will find that religion spins out of control and turns violent and death-dealing. Wishing God dead is fairly pointless insofar as religion often incorporates an irrepressible Dionysian excess that sooner or later will break through even the most puritan defenses.

Bell thinks that Vaughn's narrator at last realizes this. "If religion nearly drives her crazy it finally helps to heal her too, and this process constitutes the novel's conclusion."[24] It is actually not all that apparent that religion does aid in her healing at the end—indeed, whether healing takes place at all—but she does, in the last two pages, forgive herself for her many failures and then prays to God for the success of her manuscript (the narrative we have read), that it will be published.

More important than that contrived ending, though, is the impression of pain left by the pervasive violence of the narrator's life. Eder says that "the pain is revealed, of course, through the detours, the diversions, the concealments," and indeed it is, but it is also disclosed openly and even blatantly.[25] One such typical pain and violence scene late in the novel—another *sparagmos* scene where the narrator is "eaten"—is a dream in which she experiences the birth of her son as a rendering and devouring: "I was a roast turkey. Everybody was sitting around me at a banquet table watching TV fixing to take the stuffing out of me but then a warning beep like for bad weather flashed on the TV and then the mouth started screaming acute distress doctor the heartbeat has dropped to sixty-one acute distress and I sat up and looked at the mouth it tried to bite me and everybody at the table jumped up to get a piece of me and I woke up" (244).

The banquet table is obviously the hospital bed in the delivery room, the stuffing is the child to be delivered, who has "wrapped the umbilical cord around his neck and almost killed himself" (244), the television is the monitor, and everybody trying "to get a piece of me" is the team of doctors and nurses working to save the child. Pain is not mentioned, but it is so manifestly a part of this scene that it need not be. The pain that the narrator suffers here and elsewhere from the violence of her life ought to be worth something; it ought to be translatable into wisdom, satisfaction, peace of mind, happiness, or some other good. As David Morris reminds us in his remarkable *The Culture of Pain,* "Pain once possessed redemptive and visionary powers" now largely forgotten because

[The] secular scientific spirit of modern medicine has so eclipsed other systems of thought. We need to recover this understanding partly because it shows so clearly how pain inhabits a social realm that sprawls well outside the domain of medicine. . . . Many people today experience pain within systems of belief that Western doctors have long dismissed or forgotten. The religious and prophetic uses of pain are at odds not with medicine alone, however. They stand in conflict with almost all ordinary ways of seeing. In effect, visionary experience tends to demand a full-scale reinterpretation of the everyday world. Further, in its call to reinterpret the world, it is also implicitly political. . . . This political and visionary pain, no matter how alien to the dominant system of medical thought, is still actively at work in the modern world, like a neglected but potent sacred text.[26]

Devouring the Go(o)ds

A primary irony of *Many Things* is that although the narrator and her environment are deeply religious, she and her family do not manage to transform their pain into anything redemptive. They are not deeply religious, only broadly so, and it is their shallow religiosity that in part causes pain rather than transforms it. That religiosity is part of the cliché of the young woman's life. The violence and the pain it produces are dealt with instead in another traditional American fashion: in terms of consumerism—or more exactly, in terms of the confusion that persists in America between religion and consumerism. The young woman exemplifies that confusion. She wishes both to be obedient to Christ and to enjoy wealth: "Malone sees and helps me to see that Christ came to set us free, not to restrain us. My highest calling is to be a helpmeet for him, to obey him, to submit my desires to his, since only in losing my life shall I find it. Someday Malone will be very rich" (6). Such crass conniving, done with a play on Pauline subservience, informs much of the novel's plot. It is not always the young woman's initiative; Malone suspects, after his father-in-law's suicide, that the narrator's mother has kept a $100,000 insurance payout for herself rather than turn it over to her daughter, and he bullies the narrator into legal action against her mother. As it turns out, of course, no such money exists, because the narrator's father died in debt, but the mental pain of estrangement between mother and daughter, as well as the physical pain perpetuated by Malone on his wife, cannot be retracted.

The marriage renewal weekend also employs consumerist tactics that are ludicrously embodied in the analogy that the counselor uses to describe the roles in her own marriage: "Carolyn says it's like a food processor and a microwave oven—Kenny is a food processor and she is a microwave oven" (109). This revelation comes after the assertion that "the whole Christian life is one of submission; being submissive to your husband doesn't make you less than him it just means you just have different functions" (109). This makes as little sense to the narrator as to the reader, but she "submits" for the time being, trying to comprehend her place in this dangerous liaison in terms of high-tech appliances for the literally consumption-obsessed society. It is not surprising that the delivery room dream involves a screaming mouth that tries to bite her. Modern consumerism is also a form of *sparagmos,* a frantic and sometimes ritualistic devouring of superfluous "goods" and a tearing apart of communal fabrics that must be paid for, and the payment for which accrues to the wealth of a few.

The narrator yields to this seduction. Certainly, her church does not warn her against it but is complicit. Her solution to her mounting problems is to exploit her life and try to turn her misfortunes into fortune by writing and selling her life story thus far as a novel. This, too, is the American success story. Scandal and sensation sell; the value of pain is its cash value. Seen this way, *Many Things* challenges a reviewer's assessment of the dramatized version: "If all the character's hardships amount to is some Oprah-bound opportunism, real or imagined, then this is no tragedy."[27] The tragedy is that late-century America in its frenzy of spending and consuming does not see—ironically—its accelerating fragmentation but still hopes for wholeness through marketing its very deterioration. Vaughn's novel lays bare the lure of that false hope.

Notes

1. Elizabeth Dewberry Vaughn, *Many Things Have Happened since He Died* (New York: Vintage Books, 1992), 67. The author now writes under the name of Elizabeth Dewberry, but to avoid confusion I refer to her in connection with this novel as Vaughn.

2. Arthur Koestler, *The Act of Creation* (New York: Macmillan, 1964), see especially chapter 1, "The Logic of Laughter."

3. Madison Smartt Bell, "Meanderings of a Twisted Mind," *Washington Post*, April 19, 1990, E3. The hardcover edition of Vaughn's novel had the title *Many Things Have Happened since He Died and Here Are the Highlights*, and this excessive title is surely what Bell had in mind when he criticized it. The last phrase of the title was dropped in the paperback version.

4. Bell, "Meanderings of a Twisted Mind," E3. Elements of hysteria also inhabit the young woman's mind, and one could interpret the novel in terms of her hysterical behavior. For examples of studies that undertake this kind of approach see Diane Price Herndl, *Invalid Women: Figuring Feminine Illness in American Fiction and Culture, 1840–1940* (Chapel Hill: University of North Carolina Press, 1993), and Sander L. Gilman et al., *Hysteria Beyond Freud* (Los Angeles: University of California Press, 1993). I am indebted to Tanya Augsburg for introducing me to these studies.

5. Charles B. Strozier, *Apocalypse: On the Psychology of Fundamentalism in America* (Boston: Beacon Press, 1994), 5.

6. Allene Stuart Phy, "The Bible and American Popular Culture: An Overview and Introduction," in *The Bible and Popular Culture in America,* ed. Allene Stuart Phy (Philadelphia: Fortress Press, and Chico, Calif.: Scholars Press, 1985), 1–2, 5. The paragraph continues: "If the thesis of Egerton and others is correct, much of the rest of the country has been southernized by the black and white migrations, by the ghettos that both races have established in major cities, by the California exodus, by the spread of southern country and western music, by Billy Graham evangelism, and by the flowering within Protestantism of an evangelical emphasis that is actually an urbanization of the older Fundamentalism." The thesis to which Phy refers is in John Egerton, *The Americanization of Dixie: The Southernization of America* (New York: Harper's Magazine Press, 1974).

7. Bessie W. Jones and Audrey L. Vinson, *The World of Toni Morrison: Explorations in Literary Criticism* (Dubuque: Kendall/Hunt, 1985), 137.

8. In *Religion and Sexuality in American Literature* (Cambridge: Cambridge

University Press, 1992), Ann-Janine Morey points to a sublimation of sexual desire to language in nineteenth-century novelists, mostly women, who conjoin sexuality and religion: "Christ himself is translated through the radiant model of the religious body of woman, while sexual passion is effaced in favor of its ecstatic translation as passionate religious speech" (237).

9. The narrator's church has, as Gadamer might put it, no comprehension of the *sensus communis*. Hans-Georg Gadamer, *Truth and Method* (New York: Seabury Press, 1975), 19–29.

10. Phy, "The Bible and American Popular Culture," 22.

11. For an excellent, popularly written book on American evangelicalism and religious fundamentalism see Randall Balmer, *Mine Eyes Have Seen the Glory: A Journey into the Evangelical Subculture in America* (New York: Oxford University Press, 1989).

12. Bell, "Meanderings of a Twisted Mind," E3.

13. Vaughn's second novel, *Break the Heart of Me* (New York: Doubleday, 1993), deals more extensively with the young protagonist's sexual abuse at the hands of one of her relatives.

14. For contemporary thinkers reflecting on death see, for example, John Hick, *Death and Eternal Life* (San Francisco: Harper and Row, 1970); Edith Wyschogrod, *Spirit in Ashes: Hegel, Heidegger, and Man-Made Mass Death* (New Haven: Yale University Press, 1985); and Martha C. Nussbaum, *The Fragility of Goodness: Luck and Ethics in Greek Tragedy and Philosophy* (New York: Cambridge University Press, 1986).

15. Edgar Allan Poe's "The Philosophy of Composition" was first published in *Graham's Magazine* in 1846. I have used the version anthologized in *American Poetry and Prose,* ed. Norman Foerster et al. (Boston: Houghton Mifflin, 1970), 366.

16. Jerry Falwell, *Listen America* (Garden City: Doubleday, 1980), 150–51.

17. Joyce Sweeny, "'Highlights' Heroine Is Fool in All of Us," *Atlanta Journal/Constitution,* March 18, 1990, N8. In her study of medieval women mystics Carolyn Walter Bynum shows that they, too, had a strong sense of body fragmentation but that, unlike for modern humans, this sense was exercised out of an underlying expectation of reintegration and wholeness. See *Fragmentation and Redemption: Essays on Gender and the Human Body in Medieval Religion* (New York: Zone Books, 1989).

18. Bell, "Meanderings of a Twisted Mind," E3.

19. See also T. Mark Ledbetter, "An Apocalypse of Race and Gender: Body Violence and Forming Identity in Toni Morrison's *Beloved,*" in *Postmodernism, Literature, and the Future of Theology,* ed. David Jasper (New York: St. Martin's Press, 1993), 78–90.

20. Richard Eder, "A Shaky Voice Reveals Horror Below, *Los Angeles Times,* April 26, 1990, E7.

21. See, for example, aphorism 125 on the madman in Friedrich Nietzsche, *Gay Science* in *Basic Writings of Nietzsche,* trans. and ed. Walter Kaufmann (New York: Random House, 1968), and Thomas J. J. Altizer, *Genesis and Apocalypse: A Theological Voyage toward Authentic Christianity* (Louisville: Westminster/John Knox Press, 1990).

22. On the Jonestown tragedy see Bruce B. Lawrence, *Defenders of God: The Fundamentalist Revolt against the Modern Age* (San Francisco: Harper and Row, 1989).

23. Euripides, *The Bacchae and Other Plays,* trans. Philip Vellacott (London: Penguin Books, 1954); the quotation is from Vellacott's introduction, 33.

24. Bell, "Meanderings of a Twisted Mind," E3.

25. Eder, "A Shaky Voice Reveals Horror Below," E7.

26. David B. Morris, *The Culture of Pain* (Berkeley: University of California Press, 1993), 125.

27. Steve Dollar, "Gothic Irony Fuels Explosive 'Many Things,'" *Atlanta Constitution,* January 20, 1994, B6. The drama version played at the Horizon Theatre in Atlanta during January and February 1994. Although the play, adapted by Tom Key from the novel, necessarily leaves out a good deal, it follows the plot of the novel closely.

PART 3

The Body Apocalyptic

9

Dancing to the Apocalypse

Why have apocalyptic fantasies continued to thrive even in the
ostensibly postreligious imaginaries we have called scientific
and postmodern?

—Martin Jay, "The Apocalyptic Imagination
and the Inability to Mourn"

It's the end of the world as we know it, and I feel fine.
—R.E.M.

American sexuality interacts with the public realm, or with public realms,
to constitute a body erotic akin to the body politic. In *Agnes of God, Mariette in Ecstasy,* and *The Company of Women* this corporate entity is shaped
within the framework of the Roman Catholic church (itself a massively
influential public sphere) and is in conflict with the church's authority.
The actual lived bodies of three young women, consecrated to Christian
chastity (formally so in the instances of Agnes and Mariette), become the
sites of a struggle between individual and church to assert or suppress
precisely that sexuality that makes the body erotic erotic or that makes
possible a religiously colored sexual public realm. For its members in orders, the church in these fictions only wants this realm to exist in a form
so sublimated that the sexual dimension is "spiritualized," made nonphysical. For the rest of the faithful, this realm should exist only within the
context of marriage, where the stress is on procreation and family.

The ventures of Agnes, Mariette, and Felicitas toward negotiating a
more liberal religious-sexual space for themselves that would permit a full
exercise of passion are thwarted by the church. To tolerate them would
mean the endorsement of a sphere that the church cannot control. In all
three cases the girls' sexuality is not merely thwarted; it is manipulated
by representatives of the church (and by others), and the young women
are, as a result, badly damaged. Agnes becomes a murderer, suffers madness, and dies. Mariette is forced out of her Christian vocation and spends
a life of faithful but frustrated "abeyance." Felicitas, following a traumatic
affair and a pregnancy, settles into an outwardly submissive domestic life

but rebels inwardly against God. A public sphere that combines sex and religion is an abnormality in these texts: at Agnes's abbreviated court trial for infanticide, in Mariette's convent when her purported or real stigmata cause a sensation among the sisters and in the surrounding village, and in Felicitas' marriage infiltrated by a reactionary priest and a group of anxious elderly women.

In *Quicksand* and *Beloved* the public realm is the lacerated black community in the aftermath of slavery and experiencing a continuing racial prejudice. Its sexual aspects consist of black women's endeavors to find fulfilling, "normal" love relationships in a culture where whites view them as primitive and instinctually lustful creatures and black men often misunderstand and exploit them. Its religious dimensions consist not only of a Christianity that promotes or at least condones prejudicial treatment of blacks, particularly black women, but also of a supernaturalism at odds with a more rationalist white Christianity and derived from African spiritism. Helga in *Quicksand* enters that sphere as a relative outsider, a mulatto not at home in the black world of Harlem nor in the white world of Copenhagen. Seeking some sort of haven, she is instead swallowed up by the sectarian black community and disappears into a miserable life as a preacher's wife in the poor, rural South—absorbed into that isolated public realm.

Sethe in *Beloved,* on the other hand, influences the public realm by her impact on the white and black communities. Her mad, defiant act of infanticide in 1855 not only liberates her and her family from a return to slavery, thus anticipating the nation's formal repudiation of that outrage less than a decade later, but it also estranges her, understandably, from black fellowship for another decade beyond that. She is rejoined to it through the intervention of the community of strongly religious women. Their action—the exorcism of Beloved as ghost—suggests another powerful public realm, the uncanny world of "spirit" that impinges on everyday life and turns it uncontrollable, just as the blacks have been politically and economically unshackled and made to stand as a threat to the old white order. Curiously, though, this unnerving realm of spirit is closely aligned to a sphere of the fleshly, as celebrated by Baby Suggs's sermons, and this enfleshment likewise threatens the whites through its erotic passion.

The young secretary of *Many Things Have Happened since He Died* inhabits a strange yet familiar public realm of biblicist fundamentalism joined to a high-tech consumerist culture. It is an environment of fragments spinning centrifugally, its components of sex and religion disintegrating into a chaos that gets ordering definition only as a vision of apocalypse.

Although these six texts are not directly connected to any single traumatic moment in the American public political realm, they probably have had—and are having—a greater impact than the texts I discussed in the first part of this volume. One can only conjecture about this, of course, but I would guess that the American public is somewhat less attentive to Miller's play and two difficult novels on the Rosenbergs than to Pielmeier's drama, and its cinema version, and the moral suasion of Toni Morrison. Although neither the fictions of political strife nor the erotic body have much effect on the broad American audience (most of which neither reads nor views plays), the texts of Pielmeier, Gordon, and the others on abuse, abortion, and murder, along with Morrison's "civic" voice, are probably better known because of the power of the Catholic church, Bible-based fundamentalism, and race relations dialogue in American life.

Such inattentiveness is less the case with the following subject matter: American apocalyptic and violence in and as a public realm. It is evident that awareness of these (and involvement in them) is widespread. Consider the execution and gang rape in the Rosenberg texts; the murder, sexual abuse, and gross maltreatment of slaves in the sexual embodiment texts; and the strong apocalyptic elements of *The Book of Daniel, The Public Burning, Beloved,* and *Many Things*. Violence is, obviously, so ubiquitous in American life, as in much of the rest of the world, that we cannot escape its physical or literary expression, and it is not surprising that it receives a religious shaping in various apocalyptic motifs and projections.

According to a survey reported by Charles Strozier, almost one-third of Americans believe in the rapture (which Strozier calls "probably the single most significant theological innovation in contemporary fundamentalism"), and four-fifths expect to appear before God on Judgment Day.[1] Billy Graham, Pat Robertson, and thousands of lesser-known evangelists preach and write on the Second Coming as a literal event, and Ronald Reagan's apocalyptic reflections are still familiar.[2]

A good deal of apocalyptic violence has a sexual orientation that relates it to the concerns of embodied sexuality. Strozier refers to the sexualization of the rapture "in the minds of fundamentalists," how in that moment of massive doom for those left behind, the "meeting in the air . . . becomes a kind of heavenly sexual intercourse" between the returning Christ as bridegroom and the faithful of the church as bride.[3] In academic context, we recall that the subtitle of Catholic critic Judith Wilt's book on abortion in recent American fiction is *The Armageddon of the Maternal Instinct,* an inflammatory tag line that illustrates the pervasiveness of apocalyptic rhetoric even in serious scholarship on aspects of sexuality.

A more popular, and populist, example is found in the portentous language of Donald Wildmon, a busy member of the clergy known for his battles against perceived pornography. Steven C. Dubin writes, "The engine of Wildmon's diverse actions is the theory of a 'great war' between incompatible world views. On one side is Christianity, and on the other, 'secular humanism.' The stakes in the inevitable clash between these two doctrines are enormous: the future of the United States, nay, the fate of all Western civilization in the long run."[4] Wildmon's enemy, secular humanism, is significant for this study as the substitute for communism now that the cold war threat has ended, and secular humanism is the evil force Frank Peretti dramatizes in his best-selling apocalyptic fiction. Perreti's *This Present Darkness* (which in 1994, eight years after its original publication, had already gone through thirty-eight printings), for example, features an epic battle of angels and demons in the sky above Ashton in heartland America as New Age forces, led by a seductive female psychologist, try to pervert the conservative Christians of the town and take it for Satan.[5]

Knowing at All Costs

The audience for the works I will examine (except for one film) does not approach the size of that for Peretti's facile narrations. I will discuss far more demanding works of art that address violence and the dangers of mass cataclysm far more responsibly—and ultimately far more persuasively—than Peretti's popular religious entertainments. In the first part of this volume I interpreted three texts dealing with the hysteria surrounding a single incident in modern American religious-political history (indeed, I argued that each *was* a religiously infused incident); in the second part I analyzed six texts on sexual embodiment in modern America with religious connotations but not connected to a specific event such as the Rosenberg affair. In this third and final part I will connect American violence and the apocalyptic mode to two particular catastrophic events and two catastrophic conditions. The events are, first, genocide practiced against Native Americans and brought to a climax in the 1890 massacre of the Sioux at Wounded Knee in South Dakota and, second, the Vietnam War. The conditions are environmental destruction and what is now being called the epidemic of violence in America.

I intend for my primary unifying denominator, what I term the "body apocalyptic," to convey three things about American civilization. First, employing the term *apocalypse* to mean disclosure or revelation (from Greek *apokalypsis:* revelation, unveiling) refers to the characteristically American desire to receive redemptive revelation through supernatural, usually dramatic channels. This is not exclusively an American trait, of course, but it is deeply and incisively American and to be observed in the early colonial theology of Cotton Mather, the illuminations of Jonathan

Edwards, the transcendental insights of Emerson, the lyric-corporeal celebrations of Whitman, the resolute excesses of Shakers, Mormons, and Jehovah's Witnesses, the urgent impulsions toward freedom of African Americans, and the anticipations of Pentecostals. In more (but not much more) sublimated form it inspired the westward drive across the continent and the decimation of Native Americans, the American infatuation with psychoanalysis (promising revelation from the unknown within oneself), the determination to fight the secret conspiracy of communism at home and its open threat on foreign soil, the exploration of space, and our achievements in medical technology.

This passion to know—at all costs—is what Harold Bloom has labeled American Gnosticism. Bloom argues that gnosticism "is now, and always has been, the hidden religion of the United States, the American Religion proper." This gnosticism for Bloom is an overwhelming rage for self-knowledge, to find "that innermost self . . . that secret place [where] Ronald Reagan and the characters of Thomas Pynchon's fiction blend together."[6] However uncannily correct (and mischievous) Bloom may be in uncovering one prominent aspect of American religiosity, he is at best half right. As Martin Marty points out, Bloom almost totally ignores the public, communal side of that religiosity—as he ignores the mainline denominations other than the Southern Baptists—and it is through this vast omission that Bloom views American apocalyptic as gnosticism.[7] Whereas the striving toward divine or self-knowledge of gnostics is by its very nature spiritualized and basically uninterested in the body, apocalyptic is radically corporeal and obsessed with saving the body; this compulsion to redeem the body through revelatory knowledge provokes violence.

This fatal connection of apocalypse and violence is a second trait of the "body apocalyptic." It is a characteristic of apocalyptic as old as the harsh and lurid visions of the Book of Revelation and as new as the 1993 debacle of the Branch Davidians in Texas. Koresh's ill-fated sect, in fact, illustrates the dynamic of the relationship between apocalypse and violence: The believers in an apocalyptic event, looking forward to some *dies irae* that will destroy their enemies and in the process redeem the faithful, are always the victims, yet they tend to be aggressive and militant, one way or another, and incite the violence sooner or later perpetrated on them. Thomas Müntzer and his Anabaptist army annihilated in 1525 in the Peasants War in Germany are a particularly radical example. David Koresh and his heavily armed disciples defending themselves to the death in Waco against the FBI onslaught are a tragic recent case.

Third, "body apocalyptic" conveys that the devastating revelatory event not only destroys bodies but also ravages the land. As an example, the nuclear bombings of Hiroshima and Nagasaki in 1945, interpreted widely as apocalyptic occasions and prefiguring at least for some the final Apocalypse, killed hundreds of thousands and, beyond that horror, laid waste huge areas of terrain.[8]

The following chapters are concerned with a revelatory and violent American apocalyptic. It destroys humans and their environment; appears throughout our history, sometimes overtly (but even then largely unrecognized) and sometimes hidden; and always manifests itself, directly or indirectly, as religious expression. It also usually helps to constitute a public sphere as it coalesces around certain moments of political crisis (the defeat of the South in the Civil War and the end of a way of life, the Rosenberg affair, the assassination of President Kennedy, and the end of "Camelot" and the "New Frontier") and excites a sexual response in the midst of catastrophic events (the sexual abuse of death camp inmates during the Holocaust, the mass rapes of the war in Bosnia and the massacres of Rwanda, and the sexual excesses of Koresh in the Waco compound). The texts dramatize the violent political and sexual components of American apocalyptic in some of its most revelatory moments and suggest that it is one of the fundamental American reflexes.

Just what that means is complex, but this subject is the focus of considerable research these days, research inspired no doubt by something as obvious as the approaching end of the second millennium of Christian-dominated history, by the emergence of feminism and minority studies that analyze political and sexual violence from new perspectives, and by what appears to be an increase in violence and lawlessness in America and worldwide.

Strozier's psychoanalytic approach in *Apocalypse* stresses how severe personal traumas of modern life cause Americans even in an age termed secular to look for relief through supernatural intervention—or, better said, through fulfillment of a divine plan that even as it ends history will introduce a new and better era. Strozier sees apocalyptic present in America from its beginnings—for example in Hopi religion, in the mood of the nation following Lincoln's assassination, and in New Age vogues. He notes that "one could even note that the discovery of America began in a kind of phallic apocalyptic" and then quotes Catherine Keller's deconstructive analysis of Columbus as the "penetrating" and "piercing" explorer simultaneously opening the virgin new world for Christ and preparing it for the end, "the new Christ who would discover Eden and rejuvenate the faith at the moment of the world's transformation into the millennium."[9] In *When Time Shall Be No More* Paul Boyer argues convincingly that "prophecy belief is far more central in American thought than intellectual and cultural historians have recognized . . . and that in the years since World War II the prophecies of a special belief system—dispensational premillennialism—have played an important role in shaping public attitudes on a wide range of topics from the Soviet Union, the Common Market, and the Mideast to the computer and the environmental crisis."[10]

Stephen D. O'Leary in *Arguing the Apocalypse* sees apocalyptic rhetoric from ancient times to the present as part of an eschatological logic that is still very forceful in the modern era, as exemplified in the Millerite expectation of a world ending in 1840, in Hal Lindsey's prophecies, and in the New Christian Right:

> The apocalyptic tradition, founded in mythic narratives and canonical scriptures and augmented by debates about the meaning of these texts, provides the social knowledge base that enables apocalyptic movements to appeal occasionally to a wider audience than the tradition's devotees and caretakers. Such an expansion beyond the base of the tradition is possible when the conventionally accepted understanding of a culture's destiny seems unable to account for social ills that challenge and threaten normal mechanisms for dealing with life's "ultimate exigence" of time and evil.[11]

In *Arresting Images,* his study of the contemporary visual arts in America, efforts to censor them, and a defiance of such attempts by the artists and their supporters, Steven Dubin calls attention to conservative and reactionary attacks on "immoral" art as a harbinger of doom. He observes that some "cite *Roe v. Wade* as a triumph of secular humanist values over morality, and gay rights ordinances represent a legal endorsement of homosexuality as normal and legitimate. In all these instances there is the sense of apocalypse: diabolic powers of darkness have been unleashed, and they must be reined in to avert the total destruction of society."[12]

Finally, Martin Jay, in a chapter from *Force Fields* entitled "The Apocalyptic Imagination and the Inability to Mourn," offers an intricate argument that distinguishes between religious and scientific apocalyptic, the latter being the secular version represented by "such writers as Barry Commoner, Robert Heilbronner, and Jonathan Schell . . . [whose] scenarios of global destruction and the termination of life, perhaps only cockroaches aside, [are] plausible to an educated audience often contemptuous of explicitly religious fantasies of the last days."[13] Jay (whose contempt is barely concealed) thinks that the postmodern lack of seriousness about the reality of apocalypse (as expressed by Jacques Derrida, Jean-Francois Lyotard, and others) helps explain our "inability to mourn," that is, the continuing entrapment of "apocalyptic thought . . . in the cycle of depressive anxiety and manic release," and he projects one solution, following

Julia Kristeva's psychoanalytic terms, in separating from the mother: working through our ambivalent relationship to "mother earth" as that of which we both are and are not a part.[14]

A reading of director Francis Ford Coppola's *Apocalypse Now* and Philip Caputo's novel *Indian Country* will combine the topos of apocalypse with the history of conflict between Native Americans and the U.S. government and with the trauma of the Vietnam War. Then, discussion of Louise Erdrich's novel *Tracks* will continue the theme of American Indian apocalypse as it relates to the destruction of a people and the ravishing of the land.

Armageddon at Wounded Knee

Although only *Indian Country* and *Tracks* deal substantially with the role of Native Americans in the history-myth of American apocalyptic, an eloquent Indian text can provide the narrative background of these chapters—as did the history of the Salem witch trials (largely by indirection) and the mid-nineteenth-century novels *The Scarlet Letter* and *Our Nig* in the first and second parts of this volume. The account of the massacre of the Sioux at Wounded Knee in 1890, a story told many times but with no "official" version, will be used as recited by Dick Fool Bull and recorded by Richard Erdoes in 1967 and 1968 (Appendix 4).

The roots of this massacre reach back to the arrival of European settlers on the North American continent, when at least ten million Native Americans inhabited what many of the invading whites preferred to call an uninhabited land.[15] The settlers' move westward over the centuries displaced virtually all of the natives and caused the deaths of many not only through battle but also through such imported diseases as smallpox, against which they had no immunity. One of the largest Indian nations surviving in the mid-nineteenth century was the Sioux (so-named by the French, a contraction of the name *Nadowessioux,* which was what the indigenous Nadowessi called themselves) or—their preferred name—Lakotas, who inhabited the northern plains.[16] Forced by the French-armed Ojibwas out of their home between Lake Superior and the sources of the Mississippi River, they thrived on the plains and become adept horsemen and hunters of the immense herds of buffalo. But soon after the Civil War the rapid incursions of white settlers into Lakota territory led the federal government to arrange a treaty with the Lakotas that gave them sole ownership of sections of Nebraska, Wyoming, and what is now the western half of South Dakota, as well as buffalo hunting rights off the reservation.

The government soon broke the treaty and did not intervene to stop the near-extermination of the buffalo by white hunters, the arrival of

thousands of white settlers via the new railroads, or the influx of pros-
pectors looking for gold. Clashes between the Lakotas and invaders accelerated, and the government took steps to bring the "enemy" Indians,
who were defending their reservation land, under control. In 1876 General George Armstrong Custer, commanding the U.S. Seventh Cavalry's
"pony soldiers" in Lakota territory and seeking to subdue the Lakota, was
attacked by an overwhelming army of Indians led by the renowned chief
Crazy Horse. Custer's entire regiment, more than two hundred fifty soldiers, was annihilated. This was the celebrated "Custer's last stand" at Little Bighorn.

It was a short-lived triumph for the Lakotas, because the government
provided reinforcements, arrested Native American leaders, and forced the
legendary chief Sitting Bull, the inspiration behind much of the resistance,
to flee with his men to Canada. New treaties took vast amounts of land,
above all the sacred Black Hills, from the Lakotas, left them without the
means for self support (the buffalo were gone), and forced them, con-
fined to their shrunken reservations, to look to the government for food
handouts, shelter, and a poor version of the white man's education in
place of tribal customs.

The extent of the degradation to which Native Americans were subjected, and of the whites' contempt for them, is expressed in an editorial
that L. Frank Baum wrote late in 1890 in a South Dakota newspaper.
Baum, who a decade later would write *The Wizard of Oz*, commented that
the death of Sitting Bull (who was shot by Indian police on the reservation) on December 15 was the end of a proud Indian heritage and advo-
cated extermination of the remainder. "Why not annihilation? Their glory
has fled, their spirit broken, their manhood effaced; better that they
should die than live the miserable wretches that they are."[17]

Into the midst of this desperate situation came, early in 1890, the news
of Wovoka, a Christianized Piute from Nevada who reported his vision
of an Indian messiah who would return to earth, bringing a cataclysm
that would kill whites and restore pristine conditions to the old Indian
lands—action that would be precipitated by the ghost dance, an exhaust-
ing ritual danced by tribespeople wearing garments painted with nature
symbols to make them invulnerable to the white men's bullets. Wovoka
the visionary quickly became conflated with the savior he prophesied, and
the "messiah craze" he created soon swept over the Lakotas and inspired
them to dance the ghost dance en masse.[18] The activities—essentially the
rituals of a new, apocalyptic religion—alarmed the agents from the Bu-
reau of Indian Affairs responsible for order on Pine Ridge Reservation
and caused them to confuse the ghost dance with war dances and fear
armed rebellion by the reinvigorated Lakota braves. Military reinforce-

ments were sent once again, among them the Seventh Cavalry. The news of Sitting Bull's murder had frightened the Lakotas, and many had fled from the reservation to the desolate "badlands." But intense cold and hunger caused a group of some three hundred fifty to head back to Pine Ridge under the leadership of a highly respected chief named Big Foot, himself ill with pneumonia.

The group was intercepted by soldiers of the Seventh Cavalry and surrendered to them on December 28. They camped at Wounded Knee Creek overnight, hoping to be escorted by the military back to Pine Ridge the following day. But on the morning of the December 29, when cavalry soldiers attempted to take guns away from the Lakota braves (emboldened in their ghost shirts), fighting broke out and the massacre took place. According to one eyewitness account, a priest gave the group their last rites, without benefit of translation, before the killing began. Women and children were pursued and shot down. New rapid-fire Hotchkiss cannon did their part, and when the carnage was over more than two hundred Lakotas, including Big Foot, and twenty-five soldiers were dead. Two days later soldiers returned to throw the frozen bodies in a mass grave, and in the process articles of clothing, including ceremonial garb, were taken to be sold as souvenirs. The federal government awarded Congressional Medals of Honor to some of the soldiers participating in the massacre.

Wounded Knee was, for practical purposes, the last significant Native American effort in some four centuries of conflict to escape subjugation. The name struck the national consciousness again some eighty years later in 1973, when Lakota and other activists mainly from the American Indian Movement (AIM) took over the area and provoked a seventy-three-day siege by the FBI and U.S. marshals. Two AIM leaders, Russell Banks and Dennis Means, were prosecuted by the government in a celebrated 1974 trial and eventually acquitted. Then, in 1975 two FBI agents were killed during a gun battle on Pine Ridge Reservation, and a Lakota named Leonard Peltier was tried and convicted for the murders. Although evidence suggests that he is not guilty, he remains incarcerated, serving out a life sentence.[19]

Notes

1. Charles B. Strozier, *Apocalypse: On the Psychology of Fundamentalism in America* (Boston: Beacon Press, 1994), 5. Strozier's comment on the rapture is on 120. The rapture of the Christian church is a fundamentalist doctrine teaching that at Christ's Second Coming the redeemed will be abruptly taken up to meet him in the air. It is based on a single Bible verse, Thessalonians 4:17: "Then we which are alive and remain shall be caught up together with them in the

clouds, to meet the Lord in the air, and so shall we ever be with the Lord." See Strozier, *Apocalypse*, 119. The "Little Apocalypse" of the Gospel of Mark 13 (also Matthew 24–25 and Luke 21) also contains sayings of Jesus that many have taken to be descriptions of the rapture, for example, verses 25–27: "And the stars of heaven shall fall, and the powers that are in heaven shall be shaken. And then shall they see the Son of man coming in the clouds with great power and glory. And then shall he send his angels, and shall gather together his elect from the four winds, from the uttermost part of the earth to the uttermost part of heaven." For a brilliant and controversial study of the background of apocalyptic in the Jewish and Christian traditions see Norman Cohn, *Cosmos, Chaos and the World to Come: The Ancient Roots of Apocalyptic Faith* (New Haven: Yale University Press, 1994).

2. Stephen D. O'Leary thinks that Reagan has been strongly influenced by fundamentalist theologians on the apocalypse but was careful especially in the later years of his presidency not to offer end-of-the-world predictions. "Whatever the epistemic status of Reagan's meditations on Armageddon, the critical alarm over his public and private statements was apparently not shared by the voters who re-elected him. It seems reasonable to conclude that, in this area as in so many others, Reagan gave voice to thoughts that, though unpalatable to liberal pundits, are shared by millions of Americans." *Arguing the Apocalypse: A Theory of Millennial Rhetoric* (New York: Oxford University Press, 1994), 183.

3. Strozier, *Apocalypse*, 122.

4. Steven C. Dubin, *Arresting Images: Impolitic Art and Uncivil Actions* (London: Routledge, Chapman and Hall, 1992), 228.

5. Frank E. Peretti, *This Present Darkness* (Westchester, Ill.: Crossway Books, 1986).

6. Harold Bloom, *The American Religion: The Emergence of the Post-Christian Nation* (New York: Simon and Schuster, 1992), 50. For a study that addresses the concerns of the second and third sections this volume, see Richard Dellamora, *Apocalyptic Overtones: Sexual Politics and the Sense of an Ending* (New Brunswick: Rutgers University Press, 1994).

7. Martin E. Marty, "All Gnostics Here," *The Christian Century*, May 20–27, 1992, 545–48. I follow standard scholarly practice in alternating the term *apocalyptic* as a noun with the somewhat unwieldy *apocalypticism*. See, for example, John J. Collins, *The Apocalyptic Imagination: An Introduction to the Jewish Matrix of Christianity* (New York: Crossroads, 1984).

8. See Paul Boyer, *When Time Shall Be No More: Prophecy Belief in Modern American Culture* (Cambridge: Harvard University Press, 1992), 115–51, on nuclear war and apocalypse. The "revelation" of these bombings was both in the realization of how "successful" atomic warfare could be and, for some believers, that the literal end of the world was imminent. It was revelatory for the Japanese in the recognition that the religiously based myth of Japanese invincibility was untenable. See also the newsletter *Nuclear Texts and Contexts* (Spring 1994): 26–31, for a helpful bibliography of recent texts on the cold war, genocide, Vietnam, and violence.

9. Strozier, *Apocalypse*, 167–68.

10. Boyer, *When Time Shall Be No More,* ix.

11. O'Leary, *Arguing the Apocalypse,* 197.

12. Dubin, *Arresting Images,* 229. Dubin's study of apocalyptic strains in the American visual arts is anticipated by Robert Jewett and John Shelton Lawrence in *The American Monomyth* (Garden City: Doubleday, 1977), especially in chapter 7, "Apocalyptic Jaws and Retributive Ecstasy," an assessment of popular catastrophe films such as *Earthquake* and *The Towering Inferno.*

13. Martin Jay, *Force Fields: Between Intellectual History and Cultural Critque* (New York: Routledge, 1993), 86.

14. Jay, *Force Fields,* 93. My summary of Jay is only a caricature of his subtle argument.

15. For this background discussion I have relied upon *Constructing the American Past: A Source Book of People's History,* ed. Elliott J. Gorn, Randy Roberts, and Terry D. Bilhartz (New York: HarperCollins), 2:59–100, and Dee Brown, *Bury My Heart at Wounded Knee: An Indian History of the American West* (New York: Holt, Rinehart and Winston, 1970). I have also used James Mooney's remarkably resilient *The Ghost-Dance Religion and Wounded Knee* (1896; repr. New York: Dover Publications, 1973), and Peter Matthiessen, *In The Spirit of Crazy Horse* (New York: Penguin Books, 1992). A hardcover version of *In the Spirit of Crazy Horse* was published by Viking Press in 1983, but lawsuits filed by the FBI, FBI Special Agent David Price, and former South Dakota governor William Janklow blocked the publication of paperback and foreign editions. Eventually the courts ruled in favor of Matthiessen, and further publication was permitted.

According to Patrick Cudmore of Oglala Lakota College, the figure of ten million Native Americans would be far too low. Cudmore claims in an interview in the documentary film *Wiping the Tears of Seven Generations* (see note 19) that fifty million Native Americans died over twenty generations through contact with the settlers through war, starvation, and European diseases.

16. See Matthiessen, *In the Spirit of Crazy Horse,* xxv, for a more detailed account of the uses of the terms *Sioux* and *Lakota.*

17. L. Frank Baum, *Aberdeen Saturday Pioneer,* December 20, 1890, cited in *Constructing the American Past,* ed. Gorn, Roberts, and Bilhartz, 99, where the year of the editorial's publication is incorrectly listed as 1891.

18. Randall Balmer offers evidence that ghost dancing did not always triumph over white enticements: "Miss Mary Collins and Grindstone, a converted Sioux, broke up a Ghost Dance at Sitting Bull's camp on the Grand River and lured the Indians away to a Christian worship service." See Balmer, *Mine Eyes Have Seen the Glory: A Journey into the Evangelical Subculture in America* (New York: Oxford University Press, 1989), 213.

19. See Matthiessen, *In the Spirit of Crazy Horse,* for an exhaustive study of incidents on Pine Ridge Reservation during the 1970s. See also *Wiping the Tears of Seven Generations* (1991), a documentary film produced by Native Americans about the Bigfoot Memorial Ride, a sacred horseback ride undertaken by Sioux/ Lakotas and others every December from 1986 through 1989, with the culminating ride in December 1990, and covering the route Big Foot and the ill-fated Lakotas took in their effort to reach safety at Pine Ridge Reservation. Described

by one of the film's narrators as "a sacrifice, a prayer, a ritual healing," the two-hundred-fifty-mile ride was conceived and organized by Sioux educators to end "seven generations of mourning" and create a new sense of tribal identity. The film was directed by Gary Rhine and Fidel Moreno and produced by Gary Rhine; it is listed as a Kefaru Production in association with Eagle Heart Productions.

A few persons who have read this chapter in manuscript form have commented on its abrupt ending. I have intended that abruptness to convey the sense of the unresolved "plot" of the treatment of Native Americans.

10

Apocalypse Now:
Melancholia at the End

Perhaps the war had awakened something evil in us, some
dark, malicious power that allowed us to kill without feeling.

—Philip Caputo, *A Rumor of War*

The Vietnam Veterans Memorial honors the names of those
who lost their lives in the war; their names are shadows in the
stone. The names are the remembrance of stories, and the
shadows of the names wait to be touched. A Wounded Knee
Memorial would honor the names of those who were murdered by the soldiers; the shadows of the ancestors could come
to their names in the stone to hear the stories of survivance.

—Gerald Vizenor, *Manifest Manners*

Why retell the story of Wounded Knee? It is not the subject per se of any
of the fictions I interpret in this or the following chapters. It is, however,
"behind" these fictions in both obvious and subtle ways. For instance, Richard Slotkin in *Regeneration through Violence* claims that "the shaping
experience [of America] was the extended wars with the Native American Indians," an experience that mythologized the white settlers "as a new
race of people, independent of the sin-darkened heritage of man, seeking a totally new and original relationship to pure nature as hunters, ex-
plorers, pioneers, and seekers."[1] In this view the battles with the Indians
consist of apocalyptic violence that, ironically, cleanses the victorious invaders and encourages them to comprehend themselves, postapocalypti-
cally, as the inheritors of a pristine new earth. It is the exact opposite of
the apocalypse that Wovoka envisioned for Native Americans, who again
serve, ironically, on the one hand as symbols of the satanic old order that
must be purged and on the other as the models of the new race, pure
and in harmony with nature, that the whites wish to become.

Edward Said, arguing the persistence of that paradox in the late twentieth century, describes a 1991 exhibition called America as West at the
National Gallery of Art in Washington, in which "the conquest of the West

and its subsequent incorporation into the United States had been transformed into a heroic meliorist narrative that disguised, romanticized, or simply eliminated the many-sided truth about the actual process of conquest, as well as the destruction of both native Americans and the environment. Images of the Indian in nineteenth-century American paintings, for example—noble, proud, reflective—were set against a running text on the same wall that described the native American's degradations at the hands of the white man."[2] Members of Congress, journalists, and others were indignant over this "unpatriotic" denigration of the story of the whites' subjugation of the West.

Gerald Vizenor (himself of Chippewa ancestry) makes a still more audacious claim: "The Vietnam War, and the horrors of racialism recounted in the literature of survivance, aroused the nation to remember the inseparable massacres at My Lai, Sand Creek, and Wounded Knee."[3] I think, regrettably, that this is overstated: Most Americans did not, and still do not, know about the Wounded Knee and Sand Creek massacres in the first place. It is only in recent years that Native American artists such as James Welch and Wendy Rose, along with such sympathetic non-Indians as Thomas Sanchez, have depicted these tragedies dramatically. *Thunderheart, Black Robe,* and *Dances with Wolves* (films with varying degrees of authenticity) have also been educating the public about the horrendous treatment of American Indians.[4]

Vizenor believes, though, that even this new attention to Native Americans is corrupted by a consumerist-media culture generating a simulation of Indian tradition, in which its members are complicit, rather than a genuine recollection of it.[5] Nevertheless, the Native American-Vietnam war connection has been made, stimulated also by the recognition of the many American Indians who fought in the war there, usually in the infantry. Many Vietnam novels and memoirs have at least one Indian among the "grunts," valued for his outdoorsmanship that rivals the tracking and survival skills of the Viet Cong.[6] There is also historical irony in the fact that in the 1965 battle of Ia Drang, "the bloodiest campaign of the entire war," it was the Seventh Cavalry that bore the brunt. "The Seventh Cavalry, the descendant of the unit that perished at the Little Big Horn, had ample opportunity to think about . . . 'Custer's luck.' . . . By close of business on Nov. 17, more than 230 American soldiers were dead and another 240 or so wounded."[7]

Beginning with this Native American-Vietnam war coincidence, the argument that follows is a version of one that Richard Slotkin articulates brilliantly in *Gunfighter Nation: The Myth of the Frontier in Twentieth-Century America.* It consists first of the proposition that the Vietnam War was for Americans a postmodern version of the eighteenth- and nineteenth-century Indian wars. American GIs who fought in Vietnam saw instinctively the parallels in the term *Indian country* ("to designate territory under enemy control or any terrain considered hostile or dangerous"), which they used to label terrain controlled by the Viet Cong or North Vietnamese.[8] Like the American Indians, the North Vietnamese and the Viet Cong, badly outgunned, did not "fight fair," choosing for the most part ambushes, night attacks, and attritional small encounters rather than large, static battles of massed forces. Like the Indians, they had the advantage of fighting in and using to great advantage the rugged terrain with which they were familiar and the enemy was not. Like the Indians, they practiced hideous atrocities on the Americans and provoked equally gruesome ones in return, leaving their villages of women and children vulnerable to the vengeful U.S. troops. Like the Indians, they were defending themselves against foreign invaders who had no business being there—invaders whose armies were far-flung, poorly led, and made up for the most part of conscripted young men who did not wish to be there.

For American policymakers and "hawks" among the citizenry, the war was, like that against the Indians, a conflict with the powers of evil—the communists who, if not checked, would continue their planned "takeover" of the world. In fact, the American presence in Vietnam was to protect American interests in the East, a modern application of Manifest Destiny, the doctrine invented to justify Anglo-Saxon expansionism in the Western Hemisphere. More subtly, like the wars against the Native Americans the Vietnam War was for some a testing of American mettle (and of metal, as new weaponry was put to use) in the heady era of John F. Kennedy's "new frontier" presidency and then in Lyndon Johnson's "great society."

To be victorious in Vietnam, it seemed at the start, would mean to end the communist nightmare, with its threatened apocalypse, and turn with redoubled energy to the task of creating racial and social justice at home. What happened instead, following a fourteen-year-long war of attrition that ended in humiliation and frustration, was not altogether unlike what happened to Native Americans after Wounded Knee. The United States slid into conditions of negativity that the majority still has not acknowledged. Just as the Lakotas have not properly come to terms with Wounded Knee and have not been able (until recently), for many reasons, to mourn it and transcend it, the United States has not fully faced the debacle of Vietnam but has tended to thrust it aside and deny its influence.[9]

The fiction discussed in this and the following chapters shows the traits of post-Vietnam War sensibility in the United States. Where we are and how we are as a nation is not solely or mainly the result of the war in Vietnam. That war somehow coalesced and crystallized the country's ills, which are as old as the country itself but developed in especially virulent form late in the nineteenth century—toward the end of our last apocalyptic turn—and carried over into the most violent century of human history. Even to consider the source of these ills demands something like a theological leap of faith, or at least a moral openmindedness, for it involves a moral-theological diagnosis. The postwar condition reflects the trauma of recognizing the immoral nature of the nation's expansion: as a country built on conquered and stolen land. The fact that most, if not all, civilizations have emerged thus, or that in the case of the United States it has resulted in a haven for the oppressed of the world, does not alter the truth. We live in a land that our ancestors took from someone else, and we are still reluctant even to acknowledge that usurpation.

Yet this acute awareness underlies the fictions that follow, which are far more concerned with depicting the present traumatic situation than with reflecting on how the tragic dilemma came about. It is as if the relatively newly named condition of post-traumatic stress disorder (at the heart of Caputo's *Indian Country*) was allegorized to refer not just to Vietnam veterans suffering the delayed effects of what we once called shell shock or battle fatigue but to a whole country experiencing the puzzling and frightening symptoms of that phenomenon.

An Archetype for Apocalyptic

The fiction of the body apocalyptic is approachable through a connection to what I have termed the archetypal narration of seduction-abuse-abandonment. That sequence applies, in nominally altered form, to the history of white treatment of Native Americans and to the history of the Vietnam War—not in the context of love relationships but in the framework of relationships (in many cases contractually formalized) of trust, reliance, and cooperation. American history abounds with examples of Indians seduced or outright tricked into signing treaties with the federal government, entering into agreements whereby they usually sacrificed control over land in exchange for promises of protection, noninterference or relative autonomy, and nurturance. The treaties were routinely broken, often through the actions of members of Congress hostile or indifferent to the Indians' state of affairs.

This seduction was exacerbated by abuse, when in the wake of broken or ignored treaties Native Americans of many groups were removed from their lands, forced to accept white systems of land ownership, deprived of adequate food and shelter, made to abandon tribal ways, and encouraged into alcoholism. Abandonment occurred during and after the abuse as Native Americans were more and more left to suffer degradation and deprivation on reservations that had scandalously inadequate funding for even basic decent survival.

A similar pattern obtained for the American treatment during the sixties and seventies, both of the South Vietnamese citizenry and of the American soldiers who fought there. The record of official American involvement, including that of the CIA, is so shadowy that the truth may never be known about the deaths of South Vietnam president Ngo Dinh Diem and his close advisor, his brother Ngo Dinh Nhu (husband of the notorious, puritanical "first lady" Madam Nhu), during the coup led by rebel chief Duong Van Minh in 1963. It is apparent, however, that American efforts to have Diem toppled when it became clear that his regime would no longer accede to American demands were part of a pattern of seduction and betrayal (however inept) that lasted throughout the war. Seduction came in the form of bribes and promises of support to various Vietnamese strongmen who might help carry out American policy— whatever it might be at the moment. Abuse took place in the wide-scale mistreatment of innocent civilians—justified as inevitable during the confusions of a conflict in which Viet Cong infiltrated the population—and in the extensive destruction of the land. The final abandonment occurred when the United States gave up the whole agonizing struggle and withdrew its personnel as North Vietnamese troops were advancing on Saigon in late spring of 1975, leaving the South Vietnamese at the mercy of the triumphant communists.[10]

The sequence is still more patent in terms of U.S. treatment of its soldiers who fought in Vietnam. The most unpopular war in the country's history, it was presented nevertheless as a necessary battle against the ruthless incursions of communism and thus used to seduce thousands of young men to enlist or be conscripted willingly. After they had fought an incredibly brutal campaign under nightmarish conditions, they were exploited to seduce a public at home into believing, even into the midseventies, that it was a conflict that should have been fought and could have been won.[11] The massacre of My Lai in 1968 stands for the abuse that American soldiers, enraged and frustrated over the deaths of their comrades in vicious jungle warfare, exercised on indigenous people, but it is only one of a huge number of atrocities practiced by both sides. Yet those very soldiers were abused by their own leaders. Caputo's story, related in A Rumor of War, is a case in point. An officer in charge of a platoon on active duty in Vietnam in 1965, Caputo was arrested and charged with the murder of a Vietnamese boy whom he and his men believed to be a Viet Cong. Only by pleading guilty to a lesser charge of lying (Caputo had claimed that the boy walked into an ambush) could he avoid a court martial.[12]

Perhaps most dramatically, American veterans of the Vietnam War endured abuse after they returned home, largely as a result of the powerful antiwar movement, and were essentially abandoned by their government. Promised jobs did not materialize, those suffering drug addiction received inadequate treatment, and those complaining of illness caused by exposure to defoliants used in Vietnam (above all the notorious Agent Orange) were either ignored or subjected to bureaucratic obfuscation. For years, those experiencing post-traumatic battle stress found little understanding or sympathy. It was as if the government and most of the rest of the nation wanted evidence of the war simply to vanish.

The archetypal narrative of American love relationships thus applies, modestly transposed, to key events of war and attempted conquest in American life. Still more significant is that the quartet of elements I adopted in the context of that narrative—shame, pain, awe or mystery, and ecstasy—can be applied to read my texts of apocalyptic. They can be modulated into closely related concepts that help explain the behavior of those caught in the tensions of anticipated cataclysm. Shame, which figured prominently, for example, in the misfortunes of the protagonist of *Agnes of God* (as well as in the lives of the characters discussed in the fictions of the Rosenberg affair), in the fictions of apocalypse evolves—or degenerates—into paranoia, a reaction often justified because those who display it are persecuted or harmed outright. Shame, which *Webster's* defines as "a painful sense of having done something wrong, improper, or immodest," slips into paranoia when others manipulate that painful sense and turn it against the shamed one. Pain, so central in the ordeals of Mariette and the *Many Things* narrator, deepens in the apocalyptic texts into a condition of trauma. Pain accompanies trauma, "an injury or wound violently produced" or "the condition or neurosis resulting from this," to quote again from *Webster's*. In these texts it is the trauma that is emphasized over the pain, not least also in the sense of a third definition, "an emotional experience, or shock, which has a lasting psychic effect."

Something more complicated happens in the case of awe or mystery, the element that is so strong in *Beloved*. In the texts of apocalyptic it is transformed into simulation. Instead of experiencing the authentic confrontation with the ineffable or inexpressible, characters find intensely and self-consciously acting out what they conjecture that experience to be. Sometimes it is an avoidance of the fearful—the awesome—force of the mystery that engenders simulation. Sometimes it is the inability to respond to such mystery. Finally, the element of ecstasy, at the center of the postulant Mariette's real or feigned encounter with divinity, in the apocalypse texts becomes its near-opposite: melancholy.

"This Is the End"?

Apocalypse Now opens with the music of rock star Jim Morrison and The Doors singing "This is the end," and they are heard again singing the same lyrics near the film's conclusion. But the film does not end with the degree of apocalyptic overload that one might expect. It departs dramatically, in fact, from the John Milius and Francis Coppola script at this point, for the script does offer a stunning final battle that has all the trappings of Armageddon in Cambodia except that one cannot tell which are the forces of good and which of evil.[13] Such confusion typifies *Apocalypse Now*, a cinema production of epic confusion that was confused during its wildly expensive four-year gestation and that surely reflects the confusion of American involvement in Vietnam. As Ward Just says, "Francis Ford Coppola made his movie the way Americans fought the war, with no restraint," and Jean Baudrillard is still more negatively effusive: "Coppola makes his film like the Americans made war—in this sense, it is the best possible testimonial—with the same immoderation, the same excess of means, the same monstrous candor . . . and the same success."[14]

Flawed it is. The problems that attended its filming in the Philippines are nearly as legendary as the film itself: Marlon Brando's irascibility, Martin Sheen's near-fatal heart attack in mid-filming, Coppola's bad health, wretched weather that demolished the sets, the dissolution of director Coppola's and his wife Eleanor's marriage caused in good part by on-site tensions, and other difficulties with temperamental actors and writers (Michael Herr, author of *Dispatches*, was brought in to rewrite sections of the script).[15] Although critics have severely panned what resulted, it has taken on mythic qualities. The actor Brian Dennehy, who fought in Vietnam (and who knows his Aristotle), articulates that sense: "The implication in war movies is that war has a rational beginning, middle and end. And of course none of it does. It's absolutely fucking chaos. *Apocalypse Now* is the movie. Even more interesting is that it was made so soon after the war was over. It was about the war and a parable about the war. It was and is the most sophisticated overview of the experience."[16]

But the critics reacting to the film upon its initial showings in 1979 saw more of the "fucking chaos" than any effective artistic order that Coppola might have imposed on it and thus on the war. Most of the criticism focuses on the last third of the film, the scenes in the Cambodian jungle where the renegade Colonel Kurtz, played by Brando, waxes philosophical (and theological) to Captain Willard (Martin Sheen), sent to kill him, about the nature of evil. Vincent Canby remarks snidely, "When we arrive at the heart of darkness we find not the embodiment of evil, of civilization junked, but of an eccentric actor who has been given lines that are unthinkable but not, unfortunately, unspeakable."[17] Michael Wood lays the blame for the failure on Coppola's skewed vision: "Kurtz . . . becomes a name for a hyperbole that can't be had, a bulky ghost lost in a forest of symbols, floundering among suggestions of romantic evil and primordial lusts."[18] Ward Just thinks that "what began as an original and intellectually and visually rich view of the war becomes bloated and pretentious, a kind of hip *Patton,* ending with Kurtz strolling in his necropolis reciting T. S. Eliot before being hacked to death by the assassin Willard. Mistuh Brando, he dead."[19]

That last phrase refers to the scene announcing the death of the monstrous character Kurtz in Joseph Conrad's novella *Heart of Darkness,* on which text of *Apocalypse Now* is, after a fashion, based. As in Conrad's narrative, a man travels to the mysterious, savage, and lush interior to find a powerful white man who has "gone native" and seduced or coerced the local inhabitants to commit all sorts of atrocious deeds. But in the film, instead of Marlow heading up the Congo to find *his* Kurtz, the Vietnam veteran Captain Benjamin Willard is assigned the mission of locating Colonel Walter Kurtz, a Special Forces operative who has set up his own army in the Cambodian wilderness, an army consisting mostly of indigenous Montagnard tribesmen and American deserters. Kurtz runs his outpost ruthlessly (one sees hanged bodies and heads on poles in the encampment on the site of temple ruins) and leads forays against a shadowy enemy, North Vietnamese crossing the border but more recently against South Vietnamese as well. Clever adaptations of Conrad's actions appear, such as, instead of "the French man-of-war 'firing into a continent' . . . a formation of jets burning an empty tropical landscape."[20] Willard is taken upriver on a heavily armed patrol boat with a crew of four Americans, finds Kurtz, is tormented physically by him and made to endure his monologues on violence and evil, and finally completes his mission and chops Kurtz to death with a machete as aroused tribespeople outside on the temple grounds hack a water buffalo to pieces in a ritual sacrifice.

Kurtz exemplifies perfectly the apocalyptic version of the seduction-abuse-abandonment sequence. A brilliant officer who could have "made general," he is seduced by what one can best describe as the erotic attraction of violence, of living beyond the bounds of normal civilization; already in his late thirties, he endures the strenuous Special Forces training and takes command of a unit in Vietnam, which responsibility he distorts grotesquely into his role as the demonic leader of killers in Cambodia. That mentality is described in, among many other places, Mark Baker's best-selling *Nam: The Vietnam War in the Words of the Men and Women Who Fought There.* One of the anonymous voices reflects on the soldiers who developed an appetite for the war. "They got there and found out that their talent was killing and they were damn good at it. They had a taste of killing and they all liked it. Now when the war ended, what were they going to do?"[21]

It is clear that for Kurtz there can be no return home, even though he has a family back in the United States (in the Milius script Willard visits Kurtz's wife in a final scene much like that of Conrad's Marlow meeting Kurtz's betrothed). In love with carnage, Kurtz abuses those subordinate to him and abandons himself to a life of destruction—insane by normal standards but guided and justified by his glimpse into the "horror" of existence. The American military, however, will not abandon Kurtz. They need to have him dead—"terminated with extreme prejudice" as a CIA agent in the film puts it—because his killing is not done under their auspices, and Willard is appointed the executioner. His trip upriver, culminating in the meeting with Kurtz, provides the scenes that demonstrate how awe, shame, pain, and ecstasy are transmuted into simulation, paranoia, trauma, and melancholy to convey this cinematic fiction of war's senseless anomie.

To the Heart of Nothing

The first of these scenes occurs, however, before Willard and the crew of the patrol boat set out on the crucial part of their voyage. Their boat needs to be air-dropped by helicopter into the mouth of the Nang River, whence they will begin the search for Kurtz, and this maneuver introduces them to Lieutenant Colonel Kilgore (the name symbolism is blatant), commander of an air cavalry unit of helicopters and played with manic relish by Robert Duvall. One of the best spots to put in the boat is near a beach held by the Viet Cong and also ideal for surfing. Because Kilgore is a surfing enthusiast, he determines to secure the area both to surf and to launch Willard on his way.

Some critics (Wood and Canby) thought that the sequence outshines the film's ponderous conclusion and that Kilgore is more apt than Kurtz to embody the lunacy of American behavior in Vietnam.[22] But Ward Just disagrees: "There weren't any surfing lieutenant colonels in South Vietnam and the idea of securing a fortified beach [for] . . . whatever the hell it is that surfers do, is ludicrous and I don't believe it for a minute. . . . It's a California cliché that has nothing to do with the reality of South Vietnam. The war was many things, but it was rarely a ludicrous thing."[23] The scenario is in any case breathtaking. The helicopters attack the beach and the village beyond it with spectacular firepower, flying in like gigantic sci-fi insects, with a loudspeaker from Kilgore's command craft blaring Wagner's "The Ride of the Valkyries." That assault is followed, as Kilgore and a California surfing ace prepare to take to the waves, by jets swooping in to incinerate the terrain with napalm, provoking Kilgore's often-quoted line, "I love the smell of napalm in the morning. . . . The smell of gasoline smells like victory."

This fearsome and lethally beautiful sequence (the billowing orange flames against the blue sky, the sleek jets, the clear morning sea) is an arresting example of how awe over an evocation of mystery turns into simulation, more or less as Jean Baudrillard developed the concept in texts such as "Simulacra and Simulations."[24] Some consider the Vietnam conflict to be the first "postmodern" war, and one of the traits that made it thus was its quality of "hyperreality" on the one hand and, on the other, of an intensified self-consciousness in those caught up in it that expressed itself as an extreme objectification, a sense of noninvolvement.[25] Some of this was certainly part of other wars. Stephen Crane portrays such a combined sense of hyperreality and of disengagement in the protagonist of *The Red Badge of Courage* in the Civil War, and the surreal nature of World War I trench and gas warfare is also familiar.

But in the Vietnam War the addition of the extensive use of drugs (it was labeled widely as a psychedelic war fought by stoned soldiers) and the deployment of high-tech, sometimes computerized weaponry (which both distanced its users from their victims and increased the carnage) contributed to the experience of a simultaneous super- and unreality.[26] The awe inspired by the mystery of any profound experience seemed under the peculiar circumstances of Vietnam to ricochet back on itself to produce a simulation, an effect of the real that replaces the real because it has become too stupendous to apprehend. Michael Herr, struggling to comprehend that experience, makes a connection to another historical outrage committed on Native Americans, this one suffered not by the Lakotas but by the Cherokees: "Might as well say that Vietnam was where the Trail of Tears was headed all along, the turnaround point where it could touch and come back to form a containing perimeter."[27]

This is not quite the same as Baudrillard's simulacrum, which he defines as the code or symbol that substitutes for a truth (a solid referent) that can no longer be believed so that we exist in a world of simulacra that has no basis in an absolute. In Coppola's version Kilgore's air cavalry attack combined with the surfing generates a kind of terrible play, a grotesque ludic excess that transforms the "reality" of the war into apocalyptic simulation—a savage, revelatory moment that shows forth, at heart, its vicious vacuity.[28] The assault on the village, further, reminds one of the My Lai massacre, where, as Slotkin glosses it, the Americans behaved like "savages" reminiscent of "Mary Rowlandson's description of the Indian massacre of Lancastrer in King Philip's War."[29]

A scene—one that Coppola calls "the most important part of the movie"—that exemplifies how shame and paranoia interact takes place as the boat heading upriver encounters a sampan filled with peasants and their animals and produce.[30] Suspecting Viet Cong among the passengers, the Americans stop the craft to inspect it, their rapid-fire guns trained on the peasants. When a Vietnamese girl suddenly darts away, the nervous men open fire and kill everyone on the boat, then discover that the girl was moving to protect a hidden puppy. At that point the four Americans (Willard has not participated) show deep shame, and when they see that the girl is still alive, they plan to take her to a friendly village where she might be saved. But Willard then intervenes, finishing her with a shot to the head, and the journey continues. The paranoia, the justified but obsessive fear of Viet Cong lurking everywhere, had lead to the mistake that produces shame. But before that it is the felt shame of being there in the first place, aggressors amid a peaceful people trying desperately to lead normal lives, that causes the American paranoia, and then it is that paranoia that fuels the excessive, violent actions accruing to apocalyptic climax.

It is noteworthy that Captain Willard (played with skilled understatement by Sheen) appears to be normal in contrast to the manic Kilgore and beyond-the-pale Kurtz. Appalling events register on his haggard face: disbelief that shifts to resignation, recognition of things horrifying that become still worse. Above all, he appears to be a man who has endured great pain and is on the verge of traumatic collapse. According to persons involved in the filming (and representing another twist to my discussion of simulation), Coppola manipulated—abused—Sheen into a performance, an acting-out of pain and trauma, that moved beyond acting into embodiment. As a *Rolling Stone* piece on Sheen puts it, "[Coppola] would tell Martin, 'You're evil. I want all the evil, the violence, the hatred in you to come out.' You tell that to a guilt-ridden Irish Catholic and he hasn't got a chance."[31] According to Eleanor Coppola's diary, such pressures during an early scene sent Sheen into a psychotic episode: "Marty was lying on the bed really drunk, talking about love and God. He was singing . . . *Amazing Grace.* . . . Marty asked the nurse to pray and sing and I could see she was praying dead seriously."[32] Such emotionality does not guarantee a great performance (it can hinder it), but in Sheen's case it seems to have prompted a persuasive and compelling articulation of pain verging on trauma. The scene in which Sheen broke down is the initial one of the film, where Willard in his hotel room, drunk and waiting for his mission, smashes the mirror, lacerating his fist, then smears his body with his blood, foreshadowing the film's blood-drenched final scene.

Kurtz recalls a time of innocence and even evokes a moment of youth on the Ohio River with overtones of Huckleberry Finn. But he is usually described as a monster like his counterpart in *Heart of Darkness,* someone who has seen so deeply into the underlying savagery of existence that he loses his civilized restraints and turns savage himself. A good case could be made for diagnosing him as traumatized, however, emotionally crippled through experiences of overwhelming pain; Willard comprehends him because he himself is rapidly approaching that condition. Kurtz, who suffers and is possibly dying from a festering wound (mythic Fisher King overtones here), relates to Willard just such a traumatizing painful moment, the emphasis he gives it suggesting its centrality to what he has become. Long before his self-exile in the Cambodian jungle, he was with a Special Forces unit that inoculated the children of a Vietnamese village (they might have been Montagnards) against polio. An agitated old man calls them back and shows them a pile of the inoculated arms of all the children hacked off by Viet Cong. Kurtz tells how he wept in grief and frustration then comes to see the incident, in a sort of conversion experience, as an act of transformational moral courage on the part of the perpetrators, an aspect of the code of "horror and moral terror" by which he himself has learned to live and act.

His logic is muddled, of course, although he declares that his thinking is clear even if his soul has gone mad. He has been able to incorporate that terrible traumatic encounter only by going deeper into its mystery, but he has not gained enlightenment, only suffered a massive, permanent blow to his sense of conventional morality. In this he is hardly different, in spite of his philosophizing and mythicizing (Wood is right in suggesting that a romanticizing of evil is involved), from the GIs, described by Mark Baker and others, who fell in love with killing in Vietnam and could not overcome that infatuation once they were back home. This is the fearful face of trauma.

What bothers the critics most about the last third of *Apocalypse Now,* along with Brando's eccentric performance, is that Coppola tries and fails to express what is not expressible. The temptation surely was strong. As Just says, "In so many ways Vietnam became a furious search for myth and metaphor."[33] The scene showing Frazer's *The Golden Bough* and Jessie Weston's *From Ritual to Romance* on Kurtz's table bears him out in the case of this film. Wood declares that Kurtz represents (although Kilgore does it better), "what Mary McCarthy once called the metaphysical element in the American involvement in Vietnam. Not the unwillingness to admit defeat, and not the doctrinal attachment to our system of production and consumption which McCarthy herself defined as metaphysical, but the enormous charm of the inexhaustible enemy, an endless, heartless darkness where a madman could go looking for victory, never finding it, and never having to give up the search."[34]

The charm lies in tangling with the metaphysical when it gives off the scent of evil, in trying to express an inexpressible that seems demonic. This seduction pervades almost all attempts to comprehend the lust for destruction that so many ordinary people turned killers in Vietnam exhibited. Wood thinks that Coppola actually brings off a fleeting articulation of the inexpressible but that it is neither appropriate nor worth the effort. "There *is* something there, a sense of a condition beyond our power to name it, and when Willard, on his way to kill Kurtz, emerges red-eyed and mudstained from a swamp, like a creature from an ancient, pre-human world, we glimpse, briefly, the film's other subject: the absolutely unimaginable, caught by miracle in a camera. But this is not a political subject, it has nothing to do with Vietnam, and Coppola in any case can only hint at it, a faint touch of the authentic in a pile of maudlin fakery."[35] Such a judgment seems a misguided conclusion to an otherwise brilliant review. This glimpse of the "unimaginable, caught by miracle" is ultimately political and has everything to do with Vietnam. Governments exist to safeguard the quotidian in which "miracles" can occasionally be performed by our best artists, and the Vietnam War happened as it did, as a traumatic ordeal, because governments, above all the American government, thought they could identify and overcome the evil in the other without succumbing to its power in the self.

But the infatuation with violence infecting Kilgore, Kurtz, and finally even Willard shows up at last in the maligned last part of *Apocalypse Now* as an ecstasy that has turned to melancholy. Those who love to kill get weary if not sated; they cannot grieve but do become dejected. Martin Jay argues that the permeating apocalyptic mood of postmodernism displays the same symptoms of melancholia Freud identified: "deep and painful dejection, withdrawal of interest in the everyday world, diminished capacity to love, paralysis of the will, and most important of all, radical lowering of self-esteem accompanied by fantasies of punishment for assumed moral transgressions."[36] According to Freud, the melancholy can change into "manic elation," actually "two sides of the same coin," similar to what I am calling ecstasy, and these together in Jay's analysis characterize "apocalyptic thought [that] remains caught in the cycle of depressive anxiety and manic release."[37]

"The complex of melancholia behaves like an open wound, drawing to itself cathectic energy from all sides . . . and draining the ego until it is utterly depleted," Freud maintains.[38] Kurtz has the open wound, literally, and exhibits the melancholy following manic elation as well as the extreme narcissism of the individual who cannot exercise normal grieving because he will not let go of the departed love object. That lost object for Kurtz is nothing less than Western civilization or the Christian heritage. He thinks he has seen "the horror" that propels him beyond that heritage, yet he cannot truly give it up for it is too much a part of him. His rage for destruction is apocalyptic; possessed by a vast ego, he wishes to take the world down with him as he is overwhelmed by "the horror." His rage is also an effort to liberate himself, to separate himself from the symbolic mother (the locus, finally, of narcissistic desire) by ravaging the surrogate mother earth.[39]

Mr. God, He Dead

I have borrowed Jay's psychoanalytical strategy to plumb the metaphysical as it pervades *Apocalypse Now* and to "rehabilitate" Kurtz's role as more understandable and less murky than the critics have taken it to be. It is an analysis that may be hard to swallow, however, and it can be balanced by attention to religious aspects of the film. One that is prominent concerns the figures behind the film: the Catholicism of Coppola and Sheen that was mentioned in the *Rolling Stone* account of the director tormenting his main actor into a Christian guilt-ridden performance. A knowledge of such motivation matters far less than the evidence of a Christian dimension in the film, and there is relatively little such evidence: a chaplain holding a service with American soldiers (in ironic juxtaposition with the carnage), some ruined structures outlined crosslike against the sky, and the evocation of Eliot's and Weston's once fashionable Grail-myth ruminations. Most interesting in this context is the borrowing of Wagner's "pagan" opera music when Kilgore blasts out "The Ride of the Valkyries" during the air cavalry assault. The Valkyries in Nordic myth, Odin's maidens who guide fallen heroes to Valhalla and serve them there, seem to be misunderstood by Kilgore (and Coppola) as vengeful furies who attack a terrified enemy, but the confusion is instructive. Wagner, for all his obsession with heroic "German" mythology, could not rid himself of his Christian heritage; it pervades his work, and, similarly, the helicopter assault in the film has overtones not of Nordic or Greek heroism but of judgmental American evangelistic fervor as old as the colonies: demolishing the demonized enemy with apocalyptic force.

Kurtz is caught between Eastern and Western religiosity as well as between ancient belief and modern skepticism. His reading of Eliot, among other things, suggests an intellectual Christian orientation, but he has established his heavily fortified outpost in the ruins of what appears to be an ancient Buddhist temple.[40] Whether or not the background of the setting is Buddhist, the emphasis is on blood sacrifice, and Kurtz is an absolute ruler who destroys his enemies and kills his subjects at will. The site is littered with bodies of the dead from a recent battle and of those executed by Kurtz. He is also worshiped by the tribespeople and the American deserters.[41] In this role he becomes the vulnerable deity-king of Frazer's *The Golden Bough* who defends himself nightly in the sacred grove until he is at last deposed by an assassin who becomes the next king.[42] For Frazer this killing is sacrificial, the king expiates the sins of his people with his life and keeps the land—their livelihood—fertile for them, and the film carries through the sacrifice motif. As Willard hacks Kurtz to death in his quarters, Kurtz's subjects just outside decapitate a water buffalo and hack the animal to pieces. It is a "mythopathic moment," a double *sparagmos* that is intended to cleanse.[43]

Kurtz forces Willard to share his suffering, but Willard is not, at last, seduced—or if he is, it is to fulfill Kurtz's own need for self-destruction. The ordeal that Kurtz puts Willard through is a purification ritual that readies him to perform Kurtz's execution. Kurtz, in the midst of his hubristic savagery, appears to recognize the extent of his excess, that he is a beast who needs to be put down and that he has usurped the prerogatives of the gods and must pay for doing so with his life. By rights (and rites), Willard should become the next deific ruler, and it is clear when he emerges blood-smeared from the killing and stands above the waiting crowd that he is tempted. But that is not his role or destiny. He throws down his machete, and as he walks through the mass of people toward the patrol boat (taking with him the one surviving crew member), they too drop their weapons—a hopeful gesture in the midst of carnage.

In the script Kurtz dies on Willard's boat, returning to Vietnam, apparently of wounds, illness, and exhaustion, following a tremendous battle at the fortress-temple that includes an air strike: "Balls and rain of fire sweep down on the temple, the enemy, everything. It is the biggest firework show in history."[44] Afterward, "The entire temple is devastation. Vultures by the hundreds circle overhead. There are few survivors. Everywhere is smoke and heaps of bodies."[45] But Coppola rejected this apocalyptic orgy, choosing instead to have Kurtz expire, relatively speaking, more quietly. It was the proper choice, providing a symbolic vehicle for expressing what is finally the death of God—not Nietzschean style but more in terms of a Holocaust nihilism.

The horror that Kurtz sees and that Coppola glimpses and brings miraculously to the screen is not the bestiality of human and natural existence, but something—the nothing—beyond that. It is the nothing that cannot be mourned because nothing can connect—"cathect"—to it. It is the blank face of abandonment (like the face of the huge stone deity we see near the film's end, whose empty eyes merge briefly with Willard's), of utter desertion even beyond apocalyptic spectacle, and it is the price that a civilization pays for its abuse of other cultures in the name of God.

How can one think of *Apocalypse Now* as a work belonging to the public sphere? And to which public sphere? Since the war in Vietnam ended, Americans, in spite of public rituals of closure and reconciliation, have tried to put it out of their minds and memories. It surfaces frequently, however, evidence of the existence of the return of the repressed. Often it is part of the continuing and unresolved neurosis that belongs to the centuries-old trauma rooted in crimes against the native inhabitants of the American continent and its terrain. We have no public realm dedicated to remembering Vietnam in this fashion, certainly nothing like the place in Western, including American, consciousness for the remembrance of the Holocaust.[46] Vietnam is, nevertheless, an element of the body apocalyptic, a growing (and not necessarily healthy) aspect of a public realm that encompasses a polyphony of voices from, among other areas, religion, science, education, and politics.

One might think that *Apocalypse Now* plays a negligible role in this ferment. It played in the theaters during the late seventies, was harshly criticized, and never found more permanent form as a literary text other than its partial inspiration, *Heart of Darkness*. Yet it probably exerts an influence today far exceeding that of any of the other works discussed in this volume. It is in thousands of video stores and libraries, and it is shown in cinema, history, journalism, and literature classes in colleges and universities. Available now as a work that can be viewed repeatedly and studied, it reveals a depth and achieved vision that transcend the flaws on which its early reviewers focused.[47] As Dennehy remarked, it is *the* movie of the Vietnam War, and because its religious dimensions mirror the political-spiritual dilemmas of postmodern American life, it can be comprehended as a text at the core of public and private consciousness.

Notes

1. These are the words of Edward W. Said summarizing Slotkin's position in *Culture and Imperialism* (New York: Alfred A. Knopf, 1994), 288; Richard Slotkin, *Regeneration through Violence: The Mythology of the American Frontier, 1600–1860* (Middletown: Wesleyan University Press, 1973), 557, quoted in Said, *Culture and Imperialism*, 288.

2. Said, *Culture and Imperialism*, 314.

3. Gerald Vizenor, *Manifest Manners: Postindian Warriors of Survivance* (Hanover: Wesleyan University Press, 1994), 149. In *Gunfighter Nation: The Myth of the Frontier in Twentieth-Century America* (New York: Atheneum, 1992), Richard Slotkin refers to a Native American letter writer who responded to *Life* magazine's coverage of the My Lai massacre and reminded other readers that "this is not the first time that American soldiers have murdered women and children . . . how about Wounded Knee [?]" (589).

4. James Welch, of Blackfeet and Gros Ventre ancestry, is the author of *Fools Crow* (New York: Viking, 1986), a novel that presents scenes like those of the Wounded Knee killing. Wendy Rose, of Hopi and Miwok lineage, has written poems such as "I Expected My Skin and My Blood to Ripen" on the exploitation of the Wounded Knee event in modern times through the selling of Lakota clothing from the massacre as memorabilia. Thomas Sanchez is the author of the novel *Rabbit Boss* (New York: Knopf, 1973), in which a Wovoka-like character, Hallelujah Bob, figures prominently. Slotkin in *Gunfighter Nation* calls attention to "the re-emergence of a new 'Cult of the Indian,' represented in movie-mythology by films like *Little Big Man* and *Soldier Blue* (1970), which invoke parallels between Mylai and the Washita and Sand Creek massacre of Indians by Whites. . . . At least since 1966, Native Americans and their culture had become important symbols of rebellion in the so-called 'counter-culture' of college-age White Americans" (590).

5. Vizenor, *Manifest Manners,* 149. Slotkin describes the many ways in the seventies in which "Native Americans were also pressed into service as symbols in political and cultural controversies that chiefly concerned non-Indian groups" (*Gunfighter Nation,* 629).

6. Examples of Native American soldiers in Vietnam War literature are the "devout Baptist" Kiowa in Tim O'Brien's *The Things They Carried* (Boston: Houghton Mifflin, 1990); Corporal "Chief" Eagle, "one-half Chiricahua and one-half Blackfoot," in William Turner Huggett's *Body Count* (New York: Putnam, 1973); and the Ojibwa Boniface George St. Germaine in Philip Caputo's *Indian Country* (New York: Bantam Books, 1987).

7. Nicholas Proffitt, "Pride and Anguish" [review of Harold G. Moore and Joseph L. Galloway, *We Were Soldiers Once . . . and Young: Ia Drang: The Battle That Changed the War in Vietnam*], *New York Times Book Review,* November 8, 1992, 65. Proffitt and Caputo were together in Saigon as correspondents during the fall of the South Vietnam capital in 1975.

8. This definition appears as a prefatory quote in Caputo, *Indian Country.* Michael Herr in *Dispatches* (New York: Vintage Books, 1991), reports on an American officer in the Vietnam War zone who says, matter-of-factly, "Come on, . . . we'll take you out to play Cowboys and Indians" (61).

9. On Lakota mourning see note 19 of chapter 9. For a moving fictional account of mourning at the Vietnam Veterans Memorial in Washington, see the closing pages of Bobbie Ann Mason, *In Country* (New York: Harper and Row, 1985).

10. My sources for this information are chapter 14, "The Morality of Power: Disposing of Diem," in *Constructing the American Past: A Source Book of People's History,* ed. Elliott J. Gorn, Randy Roberts, and Terry D. Bilhartz (New York: HarperCollins, 1991); Philip Caputo, *A Rumor of War* (New York: Ballantine Books, 1977); and *The Vietnam Experience: A Nation Divided,* ed. Clark Dougan and Samuel Lipsman (Boston: Boston Publishing, 1984).

11. In *A Rumor of War,* 340, Caputo states that even in late April 1975 personnel at the American embassy in Saigon "refused to surrender its illusions that the ARVN could stop the North Vietnamese advance."

12. Ibid., 314–37. See Slotkin, *Gunfighter Nation,* chapter 17, "Cross-over Point: The Mylai Massacre, the Wild Bunch, and the Demoralization of America, 1969–72." I have learned a great deal from Slotkin and use his discussion in mine.

13. I have used the script that lists the following information on the first page: *"APOCALYPSE NOW,* Original Screen Play by John Milius. Inspired by Joseph Conrad's *Heart of Darkness.* This Draft by Francis Ford Coppola. December 3, 1975." It is available from Coppola Cinema Seven, Samuel Goldwyn Studios, Los Angeles, California.

14. Ward Just, "Newspaper Days," *The Atlantic* 245 (December 1979): 64; Jean Baudrillard, "Apocalypse Now," in *Simulacra and Simulation,* trans. Sheila Faria Glaser (Ann Arbor: University of Michigan Press, 1994), 59–60.

15. Much of this information comes from Eleanor Coppola, "Diary of a Director's Wife," *New York Times Magazine,* August 26, 1979. Her account is entertaining. She reports, for example, that Al Pacino, James Caan, and Robert Redford turned down the Captain Willard role before Harvey Keitel accepted it (who was replaced after a few weeks by Sheen) and that the Kurtz role was discussed with Steve McQueen. Eleanor Coppola also directed a documentary about the making of the film: *Hearts of Darkness: A Filmmaker's Apocalypse* (ZM Productions, 1991), which relies heavily on clips from *Apocalypse Now* and on rambling statements from Coppola, Sheen, Dennis Hopper, and others.

16. "Twenty Questions," interview with Brian Dennehy, *Playboy* 40 (November 1993): 166.

17. Vincent Canby, "Apocalypse Is 'Extremely Misty,'" *New York Times,* August 19, 1979, sec. 11, 1.

18. Michael Wood, "Bangs and Whimpers," *New York Review of Books,* October 11, 1979, 18.

19. Just, "Newspaper Days," 64.

20. Wood, "Bangs and Whimpers," 17.

21. Mark Baker, *Nam: The Vietnam War in the Words of the Men and Women Who Fought There* (New York: Berkeley Books, 1983), 156; see also Wallace Terry, *Bloods: An Oral History of the Vietnam War by Black Veterans* (New York: Ballantine Books, 1984).

22. According to Wood, "Bangs and Whimpers," 17, Coppola while the film was in the making believed this himself. Wood quotes him as writing, "The film reaches its highest level during the fucking helicopter battle."

23. Just, "Newspaper Days," 64. The witness of Caputo in *A Rumor of War,* of the many voices in Baker's *Nam,* and others, however, is that it was indeed often a ludicrous thing.

24. Jean Baudrillard, "Simulacra and Simulations," in *Selected Writings,* ed. Mark Poster (Stanford: Stanford University Press, 1988).

25. An example of playful postmodern self-referentiality in *Apocalypse Now* is the scene in which Coppola plays a cameraman who tells Sheen not to look at the camera.

26. Baudrillard in "Apocalypse Now" reflects on "the war as entrenchment, as technological and psychedelic fantasy; . . . it is necessary for us to believe in

this: the war in Vietnam 'in itself' perhaps in fact never happened, it is a dream, a baroque dream of napalm and the tropics, a psychotropic dream that had the goal neither of a victory nor of a policy at stake, but, rather, the sacrificial, excessive deployment of a power already filming itself as it unfolded, perhaps waiting for nothing but consecration by a superfilm, which completes the mass-spectacle effect of this war" (59). Baudrillard's overheated two-page critique of the film is worth reading in full.

27. Herr, *Dispatches*, 49. The sentence continues, "Might just as well lay it on the proto-Gringos who found the New England woods too raw and empty for their peace and filled them up with their own imported devils" (49).

28. Another striking simulation scene occurs at an "advanced staging area" for "Operation Brute Force" along the river when a Playboy helicopter flies in with centerfold models (one dressed in a scanty Native American costume) on board to entertain the troops. The Playmate of the Year prances onstage clad in a skimpy cowgirl outfit (the game of cowboys and Indians is in the background of American pop consciousness), shooting her imitation-Colt cap pistols against a nightscape of looming phallic structures. The men, excited by the women's moves simulating sexual acts, storm the platform, but the women are whisked off in time by helicopter; they are not available for "real" sex. In the Milius script, however, they are coerced into intercourse with Willard and the patrol boat crew in exchange for helicopter fuel.

29. Slotkin here quotes Jay Roberts describing American behavior at My Lai, specifically a soldier stabbing a calf, then compares the scene to Mary Rowlandson's 1682 depiction of Indians slaughtering both people and farm animals; see *Gunfighter Nation*, 586, 754. The Roberts material cited by Slotkin is in Hal Wingo et al., "The Massacre at Mylai," *Life*, December 5, 1969, 36–45.

30. Greil Marcus observes that the sampan scene is the turning point of the film because in it Willard shows his ruthlessness and loses audience sympathy. Coppola more or less agrees. Greil Marcus, "Journey up the River: An Interview with Francis Coppola," *Rolling Stone*, November 1, 1979, 55.

31. Jean Vallely, "Martin Sheen: Heart of Darkness, Heart of Gold," *Rolling Stone*, November 1, 1979, 46.

32. Quoted by Vallely, "Martin Sheen," 48.

33. Just, "Newspaper Days," 63.

34. Wood, "Bangs and Whimpers," 17.

35. Ibid., 18.

36. Martin Jay, "The Apocalyptic Imagination and the Inability to Mourn," in *Force Fields: Between Intellectual History and Cultural Critique* (New York: Routledge, 1993), 92. Jay is working from Freud's essay "Mourning and Melancholia" and his later *Group Psychology and the Analysis of the Ego*. A version of the inability to mourn and resulting melancholia is at the heart of the Sioux Bigfoot Memorial Ride portrayed in the documentary film *Wiping the Tears of Seven Generations*.

37. Jay, "The Apocalyptic Imagination," 91, 93.

38. Ibid., 93–94.

39. Jay uses Julia Kristeva's *Black Sun* as inspiration for this notion of over-

coming melancholia and apocalyptic thinking by attempted separation from the symbolic mother. See "The Apocalyptic Imagination," 96–97. In *Gunfighter Nation,* Slotkin, reflecting on a *Life* magazine depiction of the American soldiers' behavior at My Lai, writes, "Instead of protecting women and children from 'the horror,' they have themselves *become* 'the horror'" (585).

40. The script describes it as "the temple at Nu Mung Ba, a fortified encampment, built on the ruins of a former Cambodian civilization" (121).

41. Dennis Hopper plays a mad, drugged-out photojournalist who raves about Kurtz's godlike qualities.

42. Sir James George Frazer's *The Golden Bough: A Study in Magic and Religion* was first published in two volumes in 1890, then in twelve volumes from 1911 to 1915. A one-volume abridged version was first published in 1922 by the Macmillan Company. It is this version, of course, that Kurtz possesses. The sacrificial king is treated by Frazer at the start in chapter 1, "The King of the Wood." Coppola has said that the animal sacrifices can be understood in terms of Frazer's study. Marcus, "Journey up the River," 54.

43. Earlier in the film Kilgore has a cow or steer airlifted in by helicopter to be slaughtered to supply a barbecue feast for his men. It is a moment of cinematic "intertextuality" that causes one to recall the classic scene in Federico Fellini's *La Dolce Vita* in which a statue of Christ dangles beneath a helicopter that passes overhead. The term *mythopathic moment* is from Herr, *Dispatches,* 46, who uses it in comparing American military attitudes in Vietnam to those of a John Wayne film, *Fort Apache.*

44. *Apocalypse Now* script, 145.

45. Ibid., 146. Coppola makes much of the fact that this ending is also not the one he wanted. The one he preferred has "Willard up on the steps after killing Kurtz. He's in front of the people. The people all bow. He looks, he looks back, he looks again—then it goes to the [Willard's painted] green face, and 'the horror, the horror.' . . . I thought that the film should end with a choice, which was: 'Should I be Kurtz? Or should I be Willard'?" Marcus, "Journey up the River," 56. One version of the film did portray (I do not know how long after its release) the apocalyptic ending as called for by the script.

46. We do have a public place, the Vietnam Veterans Memorial, designed by Maya Ying Lin, in Washington, D.C., which has become a national sacred space. Conrad Cherry has remarked, "It's an altar. . . . You approach it with reverence and respect and silence. The supreme sacrifice is very much there." Quoted by Gustav Niebuhr, "More Than a Monument: The Spiritual Dimension of These Hallowed Walls," *New York Times,* November 11, 1994, A8.

47. Coppola has stated, though, "I don't ever want this movie on television. . . . It wasn't designed to be seen that way. It was designed as a spectacle." Marcus, "Journey up the River," 54. It is true that the film is vastly more impressive on a large screen.

11

Indian Country:
Disorder and Late Sorrow

> I walked up and down the clearing, trying to draw the sniper's fire. "When he opens up, every man put five rounds rapid into the tree line," I said, walking back and forth and feeling as invulnerable as an Indian wearing his ghost shirt.
>
> —Philip Caputo, *A Rumor of War*

> You had the power to rape a woman and nobody could say nothing to you. That godlike feeling you had was in the field. It was like I was a god. I could take a life, I could screw a woman. I can beat somebody up and get away with it. It was a godlike feeling that a guy could express in the Nam.
>
> —Unidentified Vietnam combat veteran, in Mark Baker, *Nam*

In Philip Caputo's third novel the Vietnam War comes home. Its Ulysses is Christian Starkmann, a veteran from Oak Park, Illinois, near Chicago (where Hemingway grew up), but Starkmann is not one of those who discovered a taste for killing and is thus corrupted for civilian life. The son of a militantly pacifist, antiwar activist Missouri Synod Lutheran pastor, he is a decent man who enlists in the late sixties for two reasons.[1] The first is to spite his father, a motivation stronger than he himself knows and so deeply buried that he learns its full force only years later following his breakdown. He learns that beyond the spite was the desperate desire to have his stern, aloof father respond to him in love. The second reason is to be with his close friend, the young Ojibwa Boniface George St. Germaine, whom Starkmann learned to know on fishing trips he and his father took to Michigan's remote Upper Peninsula. Bonny George's grandfather Louis, a shaman, would be their guide. Christian is a divinity student and has a draft deferment, but Bonny has no such privilege. He discusses exile in Canada with Chris on a fishing trip, but his grandfather, informed in a vision, has already advised him to serve his country. As Bonny George tells it, "We're not pacifists. We're not cowards. We don't run. That was pretty much Grandpa's message" (42). On that same trip Chris is caught in a strong current, and the young Indian saves him from drowning. Soon after that, Chris, grateful and defiant, determines to enlist and fight the war with his friend. "What he was going to do was, for him, so daring, and would cause his father such pain, that he had to get used to the idea" (51–52).

The novel's chronology then shifts to 1981, about a dozen years after Starkmann has returned from the war. He now lives, estranged from his parents, with his wife June and two daughters on an isolated Upper Peninsula tract of forty acres bordering an Indian reservation near the shores of Lake Superior. He has earned a college degree in forestry and works as a timber surveyor for Great Superior Iron and Timber. Of late he has been suffering agonizing nightmares, signs of post-traumatic stress disorder (PTSD) that he does not recognize as such. These become more intense and distressing and show up particularly as paranoia (he thinks that his supervisor at Great Superior wants to have him fired), a growing inability to communicate with June and others, heavy drinking, and an episode at the local (fifteen miles away in town) bar, where he turns aggressive then collapses and relives a war experience in a half-conscious state.

Things are exacerbated by Chris's abrupt visit to Chicago to be with his father, who has suffered a severe stroke. While Chris sits alone with him in a hospital room, trying to reconcile with him, the old man dies. Eventually, following drinking and fighting while surveying in the forest, Chris is indeed fired and, instead of looking for other work, turns his energies to fortifying his property, "securing" it as if it were a battle zone. Ever more perturbed by his irrational and violent behavior and depressed herself by the harsh winter and isolation, June "bribes" him into seeing Eckhardt, a psychologist in town who specializes in post-traumatic stress disorder, but healing is not forthcoming. At a group therapy meeting, when the submerged truth of his war experiences starts to surface, he goes into a rage and runs away. Back home he dresses in combat uniform, paints his face, and prepares to die defending his home. But it is June who comes home, delayed in town and concerned for her daughters, and in the ensuing fight with her Chris rapes her anally before she escapes with the girls.

Outside in a foxhole near his "perimeter," Starkmann recalls clearly at last the battle scene that has been too horrible to remember. Filling in for a dying officer during a firefight, he called in an air strike but gave incorrect coordinates, and his friend Bonny George, not far in advance of him, was burned to death by napalm. Starkmann particularly remembers his dying comrade's final words, "*I saved you from the water, but you killed me with the fire.*" He booby-traps the house with a home-made bomb—a flip of the light switch will detonate it—and waits, but instead of the police appearing to die with him in an apocalyptic conflagration, June drives up again. He stops her in time from entering the house and then persuades her not to leave him for good by promising to undergo therapy seriously.

Now the therapy is effective, but Chris feels the need for another kind of healing and against the advice of Eckhardt sets out to find old Louis St. Germaine. He locates him on a vision quest in a remote part of the woods and tells him how he caused Bonny George's death. The old shaman does not forgive him, telling him that forgiveness is not an Indian concept, but helps him nonetheless to deal with his guilt and learn to forgive himself. Chris returns to the stream where he nearly drowned many years earlier. He undresses, swims through it, and throws away his Vietnam uniform and the decorations he has brought along.

The reviewers were generous, on the whole, in their assessment of *Indian Country*. Michiko Kakutani remarks, "Cutting back and forth between Chris' memories and the war—recreated with frightening, dreamlike power—and his current paranoia, Mr. Caputo does a brilliant job of communicating his increasingly crazed state of mind."[2] John Melmoth, less sympathetic, calls it "an odd concoction of boy's-own-story machismo, compassion, self-pity, misogyny, sexual special pleading, backwoodsmanship and myth-making" but still thinks that its evocation of the war experience is "real if unrefined."[3] Dick Roraback declares, "Yes, 'Indian Country' has been explored, mined, combed and recombed in recent years. And yes, Caputo explores it again. Better—far better—than most."[4] Frank Conroy, examining the text from a novelist's perspective, sees many flaws (e.g., the narrative is overwritten and could have been cut) but thinks that this ambitious work is effective in showing one kind of healing.[5]

Homo Furens

The novel does skirt the possibility of slipping into cliché yet escapes it. That possibility is lively because the protagonist's condition is, after a fashion, a cliché. It has been diagnosed, given a appropriately jargony label, and researched exhaustively; the literature on PTSD and on trauma more generally is large.[6] But as Conroy points out, "There are as many different forms of combatitis veteranitis as there are people suffering from it, and that makes sense. There are many different ways of healing, and that makes sense too. 'Indian Country' makes the point that we should not try to understand these things too easily."[7]

With that caveat taken to heart, my concern will be with how Starkmann's trauma is both "standard" and unique and how it can be understood as a microcosmic version of America's ancient and recent wounds. First, however, it is convenient and fitting to use the characters of Louis St. Germaine and June, Starkmann's wife, to address two of the four elements of the body apocalyptic: melancholy resulting from ecstasy and simulation deriving from awe.

Louis, whatever insignificant role he plays in the white world and among his own people the Ojibwas as they lose their heritage, views himself above all as a *mide*, a medicine man. Earning the name Wawiekumig as a shaman initiate, he has absorbed much of the ancient lore from the old masters and used it wisely throughout his long life, gaining respect on the Vieux Desert reservation as The-Man-Who-Knows-Everything. His vision quests, physical-spiritual ordeals of fasting and isolation, have afforded him much insight, and he has known ecstasy through extra-body experiences such as flying around the world with an eagle, "seeing the world as an eagle does, whole and entire" (55). But as he ages and grows feeble, with no one to train as his successor (Bonny George would have been the one, which makes his death all the more poignant), Louis drifts more and more into melancholy not so much of the sort treated psychoanalytically by Martin Jay but more a profound sadness caused by the demise of a great, sacred tradition as the younger generations take up the ways of the dominant white culture that has oppressed and ignored them for centuries. Louis/Wawiekumig's inability to accept this situation induces a melancholy like that which Freud depicts—his ego investment in the lost (or vanishing) love object is vast—and he cannot mourn it appropriately because he has been unable to distance himself from it. How he reaches a resolution, at the end, in a manner in keeping with his heritage.

Louis also exemplifies the relationship between awe/mystery and simulation and in a manner more positive (although in an apocalyptic context) than Jean Baudrillard's theorizing on simulation. He recalls the life-changing impact of his initiation into shamanhood, the literal blow from which his "new self will be born" (149). "There was a sharp blow to his temple. Without help, Wawiekumig leaped to his feet and knew the finding of the shell in his mouth had not been the work of some juggler, but a true mystery. . . . Spiritual vitality, power, the life-force of the Mide-manito [shaman of God]" (151).

Conroy (who should know better) sees all this as "mumbo jumbo" that tests the reader's tolerance, but such passages are integral to both the white and Native American plot development.[8] Aside from the evocation of war that the blow and shell (as part of a bullet) in the mouth inspire, the scene relates to simulation in other ways. Louis has suspected that he is being manipulated by a magician (a "juggler") or trickster, someone who simulates in the sense of creating illusory reality. Instead, he encounters "true mystery," a prelude to and preparation for introducing Starkmann to the mystery that reconciles him. Throughout his life Louis both creates and responds to mystery through simulation. He is awe-inspired and inspiring through his acts of simulation involving his medicine bundle, his flight with the eagle, and the ghost rites that accompany Bonny George's charred corpse (secretly disinterred by Louis from the Christian cemetery) to the "Village of the Dead."

These actions are not quite apocalyptic in Baudrillard's sense, where the simulation world of technology, out of control, hastens the global cataclysm. Yet they are Baudrillardian insofar as they are rituals seeking to ward off the technological destruction that engulfs Native Americans. Early in the novel Bonny George puts that view to Chris in apocalyptic terms when he explains "wolf time," a concept antagonistic to Indians:

> It's this prophecy a witch gives to Odin predicting the end of the world. The Twilight of the Gods. There's war all over the world. Brothers killing brothers. Fathers kill their sons. Sons kill their fathers. And it all comes down when this giant wolf leaps up and swallows the moon and the sun in his slobbering jaws. Get the picture? When white people came over here, they brought all that baggage with them, and they wiped out the wolves because they were afraid of them, not just because wolves raided livestock. . . . The Indian was killed for the same reason. (30)

There is not much simulation in the actions of Starkmann's wife, a sensible and practical social worker, apart from her putting on a face of normalcy for the sake of the daughters in a family context where the husband and father's behavior turns increasingly erratic and dangerous. June has known little awe or mystery. Of French Canadian and Finnish ancestry from Sault Ste. Marie, she was impregnated as a high school senior by an older man (the father of her eldest daughter), then abandoned by him—yet another version of the seduction-abuse-abandonment sequence that marks American lives. Her marriage to Chris, although passionate, is permeated by loneliness and his growing paranoia.

Kakutani thinks that June "initially strikes us as a stereotyped collection of male fantasies [who] . . . slowly evolves into a more and more sympathetic human being."[9] I doubt that she is a repository of male fantasies for many readers, although she surely is a survivor. She is also literally down to earth; she is a woman in love with the soil, and in the soil are her ecstasy and melancholy. Always close to depression thanks to her unhappy past, the desolation of the Upper Peninsula, and her husband's frightening behavior, she rouses herself in midspring by turning to her garden, and at one moment in the midst of her distress she creates a brief ecstasy: stripping naked and pleasuring herself in the sun's warmth above the newly seeded furrows. But this is short-lived. Melancholy, one of the four ancient humors meaning "black bile," was the one related to the element of earth, and June's joy of earth shifts quickly to sadness. It strikes her harshly just after she has barely escaped death in the bomb-rigged house and sees no cure for her husband's derangement. "A mournfulness welled up in her" (382), and she decides then and there to leave him and take her daughters with her. But that is the very incentive Chris needs. He promises to get help at last, so June relents and stays, and "joy mov[es] through her like the wind" (383).

These swift alternations of joy and sorrow, ecstasy and melancholy, are connected to unresolved loss. June's deprivations had earlier created an aura about her that attracted Chris. "He saw an expression of pain and sadness mingled with the challenge in her eyes. In that instant he knew the magic of encountering a kindred spirit. She, too, was lonely, an exile suffering from unseen wounds" (106). But sharing the pain and depression does not help this couple make it through. They turn their hurt on each other and increase it, especially the incommunicative Chris ("a reincarnation of Gary Cooper. *Yup. Nope.*" [113]), who becomes even less vocal as his stress deepens. It seems that he has never known much else than depression, a condition deriving more or less directly from his father's dour religion and personality. "Starkmann" means "strong man" in German, and the rigid father-preacher is as fiercely unyielding in his family relationships as in his antiwar activism. The father-son liaison is classically oedipal, and the fact that a reconciliation never happens, in spite of Chris's efforts at his dying father's side, prevents the son from healthful expressions of grief and increases the melancholy already at work.

A crucial encounter not long after Chris returns from Vietnam hardens the antagonism between them. When the father asks the son, who is floundering, to "resume his studies for the ministry," Chris refuses and blurts out his fateful reason: "Because I don't believe in any of those lies and bullshit you preach on Sundays. I never did" (101). It is a symbolic wounding of the father by denying validity to his vocation, and the father is unforgiving. Chris packs to leave home, and when he informs his father of his plans, the Reverend Starkmann strikes his telling, "castrating" blow: "My son left a long time ago. . . . He never came back" (102). The tormented son, trying desperately to make amends years later, to reach the dying "love object," cannot; he is left seeking and failing to mourn that from which, in spite of his efforts, he has been unable to separate himself.

It is not surprising that such circumstances propel him faster and deeper into genuine paranoia. Back from Vietnam and reluctantly out for a "night on the town" in Chicago with an acquaintance, he is struck in the face, outside a singles bar, by a bag of fast food thrown by someone in a car of cruising teenagers and spattered "with hamburger scraps, greasy French fries, and gobs of milkshake" (99). It is a portentous moment, the returned veteran assaulted with a chief symbol of the things for which he has fought, complicit in ravaging a foreign land to assure the flourishing of a wasteful consumerist society at home. He remains calm and does not give chase, knowing that if he caught them, "he would have no choice but to kill them" (99). This suppressed overreaction is part of his paranoia, which is already apparent. Following several nights of war dreams, he buys a gun, "an M-1 carbine modified for sporting use," and sleeps behind a locked door with the loaded weapon in bed. He treats it, in fact, like a lover, "nuzzling the carbine's barrel with his cheek, his hand resting on the stock" (96).[10]

The paranoia overtakes him on the Upper Peninsula, where he lives, by now married and with a family, and assumes a terrifying shape. Soon after being fired from his surveyor's job he is out in the woods again, comes upon a decaying doe killed by a poacher, and feels "the mysterious sadness," "the inexplicable sorrow," and "the sadness without object" (302). That quickly shifts to a sense that he is being stalked by some predator, perhaps a panther. He panics and runs, gets lost, and eventually finds his way back to his truck. One recalls his father telling him, in a brutal letter, that he fears his son will become "*Homo furens*, half man, half beast," and he seems to have done that, his persecution complex affecting his reason and causing him to flee the nameless beast that is, in part, himself.[11]

In *Means of Escape* Caputo mentions the "Dark Thing" that visited him after Vietnam and that he identifies as "a guilt that somehow got twisted into a black anger."[12] The beast metaphor is also part of the relationship between June and Chris that one reviewer has misunderstood. June's fantasy of being taken sexually by a bear-god, which Kakutani dismisses as male fantasizing, is her ambivalent response to the *Homo furens* that her husband becomes.[13] Indeed, Caputo makes the connection explicitly while depicting a scene of rough marital intercourse ("he thrust at her from behind like the bear-god" [218]). It also foreshadows the rape when Starkmann, out of control, savagely assaults his wife. When June actually shoots a marauding bear the scene can be read plausibly as her acted-out fantasy of killing her husband.

The stalking beast in *Indian Country* also reveals itself, later, as an emblem of guilt, a half-conscious foreboding of Bonny George's ghostly epiphany that appears to accuse Chris of killing him. It is only when the melancholy shows itself as guilt that the paranoia pushes Chris's trauma to its decisive climax—he will either die or seek a cure. He chooses life, then confronts his guilt with the shaman's aid, and, at last able to mourn, transcends melancholy. What emerges to take its place is not ecstasy but, for this veteran of apocalypse, a glimmer of peace.

But first he must act out his paranoia, and he does so in a manner that transforms his sense of awe into therapeutic simulation. His awe focuses on the terrible mystery of war and the savagery and devastation it spawns as well as its precious comradeship. These form the substance of his night-mares, his flashbacks, and, eventually, his obsessive recreation of a war zone on his own forty acres. It is both a willed (and willful) simulation and an unconscious, involuntary act, a reflex. As Starkmann erects de-fenses around his property, securing the perimeter with barbed wire, fox-holes, and, eventually, explosives, he simulates an event that, at the time, seems more surreal than real and was, in a perversion of Baudrillard's treatment of simulation, so horrifically unique as to beg a referent. When veterans of modern warfare state that it is so awful that it cannot be ade-quately described, they do not deny its reality, as Baudrillard denies the reality of the simulacrum's referent. They say the opposite: that war is too real, so overwhelmingly real that it defies description. It becomes it-self its only reference, and in that sense it shares Baudrillard's concept of hyperreality, an intensified experience that overwhelms all other referents. Here, too, is a reason why modern warfare produces acute PTSD: Those who have absorbed the horrors of it lack the language to depict it—to give it back to their community—and thus suffer the irresolution of its ineffability.

The flashbacks that Starkmann endures, like those of thousands of ac-tual veterans, are attempts of the unconscious to order the terrible or-deal by returning to it again and again. This compulsion plagues Stark-mann in the form of the three dead comrades from Vietnam—D.J., Hutch, and Ramos—disembodied voices of the men killed by a booby-trap bomb while Chris was in the hospital with malaria. Chris converses with them often, but their counsel is not good; they speak from and for death. They advise him to visit his dying father, and, much worse, they encourage him, when he is already engaged in his deranged defense of his property, to go all the way and die like a soldier while fighting his "enemies." The uncanny trio is also a simulation, a mysterious evocation of Chris's trau-matizing past. Although he half-recognizes the three as a sign of mad-ness and half as an objectified self-dialogue, he treats them as oracles, as near-sacred seers who in their pronouncements of the other purport to show him himself.

The flashbacks illuminate two other dead comrades, Captain Hartwell and Spec. 4 Pryce, killed in the foxhole with him before that fateful moment when he gave the wrong coordinates for the napalm strike that incinerated Bonny George. This simulation is ultimately positive, an effort of Starkmann's unconscious to break through the repressions, reveal to him what really happened in Vietnam (so terrible that he has hidden it from himself for many years), and offer him the choice of healing.

Relinquishing the Apocalypse

Referring to Starkmann the returned veteran as Ulysses, as I did at the start, was not only metaphorical. Eckhardt the psychologist evokes *The Odyssey* and reads to Chris the passage that moves him: "'Would God I too had died there—met my end that time the Trojans made so many casts at me, when I stood by Achilles after death. I should have had a soldier's burial and praise from the Achaians, not this choking waiting for me at sea, unmarked and lonely'" (325).

It is a risky tactic on Eckhardt's part, for Ulysses' complaint provokes Chris's attempt at a belated soldier's burial as he prepares for a final suicidal stand at his improvised fortress, an attempt foiled by June's unexpected appearance. But Eckhardt is trying to educate Chris about the nature of survivor's guilt, an affliction, part of PTSD, that torments him and appears dramatically in the voices of his dead friends. Eckhardt lays it out for him later, almost too neatly: "Do you remember that passage I read you from Homer? About Ulysses wishing he had died with his friends? Nowadays we call that *survivor guilt,* and one of its symptoms is identification with the victim. Way down deep, so far down you probably aren't aware of it, you want to be this St. Germaine. That's what compelled your move to the same county he came from, only you didn't know why, not in the front of your mind" (344–45).

Starkmann does not buy the diagnosis at the time. To the contrary, it propels him—protesting too much—into the suicidal rage from which he barely escapes. But it is nonetheless the revelation planted that eventually leads to his incipient recovery. Caputo's interweaving of the Ulysses material is prescient—as the work of good novelists often is—for it anticipates a fine analysis of PTSD and the Vietnam War in relation to warriors of antiquity: Jonathan Shay's *Achilles in Vietnam.* Shay deals with Achilles and *The Iliad* rather than with Ulysses and *The Odyssey,* but the connections are the same. A psychiatrist who treats Vietnam combat veterans in a Boston clinic, Shay sees parallels between the tribulations of the ancient Greek warriors and modern sufferers of PTSD. His listing of the disorder's traits sounds like a sketch of Starkmann's condition: "Their symptoms include chronic health problems caused by 'mobilizing' the body for danger, an inability to trust others—'persistent expectation of betrayal and exploitation'—and anger at military and governmental authorities. As a result, the most troubled veterans suffer from despair and isolation that lead to alcoholism, drug abuse and sometimes suicide."[14] Shay even refers to combat casualties from "'friendly fire'—accidental deaths caused by misdirected weapons," precisely the kind of mishap at the core of Starkmann's illness.[15] Achilles' career ends in tragedy, but Starkmann is luckier, for he receives, if belatedly (but then his disorder, as is its nature, shows up late), knowledgeable professional help.

The stages of Starkmann's treatment are provided in a wealth of textbooks. What is undertaken beyond the usual therapy is more significant in a discussion of the fiction of trauma as it contributes to a public awareness of the ills associated with violence in modern America and their possible remedies. His impulse and actions are religious, although not Christian or even Western in the usual sense. He turns to Native American religiosity, what some whites would call earth mysticism or even, disparagingly à la Conroy, "mumbo jumbo." Yet Starkmann's quest is worth taking seriously. It is keyed to the environment, it uses the apocalyptic mode to salvific ends, it uncovers a fascination with victimhood like that discussed in chapter 2, and it offers a prophetic word on how the collective postwar trauma of Vietnam may yet be employed to effect a reconciliation with the "original sin" of our nation's founding.

Starkmann is at heart a conservationist, so his job as timber surveyor, marking forests to be cut down by a large company that pays only lip service to environmental issues, puts him at odds with his principles. It is not surprising that the "execution" of the forests is portrayed in terms of the battles he has fought. He comes upon a trail "marked by the amputated corpses of maple trees. . . . We stacked the bodies like wood over there, . . . and over here we stack the wood like bodies. . . . Up ahead, a maple shuddered, gave its death shriek, and went down."[16] The dis-ease of nature that Chris feels is part of his disharmony that the old shaman Louis/Wawiekumig comprehends so well and that he can assist Chris in easing. Chris must return to nature to complete—or complete the start of—his recovery. He must strip naked, throw away his uniform and medals, and bathe sacramentally in the stream where once he almost drowned.

But all this happens to accompaniments of apocalypse. The mood is set early in the novel when Bonny George refers to Wounded Knee and educates young Chris in the process: "So, the Sioux didn't fight the last battle at Wounded Knee. The Ojibwa did. The Battle of Leech Lake, Minnesota, in the fall of 'ninety-eight. And the Ojibwa won that one. Killed eighteen troopers and their commanding officer, and sent the other ones running back to Fort Walton" (42). Late in the narrative, just after Starkmann's abortive defensive maneuvers, June, about to commit him to a psychiatric hospital, refers to his action as "Starkmann's Last Stand" (382), an obvious allusion to General Custer and the massacre of the Seventh Cavalry at Little Bighorn. What Chris had planned—going out in an orgy of flames, explosions, and bullets—is clearly apocalyptic, but it is just that grandiose self-destructive flexing of the ego that Eckhardt later belittles. Referring to Bonny George's death, he says, "Right. One guy got killed in an accident. He was your best buddy, but still one guy. It wasn't the apocalypse, was it" (397)?

Giving up the apocalypse is hard for Chris to do, yet it is necessary for his healing. At first he vehemently rejects Eckhardt's suggestion that he does not want to relinquish his suffering. The psychologist tells him, "It's not like you're guarding some deep dark guilty secret. It's like you're guarding a treasure" (398). Chris is outraged at that insinuation but gradually comes to see its truth even though to admit "that he cherished the memory of his best friend's absurd and violent death . . . would not be evidence of madness but of a moral sickness" (399). This nurturing of death is an aspect of battle trauma that Caputo stresses elsewhere in language much like that of *Indian Country.* Asked whether "some veterans are psychiatric malingerers," Caputo responded, "That's true of an awful lot of these people. They sort of make a treasure of their trauma. Our experiences are what we make of them."[17] In *Means of Escape* he discusses his traumatic Vietnam experience involving the innocent Vietnamese boy he and his men killed. He suffered flashbacks of the dead boy and the "Dark Thing" of depression. Eventually, he could forgive himself "by making a penance that would necessarily be of my own devising," that is, using his journalistic talents in the service of various moral crusades.[18]

No Words for Forgiveness

Cleansing himself of moral sickness is what Chris must do once he admits that he has been holding tenaciously onto his repressed and now revealed traumatic memories, but that involves Bonny George's grandfather: "If the story of Bonny George's death was indeed a treasure he'd been guarding, he'd been guarding it all these years for Louis, who had rightful claim to it. . . . It was Louis to whom he had to confess, Louis whose forgiveness had to be granted before he could absolve himself." But once arrived at Louis's remote campsite, Chris learns that the old man has no forgiveness for him, for the concept is not a part of Native American "theology." Louis, who now speaks of tricksters and is something of one himself, can only suggest "how to live with yourself" (410). When Chris confesses that "for a long time I was ashamed-to-be-alive" (410), Louis responds, "There's only one reason why you should be [ashamed], and that's because you want to be" (411).[19] That response leads Chris to grasp that

> the war had denied him the experience he'd sought up until that morn-
> ing he'd watched napalm boiling like a solar storm while men burning
> to death screamed in the jungle, Bonny George's screams among that
> infernal chorus. And he'd enjoyed it, for it is always gratifying to find
> what you've been looking for; he'd enjoyed it deep within himself, so
> deep he'd not been aware of his pleasure. But his conscience had been
> aware, and the secret delight in the horror that had taken his friend's
> life had been the source of the guilt that had racked him with night-
> mares and had almost led him to take his own life. . . . His own hid-
> den desire had transformed what had been, after all, a common mis-
> fortune of war into an apocalyptic vision of chaos, and himself into a
> murderer. (418)

Louis offers him no formula for salvation, only the advice to look within himself, but it is a far from simple transaction. Other things have taken place. Chris has returned the memory of his comrade to its rightful owner, the grandfather, an act that enables Louis to mourn properly, give up his unalloyed sadness and melancholy, and find peace before he dies. It is not as though Louis's ego investment in Bonny George as the lost love ob-ject has prevented his closure. This is the wrong language—white lan-guage—for comprehending the shaman's psyche, which is sufficiently in harmony with nature to obviate attachment to a tyrannizing individual ego.

But for that very reason it is important that Bonny George be "re-turned" to Louis. The old man sees his grandson as part of a continuum that even death cannot interrupt. Yet it is a continuum effective only if Louis can reconcile his complicity in Bonny George's death, for which, he tells Chris, he was at fault because of counseling the boy not to flee to Canada but to join the army. It is not that Louis can now forgive him-self, as Chris does at the end. As he says, the concept is not in his vocab-ulary. But he confirms and deepens the harmony in expressing his "blame," sharing it with Chris and demonstrating his ability to live with himself in spite of his great loss. Beyond that, he and Chris sense the pres-ence of what in Christian terms is grace. Louis invites Chris to go fishing and hunting with him, "You and me. Nobody else" (416), and therein lies the hint and hope that this white man may be the recipient of the sha-man's lore and learn the old ways in place of Bonny George in whatever time is left.

As Starkmann has killed his Indian brother, albeit inadvertently through panic and misapplied technology, and suffers for it, turning paranoidally vicious and suicidal, so white America has decimated Native Americans and is starting to feel the long-delayed stressful guilt as well as the secret delight as a result. But we cannot mourn the death of this problematic lost love object even though the ego investment in the Indian as a romantic model of natural harmony is large. And it will not do merely to admit the guilt and request forgiveness. Forgiveness is not for the Native Americans to supply, certainly not before their heritage is somehow returned to them and maybe not even then (should that miracle occur), for Native Americans' presence, still as the other, subverts the system that grasps forgiveness as a possibility or resolution. A harsher way of putting it is to say that a nation that produced the Indian apocalypse as an expression of Christian conquest does not deserve Christian forgiveness as a way out.

The lines must be redrawn. The dialogue with this uncanny dimension of our past and present must be reconceived in a way that the uncanny presence at least in part proposes. Louis invites Chris to look within himself, but in the process the white man gains insight into the Indian's ways. One could follow his example.

Caputo as a highly praised novelist and a prize-winning journalist has a more distinct public presence than most of the authors whose work is discussed in this volume. That he has chosen to interpret American violence abroad and at home in ways that include religious considerations, that he can confess his encounters with awe and mystery in situations of extreme danger and duress, makes his writing particularly valuable for shaping and reshaping the public realm of political-religious discourse.[20] He has faced, and faced down, the apocalypse of Vietnam and its traumatic aftermath as few others have, and he shows us what might lie beyond: not some escapist rapture, but a mood that would encourage communal self-examination, willingness to bear responsibility for our violent ways, the ability to mourn them, and the determination to overcome them.

Notes

1. The Lutheran Church-Missouri Synod is the conservative counterpart to the more liberal Evangelical Lutheran Church in America. It is the Missouri Synod Lutherans who tend toward fundamentalism and evangelicalism, even though the ELCA has "Evangelical" as part of its name.

2. Michiko Kakutani, "After Vietnam," *New York Times,* May 30, 1987, L17.

3. John Melmoth, "Men at Arms, Women in Love," *Times Literary Supplement,* February 26, 1988, 214. Melmoth reviews three other Vietnam novels along with *Indian Country* (New York: Bantam, 1987): Larry Heinemann, *Close Quarters* (New York: Penguin, 1977), Larry Heinemann, *Paco's Story* (New York: Penguin, 1987), and Caryl Rivers, *Intimate Enemies* (New York: Dutton, 1987). Other rep-

resentative Vietnam War novels and story collections are Tim O'Brien, *Going after Cacciato* (New York: Delacorte Press, 1978), Tim O'Brien, *The Things They Carried* (Boston: Houghton Mifflin, 1990), John M. Del Vecchio, *The Thirteenth Valley* (New York: Bantam, 1982), William Turner Huggett, *Body Count* (New York: Putnam, 1973), Robert Olen Butler, *A Good Scent from a Strange Mountain* (New York: Holt, 1992), and Tobias Wolff, *In Pharaoh's Army* (New York: Knopf, 1994). Tim O'Brien's *In the Lake of the Woods* (Boston: Houghton Mifflin, 1994) is in some ways reminiscent of *Indian Country*, with a setting in an isolated wilderness area on the Minnesota-Ontario border. It focuses on a Vietnam veteran, a member of William Calley's platoon that carried out the 1968 My Lai massacre, whose wife disappears. Two nonfiction accounts of the war, other than Caputo's *A Rumor of War* (New York: Ballantine Books, 1977) that have been very influential are Michael Herr, *Dispatches* (New York: Alfred A. Knopf, 1977), and Gloria Emerson, *Winners and Losers* (New York: Random House, 1976). See also Tim O'Brien, "Back to My Lai: A Fractured Love Story," *New York Times Magazine,* October 2, 1994, 49–57, for an account of the author's return to the scene where he had fought as a young man.

4. Dick Roraback, "Indian Country," *Los Angeles Times Book Review,* June 21, 1987, 7.

5. Frank Conroy, "Bringing the Terrors Back Home," *New York Times Book Review,* May 17, 1987, 7.

6. A basic text on trauma is *Trauma and Its Wake,* ed. Charles R. Figley, vols. 1 and 2 (New York: Brunner-Mazel, 1985, 1986); see also *Trauma, Experience and Memory,* ed. Cathy Caruth (Baltimore: Johns Hopkins University Press, 1994). For a text specifically on Vietnam combat trauma see Jonathan Shay, *Achilles in Vietnam: Combat Trauma and the Undoing of Character* (New York: Atheneum, 1994).

7. Conroy, "Bringing the Terrors Back Home," 7.

8. Ibid.

9. Kakutani, "After Vietnam," L17.

10. Caputo in an autobiographical account describes how he, recently returned from Vietnam, slept close to his hunting shotguns. They "were loaded because I could not sleep without a loaded weapon nearby." *Means of Escape* (New York: HarperCollins, 1991), 49.

11. This creature reminds one of other threatening half-mythical beasts in American fiction, such as the bear in Faulkner's classic "The Bear" and especially the panther in Walter Van Tilburg Clark's *The Track of the Cat* (New York: Random House, 1949).

12. Caputo, *Means of Escape,* 72.

13. Kakutani,"After Vietnam," L17.

14. The quotation is from a review of Shay's book by Herbert Mitgang, "Vietnam War as Link to Battles of Antiquity," *New York Times,* June 13, 1994, B4.

15. Mitgang, "Vietnam War as Link to Battles of Antiquity," B4.

16. Caputo, *Indian Country,* 283.

17. Barth Healey, "A Fling with Paranoia," *New York Times Book Review,* May 17, 1987, 7.

18. Caputo, *Means of Escape*, 70–72.

19. In *Ceremony* (New York: Viking Press, 1977), Leslie Marmon Silko's returned World War II veteran Tayo, part Laguna and part white, is healed through the ministrations of a Laguna shaman.

20. See Caputo, *Means of Escape*, especially 169–74, for an account of how the author experienced God while being held captive by Palestinian terrorists.

12

Tracks:
Trickster Hermeneutics

The Indian was an occidental invention that became a bankable simulation; the word has no referent in tribal languages or cultures. The postindian is the absence of the invention, and the end of representation in literature; the closure of that evasive melancholy of dominance.

　　　　　　　　—Gerald Vizenor, *Manifest Manners*

I don't think many of the Sioux have forgiven the Church for what it has done to us. . . . I think that some sort of public reconciliation should be one of priorities of evangelism among the Indians.

　　　　　　　　—Father Innocent Good House

Indicative of the continuing marginality of Native Americans in the American religion and culture discussion was the appearance in 1993 of a special issue of an academic religion and literature journal devoted to "Violence, Difference, Sacrifice" that ignored American Indians.[1] Four stimulating, well-crafted essays and two interviews explore violence in a context of myth, religion, and narrative, addressing and evoking Bataille, Derrida, Heidegger, Mishimi, black soldiers in the Civil War, Abraham and Isaac, and feminist theology. But apart from one brief reference to Leslie Marmon Silko and two to Geronimo, Native Americans are absent. Because the issue focuses on the influential work of René Gerard—not known for an interest in things American—one should perhaps not expect attention to Native Americans, and one should surely not single out this particular issue for the sin of omission—always a tactic that returns to haunt the accuser—but the point remains: Even now Native Americans are seldom included in analyses of culture where their involvement could be pivotal.

A 1992 omnibus review of texts on and by Native Americans is entitled "Who Gets to Tell Their Stories?" the answer to which, it is increasingly obvious, must be, "Native Americans themselves."[2] This is ironic because Indians have been reciting their stories for many centuries, far longer than the white settlers who arrived to occupy the land, but because their narrative mode did not accommodate white "chirographics," they literally did not come to word under the new hegemony.[3] If history is the "true" story from the perspective of the conquerors, then the Indians were struck doubly dumb, for they were not only the losers, the conquered, but they also lacked the language crucial to their telling. In one sense the apocalypse that Native Americans have already suffered, the genocide practiced upon them for centuries, has been an annihilation of and by language. The violence done to American Indians is not least a violence of and by language; it is a crime perpetrated many times over, for instance, by the government's making and breaking of treaties. In Louise Erdrich's *Tracks* (1988) it is exemplified by the deception of word and deed that caused Native Americans to lose their land and forced their heritage underground for generations.

The modern (and only) history of Native American writing is of Indian autobiographers, novelists and poets taking back language, not by seducing, persuading, or forcing the dominant culture into appropriating their language, as was done to them, but by taking up the conquerors' language—English, French, and Spanish—and its foundations and strategies in writing. Authors such as Erdrich and Silko and Wendy Rose, James Welch, Paula Gunn Allen, N. Scott Momaday, Louis Owens, Michael Dorris, and Ray A. Young Bear create poetry and prose fiction that derives from the oral narratives and from still vital myths and rituals and yet is accessible to—indeed, depend upon—a white readership.[4] In this way the Native American heritage appears to be mainstreamed into the dominant culture while offering enough of its uniqueness to influence, after a fashion, that culture.

Things are, in actuality, neither that simple nor that hopeful. Such mainstreaming does happen in the literary world and elsewhere, although it is channeled more by popularizers such as Brooke Medicine Eagle, whose *Buffalo Woman Comes Singing* consists of New Age bromides that would qualify her as a "kitschywoman."[5] But many Native American writers oppose such cooption and easy absorption into white society. They are the survivors of attempts, beginning largely in the nineteenth century, to eradicate the Indian heritage altogether by such "benevolent" means as sending the youth to white parochial schools or to federally funded institutions such as the Wahpeton Indian School in North Dakota and the Carlisle Indian School in Pennsylvania, where they would be properly Christianized. Vizenor quotes the proud comment of "nineteenth century reformer" Merrill Gates, Amherst College's president, on the dramatic successes of Indian education: "Christian missionaries plunge into these reservations, struggle with the mass of evil there, and feeling that bright children can be best educated in the atmosphere of civilization, they send to Eastern institutions these Indian children plucked like fire-stained brands from the reservations. They are brought to our industrial training schools. The lesson taught by the comparison of their photographs when they come and when they go is wonderful."[6] Or as Randall Balmer puts it bluntly, "Christianity became not merely another, purportedly superior, religion, but also a means for domesticating the Indians and schooling them in the superior ways of white culture."[7]

Against a background of such arrogant and destructive do-gooderism—also a version of apocalypse, a cultural death by competitive revelation—it is small wonder that contemporary Native American artists resent and resist modern attempts at amalgamation even though they are compelled to use white-controlled vehicles of dissemination. Some, foremost among them Vizenor and Young Bear, have developed and refined trickster writing, producing stories that employ unreliable narrators, mix genres, insert versions of "magical realism," parody other texts, and refuse closure—strategies that fool and intrigue readers, teasing them into a desire for the Indian's secret knowledge that is never fulfilled.[8]

The conflicts attending the Native American writers' ambivalences about revealing or concealing their message are complicated by frictions among the artists themselves, focusing on whether this or that writer is properly ethnic in his or her portrayal of the Native American heritage. One of the most vigorous demonstrations of these tensions has been Silko's attack on Erdrich.[9] In a review of Erdrich's second novel *The Beet Queen* (1986) Silko accused her of adopting a postmodern style (marked above all by autoreferentiality, that is, texts that refer to themselves) that supposedly reveals her solidarity with white society and alienation from her Native American roots, but the charge seems spurious. First, as Susan Pérez Castillo points out, Silko could also be seen as employing postmodern techniques (such as the use of the Laguna oral tradition in her novel *Ceremony* to demonstrate the reality of this "mythical" world), but beyond that, her antagonism toward postmodern fiction writing is misplaced.[10] The traits and attitudes of postmodern artists, as Linda Hutcheon among others has argued, tend to make postmodernism more an ally and instrument of the marginalized than of the dominant culture.[11] Even more, if Silko's accusation had any validity in terms of *Love Medicine* (Erdrich's first novel, published in 1984) and *The Beet Queen*, which do not focus exclusively on Native Americans, her concentration on American Indians in *Tracks* and *The Bingo Palace* (1994) should convince that she is anything but alienated from that portion of her ancestry.

Losing Ground

The fact remains, though, that the Native American ranks are not merely split, but fragmented and that the public realm of discourse between Indians and whites (and other ethnic groups) includes contentious words and acts among the Indians, a friction that is in good part the subject of Vizenor's *Manifest Manners*. I do not propose to treat this dissension in terms of its present political contours—Vizenor has already done that far better than I could hope to—but it is a major theme in *Tracks* that I will address in interpreting the narrative. It appears there in contexts of paranoia and simulation, two elements of the apocalyptic template.

Tracks takes place from the winter of 1912 through spring 1924, mostly on a Chippewa reservation in northern North Dakota. Chapters are told alternately by the old man Nanapush and the mixed-blood girl Pauline Puyat. It is not clear to whom Pauline is reciting her side of the story, but Nanapush, who begins the narration, is telling his to his legal but not biological daughter Lulu (he calls her "Granddaughter"), the child of Fleur Pillager, the exotic wild woman who lives on the shores of Lake Matchimanito. The child's father is possibly Eli Kashpaw or one of three men who raped Fleur when she worked in a butcher shop in the town of Argus, an ordeal Pauline (who had also moved to Argus) witnessed and relates in chapter 2, "Summer 1913." The relationships and interactions among characters are so intricate that it is useless to try to attend to them all. The plot deals on the public and political level with attempts to get the sick and poverty-stricken Chippewas to sell their heavily forested reservation land, mainly to a lumber company, and the harassment of those who do not wish to sell. On the intratribal level it treats the shifting rivalries and liaisons among various reservation families, and on a still more personal level it describes the struggles of Fleur, Nanapush, and Pauline to endure in an environment made largely hostile by other Indians as well as by whites.

In these often desperate circumstances, marked by illness and the threat of starvation, Fleur is the uncompromising one who stops at nothing to retain her land; Nanapush is the wily survivor, a shamanist-realist-manipulator who makes the accommodations he must to protect what he can of the tradition; and Pauline is the orphan girl beloved of no one who dedicates herself to Christ and the Catholic church and works in her psychotic ways to obliterate her heritage. These characters, and others, interact, of course. Pauline, for example, traps Fleur's Argus rapists in a meat locker and two of the three freeze to death, and Nanapush and Pauline are constantly at odds, he ridiculing and challenging her newfound Christian fervor and she defending it vehemently, even hysterically.

But the central action concerns Fleur, Nanapush, and their betrayal, which comes about through their involvement with the Kashpaw ("cash in the paw"?) clan. Fleur and Eli Kashpaw (handsome but not overly bright) fall passionately in love and embark on a stormy romance, followed by the de facto marriage of Nanapush and the widowed, cantankerous Margaret Kashpaw, mother of Eli as well as of the scheming younger brother Nector. Other reservation Chippewas exert pressure on them to sign over the tribal rights to the reservation land in exchange for small sums of money or the ownership of little tracts of their own, but they refuse. Because their recalcitrance endangers the sale of reservation land to a lumber company, some of the families connive to have the renegades lose their land rights by trickery. Fleur and her daughter, Eli, and Nanapush and Margaret scrape together money for belated payments on their land allotment fee, but when Margaret and Nector go to the government office to pay and thus avoid foreclosure, they learn that the sum will not cover the late payment penalty. They use the funds they have to cover the Kashpaw payments and leave the Pillager (Fleur's) fees unpaid, so she loses the land. In spite of this betrayal, Nanapush stays with Margaret on Kashpaw land, but Fleur frightens the weak Eli away and devises a devilish plan for the lakeside property she must abandon.

But long before that Fleur loses a second child and Pauline commits a secret murder and is involved in the death of Fleur's baby as well. Pauline, who has become a sort of reservation necroscopic (someone who sits with people as they die and then prepares their bodies after death), is alone with Fleur and Lulu (still a small child) when Fleur goes into premature labor. It is probably brought on by the exertions of bathing the filthy Pauline, who has refused to wash or change garments in order to "mortify" her flesh. Pauline does not help the struggling Fleur, cannot even bring her the proper blood stanching herbs, and stares transfixed—carrying out another version of her death watch—while Fleur herself delivers the child and tries to stop her own hemorrhaging. Little Lulu finally runs for help and sends Margaret to Fleur's cabin in time to save her but not the child.

Pauline grows increasingly crazed, and in spring of 1919 (her narration of chapter 8) she leaves the convent, where she is scheduled to take up a novitiate, for a trip to Matchimanito Lake in order to confront and defeat the legendary spirit who lives at the bottom, Misshepeshu, whom she conflates with the Christian devil. She takes Nanapush's boat, rows out in view of Fleur's cabin, and anchors there, screaming hysterically at those who gather on shore and resisting their attempts (above all by Nanapush) to rescue her. That night the boat is swept to shore, and Pauline strips naked and throws herself on a figure she takes to be the spirit-monster. It is Napoleon Morrissey, a hapless member of a reservation family who fathered a daughter with Pauline years before, a child Pauline gave to the Morrisseys. Pauline, who is maniacal, strangles Napoleon with her rosary, hides his body in the woods, and then returns to the convent to be tended once again by the nuns. When Napoleon's body is eventually discovered, suspicion falls on Fleur, who people think has led other men to drown. Pauline becomes a novice and is sent to teach at a Catholic school in Argus.

Buffalo Leave, Take Language with Them

Still offshore in her leaky stolen boat, Pauline perceives her mission as a decisive battle between good and evil: "I had determined to wait for my tempter, the one who enslaved the ignorant, who damned them with belief. My resolve was to transfix him with the cross. . . . Held upright by the hands of God, I prepared to meet him without encumbrance. I stripped off my raiment . . . I approached the low and rippling [bon]fire, on fire myself, naked in my own flesh, and finally with no shield or weapon to confront him but the rosary I gripped" (200–201).[12] She meets not Misshepeshu but the unlucky and probably drunken Napoleon and disposes of him in an orgiastic frenzy, then goes through a psychotic episode, back to a primitive condition similar to that of the narrator in a familiar scene of Margaret Atwood's *Surfacing*, except that Atwood's protagonist emerges purified and free of the gods while Pauline is made ready for a new life as Sister Leopolda, consecrated to Christ.[13]

Earlier that year Pauline has had a remarkable vision that merges Native American and Christian imagery, blending a scene of buffalo mass death with one of dead Indians walking toward heaven. Inspired by Nanapush's story of leading a buffalo hunt for whites—"I guided the last buffalo hunt," he says on page 2 of chapter 1—she tells of a huge herd turned suicidal by the carnage wrought among them by white hunters killing the animals only for their tongues and hides ("They tried their best to cripple one another, to fall or die. . . . They knew they were going, saw their end" [140]), then sees the Indians she has tended after death, "the people I had wrapped, the influenza and consumption dead . . . hoping to get the best place when the great shining doors, beaten of air and gold, swung open . . . to admit them all" (140). That is followed by a chilling interchange with Christ, "who was there, of course, dressed in glowing white. 'What shall I do now?' I asked. 'I've brought You so many souls!' And He said to me, gently: 'Fetch more'" (140).

The slaughter of the buffalo, the Plains Indians' symbiotic other, was an apocalypse of consumerism and waste that profoundly marked those who suffered it. As Luther Standing Bear lamented earlier in the century, "The white man will never know the horror and the utter bewilderment of the Lakota at the wanton destruction of the buffalo. What cruelty has not been glossed over with the white man's word—enterprise!"[14] Peter Matthiessen reports that "the great shaggy animal on which the Plains peoples depended for food, shelter, clothing, and utensils had been much reduced by the rifles of the pioneers and later the buffalo hunters for the railroads, and after 1862 were never plentiful again. . . . In 1883, when the last herd of northern bison was wiped out by soldiers and mercenaries on the Cannonball River (with the assistance of the Lakotas' old woodland enemies, the Cree), a century of utter dependence on the white man had begun."[15]

The destruction of the herds was at the same time a strategy to subjugate and "civilize" the Indians. Dee Brown records, "When a group of concerned Texans asked General Sheridan [in the 1870s] if something should not be done to stop the white hunters' wholesale slaughter, he replied, 'Let them kill, skin, and sell until the buffalo is exterminated, as it is the only way to bring lasting peace and allow civilization to advance.'"[16] What is still insufficiently appreciated is that the eradication of the buffalo was a religious atrocity. Matthiessen sees this a bit obliquely when he remarks, "It was recognized that the loss of their life-way [as a result of decimating the herds] would weaken the warlike spirit of the Indians, as would conversion to the Christian Church, and the Indian agents worked closely with their black-frocked brethren at the missions, whose interests were very much the same."[17] A Kiowa woman expressed it more directly during the sixties: "Most of all, the buffalo was part of the Kiowa religion. A white buffalo calf must be sacrificed in the sun dance. The priests used parts of the buffalo to make their prayers when they healed people or when they sang to the powers above." For a time the buffalo protected the embattled Indians, she adds, but when the professional hunters began the mass killing, "The buffalo saw that their day was over. They could protect their people no longer." The remnant determine to leave and are last seen entering a mountain where "the rivers ran clear, not red. . . . Into this world of beauty the buffalo walked, never to be seen again."[18] The implication is that with the vanishing of the buffalo goes also a substantial part of Indian—at least Plains Indian—religion.

Against this background of spiritual identification of Indian and buffalo, and of the depth of Native American bereavement, Pauline's vision assumes an even greater poignancy and meaning. It is significant that the slaughter of the buffalo for their tongues is emphasized. Apart from the appalling wastefulness that it represents, the taking of the tongues can be understood as a violent theft of language, particularly the destruction of the oral tradition. Joseph Epes Brown believes that "perhaps the greatest tragedy to come upon Native American groups has been the progressive weakening and occasional total loss of their respective languages," and he refers to the "history of the frequent brutal means by which this process of deculturation was furthered."[19] It is ironic that the Christian "word" should be proffered to replace the Native American orality, as preached and proclaimed oral word of salvation, as the Christ who incarnates that word, and as the sacred word of the Bible. It is further ironic that Christ's words to Pauline are consumerist and expansionist. "Fetch more," she hears him command when she asks for guidance, already having helped so many of her people into death. This is not the language of redemption and of reconciliation but of annihilation.

It is also a gospel of annihilation that Pauline feels compelled to spread in that it destroys sacred space. She engages in a constant war of words with Nanapush "the smooth-tongued artificer" (196) and generally loses the skirmishes, but she also struggles with him and Fleur in contests of Christian versus Native American ritual that are always somehow significantly spatial. In one compelling scene Fleur's labor begins too soon, and Pauline, alone with her, is paralyzed and unable (and probably unconsciously unwilling) to help. Fleur delivers the child herself then strikes at Pauline with the knife used to cut the umbilical cord, but she manages only to pin Pauline to the floor by the blade, which sticks in the wood between her thighs "through layers of wool and cotton" (159). Later, after Margaret arrives and the baby has died, Pauline pries the knife loose, rises, and makes a move to baptize the infant but is struck by Fleur and has to abandon administering the sacrament.

While she is still alone with Fleur, Pauline has what seems to be an extension of the buffalo apocalypse dream-vision. In it she and Fleur join a procession of Indians heading west: "We passed dark and vast seas of moving buffalo and not one torn field, but only earth, as it was before. . . . Those who starved, drank, and froze, those who died of the cough, all of the people I'd blessed, washed, and wrapped, all were here" (159–60). They arrive not at a Christian but a Chippewa heaven where Fleur joins a card game (reminiscent of the games in Argus with the butchers who raped her) and gambles for her newborn daughter's life. She loses but manages to save her own and Pauline's.

The Christian mythology of heaven clashes with that of Native Americans and reveals the specializing and objectivizing nature of Western thought aligned more to time than to space. Whereas all nature is sacred for Native Americans—with some locales more sacred than others, to be sure—in the Western traditions (Greek, Jewish, and Christian) the spatial sacrality is radically limited to certain narrowly circumscribed and historically oriented sites and structures. As Vine Deloria puts it, "American Indians hold their lands—places—as having the highest possible meaning, and all their statements are made with this reference point in mind. Immigrants review the movement of their ancestors across the continent as a steady progression of basically good events and experiences, thereby placing history—time—in the best possible light."[20] Brown, in an excellent, concise discussion, describes the difference:

> Native American experiences of place are infused with mythic themes. These express events of sacred time . . . are experienced through landmarks in each people's immediate natural environment. The events of animal beings, for example, which are communicated through oral traditions of myths or folklore, serve to grace, sanctify, explain, and interpret each detail of the land. Further, each being of nature, every particular form of the land, is experienced as the locus of qualitatively differentiated spirit beings, whose individual and collective presence sanctifies and gives meaning to the land in all its details and contours. Thus it also gives meaning to the lives of people who cannot conceive of themselves apart from the land. . . . It is perhaps this message of the sacred nature of the land, of place, that today has been most responsible for forcing the Native American vision upon the mind and conscience of non-Native Americans.[21]

This vision has never been prominent among those who are not Native American. Had it been, the obscene violation of the land that has turned much of America into a techno-environmental nightmare would not continue; the desecration of sacred Indian lands such as the Black Hills by miners of coal, gold, and plutonium, by railroad builders, and by game hunters would not have been permitted. Such land has constituted, literally, a religious public realm that the dominant, invading culture has not recognized as such and thus has profaned. It is, literally, a public realm as well as a discursive and symbolic one in the sense that I have been using the term *public realm,* and as such it has been silenced: The voices of the land, the local spirits, have sacrificed their tongues.[22]

Brown goes on to define further the nature of Native Americans' perception and experience of sacred space:

> Not only Native Americans but traditional-oriented people, wherever they may be, always found the means by which to be protected from the indefiniteness of space. The tipi, the hogan, or the longhouse—like the temple, the cathedral, or the sacred city center of antiquity—determined the perimeters of space in such a way that a sacred place, or enclosure, was established. Space so defined served as a model of the

world, of the universe, or, microcosmically, of a human being. Essential to such definition.of space, so central to human need, were means by which the centers of sacred space or place were established. For without such ritual fixing of a center there can be no circumference, and with neither circumference nor center where does a person stand?[23]

What Brown misses, however, is that the tipi, hogan, and longhouse focus the sacred in the midst of a landscape so permeated by the holy that it is awesome and thus threatening, whereas the purpose of the temple, cathedral, and sacred city center is to "collect" the sacred so it flourishes nowhere else. Native American views of the sacred are inclusionary and "democratic," whereas Western views tend toward the exclusionary and imperialistic. It is a distinction that informs the plot of *Tracks* and the plot against those characters "who cannot conceive of themselves apart from the land."

Paranoia and Sacred Space

The fact that shame modulates into paranoia in Philip Caputo's *Indian Country,* has to do with Starkmann's repressed shame over causing the death of his Indian friend in Vietnam. That shame grows into a sense of threat and being persecuted by those who do not comprehend the sacredness of the Vietnam experience. Vietnam was awesome for Starkmann and his comrades; the compounds and perimeters they defended seemed to be sacred sites, an aura that Chris in his deepening mental stress tries to recreate—and simulate—by fortifying his Upper Peninsula property against what he feels to be a hostile world bent on destroying the landscape. His healing occurs when he travels to the remote Indian sacred site, Louis's tipi, and becomes reconciled in the broader sacred space that encloses him.

Things are more complex in *Tracks*. Although Caputo in *Indian Country* treats dissension among the Ojibwas and the waning of the heritage among the younger generations, it is not a major element of the plot. In *Tracks* it is. A number of Chippewa families (the Kashpaws, the Morrisseys, and the Lazarres) have been corrupted by the lure of profit to be made from individual land ownership, and that temptation causes them to act maliciously against the traditionalists who believe the land is to be shared by and kept in the tribe. Individual land ownership was, in fact, a secular concept for Native Americans and a sign of a decline of faith in the sacred. If all space is sacred it cannot be owned by anyone, only held in common, tended, and treated with reverence. When the General Allotment Act, ceding tribal territories to individual Native Americans, was passed by Congress in 1887 it was acclaimed as a progressive step in guiding Indians toward a greater sense of responsibility, but it was in truth a device for undermining the old, religiously based culture. As Matthiessen analyzes it, "By destroying communal guardianship of the land, the Dawes Act . . . destroyed not only the unity of Indian nations but the people's tradition of generosity and total sharing for the common good."[24] Tribal leaders such as Sitting Bull and Red Cloud who saw through the scheme and refused—fruitlessly—to accept the terms of the act and receive their plots of reservation land (which should have belonged to them on their own terms in the first place) were the perspicacious and farsighted ones.

Paranoia is rife in *Tracks* not only because of mutual suspicion between those who want to own the land and those who want to share it. The ideal of sharing appears to be radically weakened; now it is mainly a matter of selling, or not selling, the tribal land in exchange for paltry sums of money or small tracts elsewhere so that it can be harvested for its lumber or otherwise exploited. Matthiessen describes the results of the Dawes Act in ways that make it sound like a depiction of the Chippewa dilemma: "Since according to their sacred instructions the Indians could never 'own' Mother Earth [and] . . . had no experience of the white economy, most of those who tried to adjust to the new system were sooner or later relieved of their land due to innocence, drink, inability to pay off mortgages and taxes, and, finally, the hard exigencies of starvation." For those such as Fleur and Nanapush, it is not a mere economic disaster. This particular space is, as Brown puts it, the home of "spirit beings . . . whose individual and collective presence sanctifies and gives meaning to the land" so that it is not to be sold or traded.[25]

Shame, out of which the paranoia grows, is pivotal here in three ways. First, the humiliating condition of the Chippewas leads many of them to a willingness, even eagerness, to give up the land. They are ashamed of the way they live, of their poverty and degradation, and view the money they might receive for the land as a way out of their debasement.[26] Second, they are ashamed of already having lost so much land to the whites over the generations, especially in recent years, and of their impotence in the face of the prospect of losing still more—most of the remaining reservation property. Nanapush's boasts about his sexual potency, and the high valuation placed on such potency by the other Indian males, seem to be an attempted compensation for the lack of power that they all feel. Third, the Chippewas are ashamed of the loss of sacred space that the selling of the land represents. In failing to maintain the traditional lands they have betrayed the spirits that inhabit them.

This sense of shameful failure, mixed with shock, anger, and frustration, must be what moves Fleur to attempt suicide by drowning herself in Matchimanito Lake after she learns that her house will be taken from her. She is rescued by Eli but the experience transforms her and takes her closer to the spirit world that she has just tried to enter permanently. Nanapush, attending her at water's edge, feels the power: "The ground beneath us was trembling, I felt it shake, and it was not the felling of the trees or a storm gathering beyond sight, it was what was in the water, which I didn't dare to name" (213). "What was in the water" that inspires awe in the old shaman is, of course, Misshepeshu, a sacred nature being who guards the lake and whom Pauline tried to vanquish. Fleur has been intimate with Misshepeshu before (people believe that he fathered her second child, the one that died, and she has nearly drowned in the lake twice before), and this latest encounter with him leads her into a "death" of her relationship with her people. Nanapush emphasizes how she is "laid out like the dead" (213), her body shrouded by the wet clothing, but she is very much alive now in a holy anger and curses those who have brought about the loss of her land.

In a significant way the Chippewa traditionalists who fear and are ashamed of losing the sacred land are not paranoid but realistic. As the saying goes, "You're not paranoid if they're really after you." Nevertheless, the relationship of trust between the traditionalists and the opportunists has been so thoroughly damaged that no positive interaction between them is possible. A similar condition obtains on many reservations today; Indian activists, for example those from the American Indian Movement (AIM), who seek to restore dignity and purpose to Native Americans are abused by those wishing to maintain the status quo. Now the traditionalists are those who abjure the tradition.[27] At any rate, in *Tracks* only Nanapush escapes the effects of Fleur's vengeful paranoia. Eli, terrified of her powers, flees, and even Lulu is sent away to a government school because her mother fears for her safety on the reservation. It is ironic that Lulu, now grown, listens to Nanapush's tale as she plans to marry a "no-good Morrissey" (218), a member of one of the families that tricked her mother out of her land.

Apocalyptic Simulation

Matthiessen tells of an apocalyptic tradition among Native Americans apart from that of the messiah craze and ghost dance:

> Most traditional communities in North America know of a messenger who appears in evil times as a warning from the Creator that man's disrespect for His sacred instructions has upset the harmony and bal-

ance of existence; some say that the messenger comes in sign of a great destroying fire that will purify the world of the disruption and pollution of earth, air, water, and all living things. He has strong spirit powers and sometimes takes the form of a huge hairy man; in recent years this primordial being has appeared near Indian communities from the northern Plains states to far northern Alberta and throughout the Pacific Northwest.[28]

Matthiessen mentions this creature at other times in his study, calling him by the Ojibwa name "Rugaru" (Big Foot or Big Man). One Native American on the Pine Ridge Reservation defines him as "'both spirit *and* real being. . . . I want him to touch me, just a touch, a blessing, something I could bring home to my sons and grandchildren. . . . We are fortunate to see him in our generation. We may not see him again for many many generations. But he will come back, just when the next Ice Age comes into being.'"[29]

The epiphanies of Big Foot not only provide further evidence of a continuing pervasive apocalyptic force among Native Americans (Matthiessen's account refers generally to sightings in the seventies) but also reintroduce the subject of Indian spirituality that I touched upon in discussing *Indian Country* and causes problems among non-Native American interpreters of Indian literature, including readers of *Tracks*. In his review of the novel Robert D. Narveson faces the problem head on: "Some of Nanapush's known facts require of the reader a willing suspension of disbelief, for these stories, magical in their telling, tell of magical events, such as Fleur's descents into the waters of a lake to mate with the god who dwells there, her leaving tracks of bear feet that change to tracks of bare feet."[30] Narveson identifies Erdrich's "unbelievable" (by Western standards) narratives as a kind of Latin American magic realism then confesses, engagingly, the limits of his indulgence:

> Does Erdrich's version of "magic realism" work because she writes about a race and culture alien to us white late-arrivals? As with West Indies hoodoo, a condition of its working is a belief in and by its practitioners and victims. . . . But I belong to a culture that has given up telepathy and other such magic as the price of enjoying the astonishing magic of radio waves, microwaves, and fiber-optic tele-conversations. Perhaps the flourishing of Western science has as its concomitant the impoverishment of the main-line Western imagination, and we can best appreciate other modes of imagining not through the cerebrations of science fiction writers but through the deeper poetic soundings of minority writers such as Erdrich, Alice Walker, and Toni Morrison.[31]

One of the problems with the evocation of magic realism to describe Erdrich's fiction is the ambiguity of the term. Fredric Jameson recalls meeting the concept "in the context of North American painting in the mid-1950s" and also discovering the related *real maravilloso* of the Cuban novelist Alejo Carpentier, a term that designates a world permeated by the awe-inspiring and mysterious.[32] By "magic," in contrast, Narveson seems to mean a superstitious faith unable to compete with "advanced" science. It is typical of the hegemonic reflexes of Western empiricism to categorize the other in language of inferiority: the magic of hoodoo is no match for the high-tech magic of applied science. But such triumphalist systematizing cannot grasp the self-understanding of Native Americans, which involves visionary nature empathy and trickster-ism. Both are at work in incidents that feature Nanapush and then Fleur.

The nature empathy that Nanapush demonstrates is like that of Louis in *Indian Country,* who has flown round with world with an eagle and seen things from an eagle's prospective. Nanapush during a harsh winter has sent Eli out to hunt game, visualizes him on the hunt, guides him via singing into killing a moose, then sings and drums the exhausted young man, under his weight of freezing meat, back home to the old man's cabin. None of this makes realistic sense, of course, according to a rational view, and the temptation is to explain away Nanapush's recital. For example, perhaps what Nanapush tells is merely what he imagines intensely, drawing on a lifetime of hunting experience, and Eli's success in killing the moose is both coincidence and a great stroke of luck.

But rational explanation is not the point. There is, in fact, no "point." To assume there is, and to look for it, are reflexes of Western logic, whereas Erdrich wishes to coerce or seduce the reader into a reading of an other, one that goes against the Western grain yet must be not merely indulged but acknowledged as truth with as much validity as the sort that Western scientific minds worship. One need not believe in this truth, but one must grant its possibility. Only through that deep gesture can one hope to intuit some sense of the awe-inspiring nature empathy by which Native Americans have lived—successfully—until the relationship was radically disrupted by the white usurpers. It may also be that Erdrich, of Native American and European lineage, composes such fiction to dramatize the epistemological dichotomy that she experiences, which has become the heritage of Native Americans unable to avoid the white world.

However that may be, one can grasp in the moose hunting episode and others in the novel how Nanapush transforms awe into a simulation quite unlike Baudrillard's although even more finely tuned to apocalyptic anticipation. Nanapush sees the hunt in his mind's eye and enacts its rhythms through song and drumbeat. In this way he simulates the hunt (he claims that he precipitates its success) not as an action that reveals the absence of foundational referents as in alienated technological-consumerist societies, but as part of a flow in which nature is its own sign and design. Not surprisingly, Joseph Epes Brown puts it more mystically: "Native American . . . shamans through the nonmaterial means of their sacred traditions are able to travel at will through the freedom of sacred space unfettered by mechanical, profane time."[33] Such imagizing, like Baudrillard's, "is its own pure simulacrum" but not because "it bears no relation to any reality whatever."[34] Rather, Nanapush's vision and action perfectly replicate the natural world. In his trance focused on Eli and the hunt Nanapush experiences a hyperreality not of groundless, alienated images forced together to form a "Disneyworld . . . whose mystery is precisely that it is nothing more than a network of endless, unreal circulation" but of intensely heightened perception inspired by his awe of the natural world.[35] This awe is grounded in an awareness of death (Nanapush and Eli are starving at this point; Eli nearly freezes to death on the way back) against a background of disease, starvation, and neglect. The tribe has already been decimated seriously, and the sense of a cataclysmic end is far stronger than in Baudrillard's theorizing.

That ending occurs, at least after a fashion, through Fleur's deception. Although Nanapush plays the trickster role more consistently throughout the action of the novel, Fleur also possesses trickster traits. It is rumored that she can change into a bear, and such shapeshifting is characteristic of tricksters.[36] She is suspected of having caused the death by drowning of some men of the tribe and is feared for such power. But the event that displays most spectacularly her gifts of deception is the destruction of the forest around her cabin. Fleur goes to work in secret when it becomes clear that she must sacrifice her land and her cabin. On the day that she is to be evicted she is prepared. As the loggers wait with their horses and wagons for her to leave, a breeze comes up and the tall trees start crashing to the ground. As Nanapush tells it, "Around me, a forest was suspended, lightly held. . . . Each green crown was held in the air by no more than splinters of bark. Each tree was sawed through at the base" (223). The results are startling: "With one thunderstroke the trees surrounding Fleur's cabin cracked off and fell away from us in a circle, pinning beneath their branches the roaring men, the horses" (223). Fleur abandons the reservation after causing this devastation (although she does return for four visits in *The Bingo Palace*). She has, in a way, kept control of her sacred space by destroying; it cannot now be desecrated by the new owners.

Fleur's feat is literally, physically impossible, an apocalyptic event that belongs as much to the world of spirit and mystery as Nanapush guiding

Eli long-distance on his hunt, and its description provokes the same real-ist-superrrealist dilemma as that of Nanapush's vision-hunt. Castillo casts this dilemma in terms of a postmodern literary esthetic proposed by Brian McHale, arising from a "shift from a modernist foregrounding of episte-mology to a postmodern poetics of ontology: paradoxically, postmodern-ism uses representation itself to subvert representation, problematizing and pluralizing the real. Thus the text emerges, not as a passive mirror of reali-ty, but as the space in which two or more distinct and often mutually ex-clusive worlds battle for supremacy."[37] It is "a highly effective, politicized text" in which the two alternating narrators, Pauline and Nanapush, incor-porate "radically diverse realities" from which "emerges a narrative firmly anchored in (often grim) extratextual reality."[38] The battle is not, Castillo insists, "between . . . two different perspectives of reality, but two diamet-rically different realities: that of a people in the grip of disease, death and spiritual despair, and that of a group of courageous and irreverent survi-vors. Somewhere in the middle of these two realities emerges the world of the Chippewa in all its power and complexity."[39]

The modifier "irreverent" reminds us that one of the narrators is a trickster whereas the other is merely a liar. Nanapush attempts to sur-vive the Native American apocalypse by a kind of calculated vulnerabili-ty, by opening himself up to all forces and even mediating among them. He is an extremely skeptical yea-sayer. Pauline is a "victim of accelerated acculturation."[40] She has sold her soul to a church that despises her race (although its members treat her kindly), and she denies validity to ev-erything except her delusional messages from Christ. She is a scheming but naive nay-sayer who tightens "the grip of disease, death, and spiritu-al despair" on her people. It is not hard to see that the author's sympa-thy lies with the embattled trickster, although she has empathy with the pathetic liar.

Tracks is a "politicized" fiction of an American public dialogue in which the victims see their oppressors as liars and the dominant culture sees the victims as tricksters—*unheimlich* even though they were here first. But the dominant culture does at last now see the Native Americans, if still vaguely, and it is beginning to hear them, not least through increas-ingly incendiary (appropriate for the apocalyptic tradition) statements by novelists such as one from Silko in 1991: "The Indian Wars have never ended in the Americas. Native Americans acknowledge no borders; they seek nothing less than the return of all tribal lands."[41] Erdrich's voice has been more moderate but no less a trickster's—perhaps more so. How does one listen to a trickster? One is alert to what *else* she says, to the signifi-cant unsaid. America has long had reservations about the unsaid. It is time to let sacred space return in sacred tongue.

Notes

1. "Violence, Difference, Sacrifice: Conversations on Myth and Culture in Theology and Literature," special issue of *Religion and Literature* 25 (Summer 1993).

2. James B. Kinkaid, "Who Gets to Tell Their Stories?" *New York Times Book Review,* May 3, 1992, 1, 24–29.

3. Chirography basically means handwriting or penmanship, but Walter J. Ong uses "chirographic" in *Orality and Literacy: The Technologizing of the Word* (London: Methuen, 1982) to designate writing cultures as opposed to those based on oral communication.

4. Representative novels by some of these Native Americans are: Paula Gunn Allen, *The Woman Who Owned the Shadows* (San Francisco: Aunt Lute Books, 1994), N. Scott Momaday, *House Made of Dawn* (New York: Harper and Row, 1968), Louis Owens, *The Sharpest Sight* (Norman: University of Oklahoma Press, 1992), James Welch, *Fools Crow* (New York: Viking, 1986), and Ray A. Young Bear, *Black Eagle Child: The Facepaint Narratives* (Iowa City: University of Iowa Press, 1992).

5. Brooke Medicine Eagle, *Buffalo Woman Comes Singing: The Spirit Song of a Rainbow Medicine Woman* (New York: Ballantine Books, 1991). In *Manifest Manners: Postindian Warriors of Survivance* (Hanover: Wesleyan University Press, 1994), Gerald Vizenor refers to Indian activists Dennis Banks and Clyde Bellecourt as "kitschymen" (43). I derive the term *kitschywoman* from his example. The term *trickster hermeneutics* in my subtitle is also from Vizenor's fine study.

6. Vizenor, *Manifest Manners,* 165. Vizenor gives no source for the quotation.

7. Randall Balmer, *Mine Eyes Have Seen the Glory: A Journal into the Evangelical Subculture in America* (New York: Oxford University Press, 1989), 213.

8. In "Who Gets to Tell Their Stories?" 25, Kinkaid refers to the claim of Barry O'Connell that a Pequot Indian autobiography originally published in 1829 uses such devices that are like "black 'signifying': 'doubling and redoubling the assumed meaning of words and concepts in a dominant discourse.'" O'Connell is the editor of *On Our Own Ground: The Complete Writings of William Apess, a Pequot* (Amherst: University of Massachusetts Press, 1992). In this connection see also Gregory Salyer's excellent "Gambling with Ghosts: Native American Literature and Postmodernism," in *In Good Company: Essays in Honor of Robert Detweiler,* ed. David Jasper and Mark Ledbetter (Atlanta: Scholars Press, 1994), 167–81.

9. Leslie Marmon Silko, "Here's an Odd Artifact for the Fairy-Tale Shelf," *Impact/Albuquerque Journal,* October 8, 1986, 10–11.

10. Susan Pérez Castillo, "Postmodernism, Native American Literature and the Real: The Silko-Erdrich Controversy," *Massachusetts Review* 32 (Summer 1991): 285–94.

11. Linda Hutcheon, *A Poetics of Postmodernism: History, Theory, Fiction* (New York: Routledge, 1988).

12. Louise Erdrich, *Tracks* (New York: Henry Holt, 1988); page citations are given in the text. Earlier Pauline refers to "the gold-eyed creature in the lake, the spirit which they said was neither good nor bad but simply had an appetite" (39).

13. Margaret Atwood, *Surfacing* (New York: Simon and Schuster, 1972). Christ's "love is a hook sunk deep in to our flesh, a questionmark that pulls with every breath," Pauline says (205), employing masochistic imagery strikingly similar to Agnes's vision, in *Agnes of God,* of the "Lady" who throws a big hook into her to pull her up while her mother drags her down.

14. Luther Standing Bear, *Land of the Spotted Eagle* (Lincoln: University of Nebraska Press, 1933), 43, quoted by Peter Matthiessen, *In the Spirit of Crazy Horse* (New York: Penguin Books, 1992), xxxix.

15. Matthiessen, *In the Spirit of Crazy Horse,* 16.

16. Dee Brown, *Bury My Heart at Wounded Knee: An Indian History of the American West* (New York: Holt, Rinehart and Winston, 1970), 265.

17. Matthiessen, *In the Spirit of Crazy Horse,* 16–17.

18. Entitled "The Buffalo Go," told to Alice Marriott by Old Lady Horse (Spear Woman), in *American Indian Myths and Legends,* ed. Richard Erdoes and Alfonso Ortiz (New York: Pantheon Books, 1984), 490–91. In the summer of 1994 "a female white buffalo, a sacred and apocalyptic symbol in Indian culture," was born "on a modest farm in southern Wisconsin." This is an event apparently far more rare than the words of Old Lady Horse would suggest. A Lakota shaman named Floyd Hand states, "'In North American Indian country we've been anticipating her coming since 1933–34. . . . The Second Coming of Christ is like this.'" See Richard Wronski, "Indian Prophecy Fulfilled," *Atlanta Constitution,* September 14, 1994, A10.

19. Joseph Epes Brown, *The Spiritual Legacy of the American Indian* (New York: Crossroad, 1991). The chapter from which these quotations are taken was originally published in 1976.

20. Vine Deloria, Jr., *God Is Red: A Native View of Religion* (Golden: Fulcrum Press, 1994), 62; see also Robert Allen Warrior, "Canaanites, Cowboys, and Indians: Deliverance, Conquest, and Liberation Theology Today," *Christianity and Crisis* 49 (1989): 261–65. Warrior shows how recent liberationist interpretations of the biblical narratives of exodus and conquest still appear oppressive to Native Americans.

21. Brown, *The Spiritual Legacy of the American Indian,* 51; see also N. Scott Momaday, "Native American Attitudes to the Environment," in *Seeing with a Native Eye: Essays on Native American Religion,* ed. Walter Holden Capps (New York: Harper and Row, 1976), 79–85.

22. On tonguelessness among Native Americans see Paula Gunn Allen, *The Sacred Hoop: Recovering the Feminine in American Indian Traditions* (Boston: Beacon Press, 1986), 138.

23. Brown, *The Spiritual Legacy of the American Indian,* 51.

24. Matthiessen, *In the Spirit of Crazy Horse,* 18; see also Dee Brown, *Bury My Heart at Wounded Knee,* 422–26, for an account of the visit of Sen. Henry L. Dawes, author of the allotment act legislation, to Standing Rock and his confrontation with Sitting Bull there.

25. Matthiessen, *In the Spirit of Crazy Horse,* 18. As Matthiessen points out, the Lakotas resisted allotment until World War I, approximately the time that

Erdrich selects for her portrayal of the land woes of the Chippewas Fleur and Nanapush. Brown, *The Spiritual Legacy of the American Indian*, 51.

26. In *The Bingo Palace* (New York: HarperCollins, 1994), Erdrich's fourth novel and part of the tetralogy that includes *Tracks*, this theme of the "quick fix" through wealth, here through legalized gambling on the reservation, is central.

27. Things are not that simple, of course. See Matthiessen, *In the Spirit of Crazy Horse*, and Vizenor, *Manifest Manners* for discussion of the complex politics and shifting loyalties on the reservations.

28. Matthiessen, *In the Spirit of Crazy Horse*, xxiii.

29. Ibid., 555. Although I have found no evidence of a connection between the "huge hairy man" and the buffalo, I wonder if one exists. The buffalo, having been virtually exterminated, might in their rare appearances have assumed the supernatural qualities that the Native American narrators ascribe to Big Foot. Gary Snyder retells the ghost dance story in a way that involves the buffalo: "If all the Indians would dance the Ghost Dance with their Ghost shirts on, the Buffalo would rise from the ground, trample the white men to death in their dreams, and all the dead game would return; America would be restored to the Indians." Gary Snyder, "Earth House Hold," in *The Portable North American Indian Reader*, ed. Frederick W. Turner III (New York: Viking Penguin, 1977), 561–62.

30. Robert D. Narveson, "Louise Erdrich, *Tracks*," *Prairie Schooner* 64 (Fall 1990): 135.

31. Narveson, "Louise Erdrich, *Tracks*," 136.

32. Fredric Jameson, "On Magic Realism in Film," in *Signatures of the Visible* (New York: Routledge, 1990), 128. Jameson advances a fascinating Marxist thesis in this essay: "The possibility of magic realism as a formal mode is constitutively dependent on a type of historical raw material in which disjunction is structurally present; or, to generalize the hypothesis more starkly, on a content which betrays the overlap or the coexistence of precapitalist and nascent capitalist or technological features. On such a view, then, the organizing category of magic realist film is not the concept of the generation . . . but rather the very different one of modes of production, and in particular of a mode of production still locked in conflict with traces of the older mode" (138). Aspects of this thesis would apply to the writing of Native American fiction in the context of a consumerist society.

33. Brown, *The Spiritual Legacy of the American Indian*, 52.

34. Jean Baudrillard, "Simulacra and Simulations," in *Selected Writings*, ed. Mark Poster (Stanford: Stanford University Press, 1988), 170.

35. Baudrillard, "Simulacra and Simulations," 170. See Jameson, "On Magic Realism in Film," 138, in this connection. He refers to Carpentier's *real maravilloso* as "not a realism to be transfigured by the 'supplement' of a magical perspective but a reality which is already in and of itself magical or fantastic."

36. Bear-Woman is a well-known figure in Native American oral narrative. Often she is a female who takes a bear as lover; when her offended family kills the bear, she changes into a bear herself and attacks her relatives.

37. Castillo, "Postmodernism, Native American Literature and the Real," 292.

McHale's book is *Postmodernist Fiction* (New York: Methuen, 1987). Regarding McHale on modernism and postmodernism, and Baudrillard's simulation, see also Robert Detweiler, "Apocalyptic Fiction and the End(s) of Realism," in *European Literature and Theology in the Twentieth Century: Ends of Time*, ed. David Jasper and Colin Crowder (London: Macmillan, 1990), 153–83.

38. Castillo, "Postmodernism, Native American Literature and the Real," 293

39. Ibid., 294.

40. Ibid., 293.

41. This statement appears in Leslie Marmon Silko's *Almanac of the Dead* (New York: Simon and Schuster, 1991) on the righthand page facing the inside front cover and again on the inside back cover. Not incidentally, an "army" of homeless Native American Vietnam War veterans plays a role in *Almanac*.

Conclusion:
The Body Poetic?

We are condemned and privileged to listen to the lives and
voices of others, adding our own voice to the discourse.
—George Aichele et al., *The Postmodern Bible*

All of the narratives I have addressed in this study are critical of the role
of religion in American public life. Sometimes the authors exercise their
criticism through satire and sarcasm. Coover in *The Public Burning* spoofs
the fulsome piousness of the Eisenhower era; Vaughn in *Many Things*
pokes fun at the southern combination of fundamentalism and consumerism; and Caputo in *Indian Country* caricatures a harsh Lutheran liberalism. Sometimes the criticism is more still direct and hard-edged. The
blacks in Morrison's *Beloved* and the Chippewas in Erdrich's *Tracks* voice
deep suspicion of what they perceive as exploitative white Christianity.
As Baby Suggs preaches, "out yonder, hear me, they do not love your neck
unnoosed and straight" (*Beloved*, 88). Most of the narratives, nevertheless, reveal a reluctance of the characters to discard religious belief and
practice, be they connected to a Roman Catholic sacramentalism or mysticism, a Protestant biblicism (black or white), a Jewish moralism, or a
Native American spatial sacrality.

This ambivalence expressed in and by these fictions typifies the American temper. We are quick to condemn our religious institutions for hypocrisy, intolerance, avarice, resistance to change, and what-not, yet many
see these failings as institutional corruptions—corruptions of religion in
the public realm—rather than as constituting reasons why religious belief itself might no longer be worth practicing. Because my chapters have
tended to emphasize the negative critique, and because this is not the
whole story, in these concluding pages I will stress more positive and
hopeful aspects, using the themes of family, confession, and language.

Families Going Public

No "normal" families are portrayed in any of the narratives I have addressed. They are all, one way or another, dysfunctional. Those in *The Crucible* are broken up by the fear of witchcraft and the theocracy's exploitation of that fear, as the families of *The Book of Daniel* and *The Public Burning* are damaged and destroyed by the fear of communism and the political-religious manipulation of that fear. The families in the Catholic texts (by Pielmeier, Hansen, and Gordon) are weakened or at least threatened by the stern authority of the church, whereas those in the African American novels (by Larsen and Morrison) are harmed by visitations of the spirit—in ecstatic and ghostly form—even while, in the case of *Beloved,* attempting to recover from their wholesale destruction under the institution of slavery. In the novels by Vaughn, Caputo, and Erdrich, families are torn apart by internal, religion-related tensions as well as, in *Indian Country* and *Tracks,* by psychotic experiences induced by war and extreme physical deprivation. Vietnamese families in *Apocalypse Now* are literally blown apart and those of the Americans harmed spiritually by the excesses of their invading fathers, sons, and brothers.

Where can familial normalcy be found? It is in these very texts, although one must search diligently for it, and in the process of uncovering it one finds the nature of "normalcy" changed. In Miller's tragic Salem drama, for example, the Proctors under great duress rediscover their loyalty, damaged by John's infidelity, to each other. Elizabeth, pregnant, will survive to constitute with her child a little family, even though her husband goes to his execution to maintain the principles of both of them. In *The Book of Daniel,* amid the fragilities and deceptions of the Isaacsons and Mindishes, the dignity and integrity of the Lewins, foster parents of Susan and Daniel Isaacson after Rochelle and Paul are executed, mark them as an exemplary couple, and even the sadistic Daniel, who torments his wife and child, reveals something affirmative in his neurotic and obsessive love for his mad sister.

One might consider the family of 124 Bluestone Road to be the most ravaged of all, suffering as they do from the mother's infanticide and Beloved's wanton destructiveness, yet here, too, are redemptive moments. Paul D appears from the ironically named Sweet Home farm, the only survivor of the slave families there, to help bring healing to Sethe and Denver, while the women of the black community, the larger family, join to exorcise Sethe's guilt and shame and take her and her daughter back into their midst. Agnes, that other perpetrator of infanticide, seems driven to her act by a vicious mother, then abetted by her weak-willed aunt, the mother superior. The church, represented by the convent's family of sisters, does not do its duty, and an effort at secular healing in the form of the psychiatrist replaces the church's failed ministrations. Dr. Livingstone succeeds only insofar as she is instrumental in preventing punishment of

Agnes by the state for the murder of her child; Agnes slips further into insanity and dies. Yet Livingstone is deeply affected by the young nun's confused faith and finds her way to a personal renewal, a rejuvenation of body and spirit that transcends her reliance on rationality. She beomes vulnerable to love relationships.

Vaughn's narrator tries to function amid spectacularly dysfunctional domesticity; she struggles to overcome two deaths—three, if one includes her own threatened suicide—and the loss of a child in a family that has been self-destructive for generations and has for support only a sectarian church that thrives on its consumerist clichés. Yet she manages to transform her multitude of troubles into an artful narrative, to turn abuse, grief, and pain into her story of survival. In Caputo's *Indian Country* the family suffers from the husband and father's war-induced psychosis, a terrifying illness that nearly shatters them, yet it is Chris Starkmann's wife June who in good part saves the suicidal veteran. Her unexpected arrival at the explosives-rigged house leads him to abort his selfish personal apocalypse and keep her and himself from the gruesome death he would have inflicted and begin serious therapy at last.

The distresses and recoveries of these persons do not happen in isolation—even when the afflicted ones think themselves alone—but always somehow in the context of families. One could argue that these are not "real," "average," or "normal" families, that people do not actually live together in such sensational or appalling circumstances. These fictions, however, invite us to contemplate how contemporary family life is not by definition normal; many families do in fact endure harrowing daily lives, and many members break under the strain. They also stress the remarkable resilience of family members and how they often, under great duress, discover or recover integrity, compassion, and sometimes even a chastened sense of reverence. The narratives suggest at the same time that little good can result from merely encouraging the nation's return to "family values" (a prominent slogan of the twentieth century's latter years) when families are, of themselves, incapable of embodying or articulating positive values. Families are entities between the private and public realms, part of both and composed of vulnerable individuals somehow responsive and responsible to the community. As such they are always liminal and transitional, always necessarily for and against themselves as individuals, and always for and against the community. Out of such confusion and ambivalence "family values" arise, and thus they can never be foundational.

The tension of private and public spheres that defines the family also displays itself in confession, a dynamic that is personal, religious, and civic. The narratives herein not only deal extensively with confession but parts of some are also cast as confession, for example, those involving various characters in *The Crucible*, Daniel in Doctorow's novel, Nixon in *The Public Burning*, both Agnes and the psychiatrist now and again in Pielmeier's play, the narrator of *Many Things Have Happened since He Died*, Kurtz in *Apocalypse Now*, and Pauline Kashpaw in *Tracks*. Confession has been prominent in literature for generations (Goethe in *Dichtung und Wahrheit* referred to his writings as "fragments of a great confession"), and one is not surprised to find it central in literary texts in the age of psychology and psychoanalysis. Confession plays certain roles that link it crucially to the public sphere in the volumes under discussion. It is used by those in power (in *The Crucible* and *The Book of Daniel*) not to reconcile the wrong-doer with the community but as a device to find or create more guilty persons by persuading the confessee to implicate others.

This is nothing new; it was, for instance, a prime strategy of the Inquisition. But the confessions by Doctorow's Daniel, Coover's Nixon, Vaughn's narrator, Caputo's Starkmann, and even Coppola's Kurtz are not of this nature; they are narrative-diagnostic attempts of the confessee to discover, by the casting of personal experience into story form, what went wrong. The reminiscences of these characters lead them to discover where they made mistakes, not so much to avoid making them again (in some cases it is too late for that) and not to express a regret that could lead to forgiveness and absolution (those terms belong to a theological vocabulary seldom used in these narratives), but in order to explain themselves, and their world, mainly to themselves. They are driven to find a pattern to their lives, even if it reveals itself as destructive. Confession becomes a major device for the attempted apprehension or outright creation of meaning.

In what sense are these confessions at all, if no confessor is present and no spiritual relief obtained? Sometimes a confessor of sorts is on hand to listen, and sometimes relief does result; Starkmann tells his story to Eckhardt, a counselor of Vietnam war veterans, and gets the momentum to make his peace with himself and his world through the guidance of the old Ojibwa shaman as a second confessor. Kurtz confesses to his assassin-to-be and, a deeply tormented man, gains the relief of death. But by and large the reminiscences in these narratives are offered to readers, who find themselves implicated as confessors to a fictional confessee yet unable to offer relief. Rather, they are led to assume the confessee role as well, to transfer the confessor-confessee relationship to their lives and study how the narrative-diagnostic search for meaning in the fiction suggests actual patterns in their historical world. Toni Morrison, although not reflecting on confession, has something like this relationship in mind when she says that novels should "urge the reader into active participation in the non-narrative, nonliterary experience of the text, which makes it difficult for the reader to confine himself to a cool and distant acceptance of data."[1]

The dynamic of confession that readers carry through happens "between" the text, play, or film and the readers' or viewers' communal or public lives. Even if they encounter the text in the company of others— say, as a viewer watching *Agnes of God* in a theater—they still must "process" the experience and comprehend the confession as a life-patterning strategy. We might call this, following one line of hermeneutical theory, the stage of recognition that one undergoes before the stage of understanding that accompanies interpretation. This confession-as-recognition is also a transitional moment that connects the reader or viewer to the text on the one hand and the community on the other, that employs the reader as enabler between the privacy of the narrator's confession and the reception of the work by the public.

This view of the reader's or viewer's confessional mediatory experience is pivotal in that complex process of relating fiction to our communal lives. Readers who absorb the narrator's confession (say, of Daniel Lewin revealing his sadism), acknowledge it as a plausible and authentic way of responding to life's vagaries (Daniel is sadistic because of the grief, guilt, and anger his traumatic past has induced in him), then mediate that confession in their communal interchanges (expresses in various contexts their opinion that sadists are the subjects of cruel actions and need treatment both as victims and victimizers), have "publicized" a private fiction and made it available for common discourse.

The value of this process becomes apparent when contrasted with what happens through the mania for commodified public confession on television and in print journalism as well as in highly publicized court trials. Persons exposing their private lives (or having them exposed), often providing details of failed relationships, abuse, obsessive behavior, or deviancy to a studio of audience-participants or a titillated readership, lack precisely the protection of fiction and the mediation of a narrator. They are in effect naked before a voyeuristic public, with the show host or journalist or lawyer only stressing their plight.

But why would persons be willing, as many obviously are, to place themselves in these positions of vulnerability? The drive to confess may well be heightened in an age when formal religious confession is less widely practiced, and perhaps the humiliation of such exposure takes the place of penance otherwise prescribed by the religious institution and thus relieves guilt. And for the audience to such exposure a surrogate relieving of guilt may occur insofar as one imagines oneself in the place of the confessee and plays through the humiliation as penance. Nevertheless, these situations reduce the dynamic of confession to a superficial and sensational entertainment; the heated and shouted interchanges between the confessees and the audience on television shows are a travesty of thoughtful civic dialogue. The mediated confessions of the fictional narratives I have addressed, however, do provide a measured space where the intensely private can be converted into communal conversation.

All this is not to say that actual religious confession has disappeared from public life. An obvious model for the religious interaction of private and public, religious confession also helps us to understand better the secular private-public relationship I described. What goes on, for example, in the Roman Catholic confessional is a mediated transformation of the intimate and personal into the public and institutional; the confessee is the narrator of his or her private story, and the priest-confessor is like the reader of the narrative who absorbs and shapes it for the communal good.[2]

The problem with the formal religious confession as model is that it has lost much of its authority as the religious institutions themselves are increasingly challenged and displaced by structures of secularism. This loss of authority is part of the plots of *Agnes of God, Mariette in Ecstasy, The Company of Women,* and *Tracks.* In all of these the representatives of the church are themselves so culpable and confused that they are unable or barely able to guide those who still wish to believe. As a result, the religious confession comes to serve less as a model of transformation of the private into a trustworthy communal mode and to look more like an instance of any private voice seeking response in a world offering myriad competing ideologies. Religious confession, at a time when persons are driven more and more to confess, joins the many discourses of language, which is suspected of being contingent, self-referential, and lacking a foundation outside itself.

The Body of Language

But what language lacks in terms of theological (long gone) and philosophical (under attack) foundation it tries to find in relationships to the body. Much of my study projects these relationships. Novelists, dramatists, film directors, and actors rely upon the language of written and spoken word and of visual image, but this language seeks body: some telos, some fulfillment and completion of itself in corporeality. Language can never have such self-completion, for were it to be totally fulfilled it would no longer be language but a transcendent expression of full incarnation. Yet in its teleological urgings artistic language strives to be bodied through its rhythms, tones, and voices, through its transparency toward the images it evokes (so that one forgets the language in "seeing" the scenes it creates), and even through the physicality of the print, page, and book of the written word. Of the narratives I have treated, one senses this striving mainly in *The Public Burning, Many Things Have Happened since He Died, Mariette in Ecstasy, Beloved,* and *Tracks.* In Coover's parodic novel the exuberant rhetoric of Uncle Sam, the boisterous songs and chants of the crowds "reproduced" by the anonymous narrator, the loud chaos of polyphonic voices of America at the execution circus, and the outrageous grim humor of the "Intermezzo" chapter (which consists of "A Last-Act Sing Sing Opera by Julius and Ethel Rosenberg" entitled "Human Dignity Is Not for Sale") all create the impression of a *furor loquendi,* a "rage for speaking" that wants to embody America itself as a grand public text.

This rage becomes hysteria in Vaughn's *Many Things.* There the compound sentences strung together and the sparse punctuation convey the narrator's precarious hold on her sanity as she pours forth a verbiage that seems designed to smother her many anxieties and repress her grim memories but only intensifies them. This very verbiage accrues to something almost palpable, a prattle that echoes the abuse its speaker suffers and in the process is transfigured into eloquence. Vaughn wants the novel to transcend "its narrator's limitations by transcending its own pain and violence into a work of art," and that is exactly what it accomplishes.[3] Even her parodic use of the Bible, whereby its grand language is reduced to cliché and to the mechanical formulas of "proof texts," provides it with a sort of magical "body" revealing the desire of biblicists to possess tangible evidence of their belief, some physically present sacred object to worship.

Hysteria may also be at work in *Mariette in Ecstasy,* but part of the novel's power is that we can never truly know this. Mariette may be mad or she may be "possessed" by Christ; her seizures of rapture and her wounds may be self-induced or actual instances of divine intercourse. Either way, the novel plays with the erotic as both a physical-sexual and a religious-transcendent force—in fact as a primary way as opposed to the long Christian tradition, in which humans experience the sacred. Hansen juxtaposes the language of the church calendar and the services (e. g., "Second Sunday of Advent" and "Mass of St. Lucy, Virgin, Martyr") to evocations of the seasons, animals, and people at work; he connects the sacred to the natural, physical world as a backdrop for the postulant's erotic spirituality.

Language is sacramental for Hansen, and not just (perhaps not mainly) religious language but the language of the tangible and concrete. He says that he "hoped to present in Mariette's life a faith that gives an intellectual assent to Catholic orthodoxy, but doesn't forget that the origin of religious feeling is the graced revelation of the Holy Being in us in nature, in the flesh, and in all our faculties."[4] He transforms the mystery of Mariette's physical afflictions—her stigmata and trances—into a reflection on "the Mystery at the heart of metaphysics."[5] This is not an approach with which a predominantly Protestant America, traditionally suspicious of esthetic language, has been comfortable, yet as Hansen employs it, it comes closer than most others to realizing a telos through the body.

Morrison's artistry in *Beloved* consists of another kind of mystery relating the spiritual and physical through eros. She conjures with "spirit" as ghost, as the incarnated past of a victimized people, and as divine power and has these converge in the mysterious reincarnated dead daughter who is simultaneously succuba, seducer, and, for a brief time, her mother's and sister's deep solace. The violated bodies (of Sethe, Beloved, the black men of Sweet Home, and millions of slaves) cry out for language, and flesh struggles to become word so that the sufferers can tell of the horrors of generations of abuse.

The lyrical prose and the poetry of the two chapters beginning with "I AM BELOVED and she is mine" especially provide an erotic connection of ghostliness, mass suffering and death, and a desperate need to be comforted.[6] The scene early in the novel in which Paul D sees Sethe's scarred, numb back has a similar effect. He is struck dumb by the permanent evidence of the vicious beating and reacts by kissing "every ridge and leaf" of the scar-tree. A compassionate silence and a passionate gesture replace language when the suffering witnessed is too awful for words.

But in *Tracks* the relentless effort to enforce silence on the Native Americans—by annihilating them—has led the Chippewas to respond with trickster language as the language of survival. The trickster not only deals in deception as a way of outwitting the invaders but he also employs the magic of words and objects to afflict the body, using incantations as medicine to weaken white usurpers. These strategies have proved to be failures in the world of Erdrich's novel. The Chippewas are dying off from starvation (because the federal government encouraged the eradication of the buffalo) and disease (imported from Europe) and stand to lose what remains of their land as well. In these straits they turn their trickster wiles against each other. Pauline, for example, jealous of the passion that Fleur and Eli feel for each other, abandons her Catholicism long enough to use a "charm dust" (made of "certain roots, crane's bill . . . and slivers of Sophie's fingernails" [80]) to inspire a lust in Eli for the teenaged Sophie Morrisey, and Eli, after he succumbs, thinks he has been "witched."[7]

That is of little consequence, however, compared to the betrayals the

Chippewas carry out on each other in the process of selling their land to the whites, and here again the deception involves duplicitous language. Because many of the tribe cannot read, they are easily duped by the legalese of the contracts and the empty assurances of their tribespeople and forfeit land that they had not intended to sell or to sell so cheaply. Yet language, for all its complicitness in the demise of these Native Americans, is also employed "intratribally" toward their survival. However crazy and confused about her past Pauline may be, she wishes to save her people by converting them to Christianity, and she engages Catholic sacramental language and actions—desperately evokes both Christ's physical presence and the tangibility of death—to do so. Nanapush, on the other hand, he of the cunning tongue, a keeper of the old ways and the other narrator of *Tracks*, tells his story to Lulu, Fleur's estranged grown daughter, in the hope that she will abandon her hostility to her heritage and come to embrace it rather than marrying the "no-good Morrisey" who has compromised with the whites.

Another way of recapitulating the aims and discoveries of this book is to suggest a fourth body: to the bodies politic, erotic, and apocalyptic add the body poetic—humans engaged in narrating artfully to themselves and each other certain unique private stories that resonate for the group. Just how this resonance occurs—how the singular private vision becomes a shared public mythos—remains mysterious, but the value of this transformation can hardly be exaggerated. Communities, whole societies, identify themselves and are bonded and changed by the common narratives that grow from personal expressions; it is a process initiated again and again by our most powerful fiction makers whose tales are absorbed and rendered definitive by the group.

But it is not really necessary to project such a fourth body, for this articulation takes place effectively in the three I have employed. Doctorow and Coover, for example, in imagining the excruciatingly private agonies of an alienated scapegoat family exposed and shamed before the nation, help define the complex antagonistic victim-victimizer dynamic of the body politic and impress on us the acute need for a cure to the conflicts that fragment the members of that body. Hansen and Gordon, among others, show how confessions by the characters of their fictions draw in readers and lead them to initiate public discourse of the body erotic as a secular version of confessional intercourse: people opening up to each other and declaring willingness to accept responsibility for their actions and for each other. Coppola, Caputo, and Erdrich adopt the language of extremity to describe lurid visions of cataclysm, yet the very extravagance of these images conveys the anxieties and urgencies of the body apocalyptic, its desperate desire to transcend the destruction it evokes.

What all of these fictions with religious dimensions and concerns offer the public realm is *apokalypsis,* a revelation, but one of language rather than impending destruction. One might even call it a revelation of impending language, for good literature, although it is usually cast in the past and present, strives toward new expression. That is its nature as metaphor, and it is certainly the nature of story as extended metaphor—always seeking via artifice to prolong itself, to postpone the inevitable end. Few of the characters I have studied here learn to live fully and artfully toward the end, but such education is what their authors fashion in their texts and offer to us as an exemplary way of embodying the public realm.

Notes

1. Toni Morrison, "Memory, Creation, and Writing," *Thought* 59 (1984): 387.

2. The difference, of course, is that the reader of the narrative can do nothing for the fictional narrator, whereas the priest as mediator does, through his office, change the narration into a healing force for its teller.

3. See Vaughn's response in Appendix 2.

4. Ron Hansen, "Writing as Sacrament," *Image: A Journal of the Arts and Religion* 5 (Spring 1994): 56–57.

5. Hansen, "Writing as Sacrament," 53: "Even secular interpretations point to the fiction writer's duty to express the Mystery at the heart of metaphysics."

6. All of the chapters of *Beloved* begin with the lead-in words capitalized, so that one cannot tell here whether it is "beloved" or "Beloved."

7. This dust is a "love medicine" like the potion that plays a central role in Erdrich's novel with that title.

Appendix 1:
Ron Hansen Responds

In an effort to nurture a public conversation on American fiction and religion, I asked a few of the novelists whose work I interpreted to respond to my reading of their narratives. Below is the generous response from Ron Hansen, author of *Mariette in Ecstasy*.

The shaming you refer to on your page 88, from page 143 of the book, was written to give as a possibility an attack by sisters in the convent, but for Mariette, and me, the hands belonged to evil spirits. I lifted that incident (and more, as well as some letters) from the life of Saint Gemma Galgani (1878–1903), a beautiful and possibly neurotic young woman in Lucca, Italy, who failed at her few tries at convent living and finally took work as a housekeeper, frequently suffering affronts, trances, and stigmata until her premature death.[1] She believed in Satan's special interest in humiliating her, and the tortures she related to her confessor, Father Germanus, seem right out of *The Exorcist*. I sought to report these happenings rather than interpret them, since fiction writers are far better at availing readers the opportunities for new thinking than they are adept at persuading their readers to think a certain way.

The stigmata are a great mystery to me, but so are fame, cancer, wealth, poverty, beauty, and human misery. The rules of the game are perpetually baffling. Why are some religious and irreligious people blessed again and again while others' prayers are seemingly ignored? But for that matter, why did Christ have to be crucified? My own perception is Mother Saint-Raphael's: "'God gives us just enough to seek Him, and never enough to fully find him. To do more would inhibit our freedom, and our freedom is very dear to God'" (174).

I would nuance your comments on the final pages in only this way:

that the pain she feels is not a form of God's abuse, but is still experienced by her as a gift, just as our own lives, for all their cares, are forms we zealously cling to. For Mariette it is a happy ending, in spite of everything, because, as with the nuns in the convent, the graces she receives are sufficient to make up for what may seem to us to be only loss, deprivation, and abandonment.

I particularly like your reading of the linkages between the body and the soul, the erotic and the religious. We are finally getting to an idea that was there in the book of Genesis but later corrupted, that sexuality is a sacrament, and in our compelling, physical relationships with others we edge ever closer to wholly expressing and interpreting God's relationship to us.

Note

1. Hansen says in "Writing as Sacrament" that "some parts of the letters that Mariette writes in the novel are paraphrased from confessions written by Saint Gemma Galgani in 1900 and included in a hard-to-find book called *Letters and Ecstasies.*"

Appendix 2:
Elizabeth Dewberry Responds

What follows is the eloquent response of Elizabeth Dewberry, author of *Many Things Have Happened since He Died.*

———

I hope I can say without sounding presumptuous that I think the biblical influence in my background must be akin in some ways to Toni Morrison's as you describe hers on your page 120. My parents were devout evangelicals when I was a child, and I was educated from kindergarten to twelfth grade in a very conservative church school where almost everyone I knew expressed themselves with biblical language, using biblical metaphors and echoing the rhythms of the Psalms and the Beatitudes in their everyday speech.

I think that's how I came to the reverence for words and stories that all writers have to some extent or another. I remember being very young, four or five, maybe, and having a clear sense that language, the language of prayers, sermons, and hymns, was what connected us to God, and that stories, specifically Bible stories, were how we came to know God and began to understand his world.

But I also remember memorizing the first verse of Genesis ("In the beginning God created") and the first verse of John ("In the beginning was the Word, and the Word was with God, and the Word was God") and thinking, "Well, which was it?" I still find the connection between God and creativity and words and beginnings fascinating and ultimately mysterious, but now I think all stories, or at least all my stories, at their best, use language to explore the presence of divine mystery in everyday life.

I think for the narrator of *Many Things . . .*, the act of telling her story is religious at its core in that way. It's part confession, part supplication, part railing against God, maybe even part praise, but throughout it,

I think, is her sense that she hopes to figure out who God really is, and she hopes to get him to notice her. She's also afraid she'll fail and that the consequences of such a failure are eternal separation from God, eternal fragmentation of the soul.

Her tendency to take the Bible's truths this literally is another reason (in addition to the several you mention) her psyche is so fragmented. If words have divine power, if as a Christian she is entitled to use that power, and if God can say, "Let there be light," and there is light, then she ought to be able to say to a mountain, "Move," and it will move. But if fiction writers are pretty much the only ones in this world who get to name people, places, things, and events into reality, then writing the novel is for the narrator an attempt to exercise divine power, a reclaiming of something she perceives as being otherwise lost.

As she uses and perceives this power, it is both creative and destructive, and her list of changes she'd like to make to the manuscript reveals her awareness of the novelist's prerogative to commit invisible acts of violence against the realities of her world by saying, for example, that certain people never existed and events never happened. And although I agree with you that the *narrator* doesn't transform her pain or her tendency to violence into anything redemptive—at best, she's transformed it into the book she hopes will make her rich and famous—it is my hope that *Many Things* . . . transcends its narrator's limitations by transcending its own pain and violence into a work of art.

Certainly not all artists see their work in religious terms, but I think there's a sense in which all art can be understood as a form of prayer, an effort to commune with God, to discover and experience who and what he is, or at least an attempt to explore that Mystery at the origin of the universe that some of us call God. And if God is the Alpha and Omega, if God is love and truth, if he's eternal, and if he is that Word that was there in the beginning, then writing fiction, creating beginnings and ends, exploring the meanings of love and the reasons we live the way we do, confronting death and eternity, good and evil, reaching out to heal and create life, and using words to do that—it's all inextricably connected to God. So for me, as, I think, for the narrator of *Many Things* . . . , finding God's grace has something to do with finding the right words and creating something good and lasting and true out of them.

Appendix 3:
Philip Caputo Responds

What follows is the immensely helpful response from Philip Caputo, author of *Indian Country.*

———

I found your interpretation of *Indian Country* interesting, perceptive, and accurate. You got it! Which is more than I can say for certain reviewers and literary critics, a couple of whom you mention in your analysis. I intentionally connected the experience of the American Indian with Vietnam and Christian Starkmann's spiritual malaise. The novel was also meant to be a story about myths, myths not in the sense of lies or fables but in the sense of narratives by which we make sense of our lives and the world. Louis is a man whose sacred myths are in danger of being lost due to the influence of an alien culture; Starkmann is someone whose myths were obliterated in the fires of Vietnam. I very much appreciated your reading of the episode between June and the bear. Her bizarre fantasy was not, as Ms. Kakutani had it, an example of male sexual fantasies, but of her subconscious emotions toward her husband, as her killing of the actual bear was a symbolic murder, not only of Christian but of all the men—her father, her first husband—who'd mistreated or abused her. But there was a mythic dimension to this episode as well. In Ojibwa culture, as in many Native American cultures, the bear is the mighty, manlike creature who guards the secrets to the "medicine" by which human life is sustained and prolonged. You'll notice that after June shoots the bear unnecessarily, her life begins to unravel, as does Christian's. That is, in places like the Upper Peninsula, "Indian Country," the ancient spirits and myths still exist and are violated at one's peril.

Finally, thanks, thanks, thanks for pointing out the fallacy of Conroy's description of the chapters written from Louis's point of view as "mumbo-jumbo."

Appendix 4:
The Ghost Dance at Wounded Knee

Dick Fool Bull

This is a true story; I wish it weren't. When it happened I was a small boy, only about six or seven. To tell the truth, I'm not sure how old I am. I was born before the census takers came in, so there's no record.

When I was a young boy, I liked to stick around my old uncle, because he always had stories to tell. Once he said, "There's something new coming, traveling on the wind. A new dance. A new prayer." He was talking about *Wanagi-wachipi,* the ghost dance. "Short Bull and Kicking Bear traveled far," my uncle told me. "They went to see a holy man of another tribe far in the south, the Piute tribe. They had heard that this holy man could bring dead people to life again, and that he could bring the buffalo back."

My uncle said it was very important, and I must listen closely. Old Unc Said:

This holy man let Short Bull and Kicking Bear look into his hat. There they saw their dead relatives walking about. The holy man told them, "I'll give you something to eat that will kill you, but don't be afraid. I'll bring you back to life again." They believed him. They ate something and died, then found themselves walking in a new, beautiful land. They spoke with their parents and grandparents, and with friends that the white soldiers had killed. Their friends were well, and this new world was like the old one, the one the white man had destroyed. It was full of game, full of antelope and buffalo. The grass was green and high, and though long-dead people from other tribes also lived in this new land, there was peace. All the Indian nations formed one tribe and could understand each other. Kicking Bear and Short Bull walked around and saw everything, and they were happy. Then the holy man of the Piutes brought them back to life again.

"You have seen it," he told them, "the new Land I'm bringing. The earth will roll up like a blanket with all that bad white man's stuff, the fences and railroads and mines and telegraph poles; and underneath will be our old-young Indian earth with all our relatives come to life again."

Then the holy man taught them a new dance, a new song, a new prayer. He gave them sacred red paint. He even made the sun die; it was all covered with black and disappeared. Then he brought the sun to life again.

Short Bull and Kicking Bear came back bringing us the good news. Now everywhere we are dancing this new dance to roll up the earth, to bring back the dead. A new world is coming.
This Old Unc told me.

Then I saw it myself: the dancing. People were holding each other by the hand, singing, whirling around, looking at the sun. They had a little spruce tree in the middle of the dance circle. They wore special shirts painted with the sun, the moon, the stars, and magpies. They whirled around; they didn't stop dancing.

Some of the dancers fell down in a swoon, as if they were dead. The medicine men fanned them with sweet-smelling cedar smoke and they came to life again. They told the people, "We were dead. We went to the moon and the morning star. We found our dead fathers and mothers there, and we talked to them." When they woke up, these people held in their hands star rocks, moon rocks, different kinds of rocks from those we have on earth. They clutched strange meats from star and moon animals. The dance leader told them not to be afraid of the white men who forbade them to dance this *wanagi-wachipi*. They told them that the ghost shirts they wore would not let any white man's bullets through. So they danced. I saw it.

The earth never rolled up. The buffalo never came back, and the dead relatives never came to life again. It was the soldier who came; why, nobody knew. The dance was a peaceful one, harming nobody, but I guess the white people thought it was a war dance.

Many people were afraid of what the soldiers would do. We had no guns any more, and hardly had any horses left. We depended on the white man for everything, yet the whites were afraid of us, just as we were afraid of them.

Then when the news spread that Sitting Bull had been killed at Standing Rock for being with the ghost dancers, the people were really scared. Some of the old people said: "Let's go to Pine Ridge and give ourselves up, because the soldiers won't shoot us if we do. Old Red Cloud will protect us. Also, they're holding our rations up there."

So my father and mother and Old Unc got the buggy and their old horse and drove with us children toward Pine Ridge. It was cold and snowing. It wasn't a happy ride; all the grown-ups were worried. Then the soldiers stopped us. They had big fur coats on, bear coats. They were warm and we were freezing, and I remember wishing I had such a coat. They told us to go no further, to stop and make a camp right there. They told the same thing to everyone who came, by foot, or horse, or buggy. So there was a camp, but little to eat and little firewood, and the soldiers made a ring around us and let nobody leave.

Then suddenly there was a strange noise, maybe four, five miles away, like the tearing of a big blanket, the biggest blanket in the world. As soon as he heard it, Old Unc burst into tears. My old ma started to keen as for the dead, and people were running around, weeping, acting crazy.

I asked Old Unc, "Why is everybody crying?"

He said, "They are killing them, they are killing our people over there!"

My father said, "That noise—that's not the ordinary soldier guns. Those are the big wagon guns which tear people to bits—into little pieces!" I could not understand it, but everybody was weeping, and I wept too. Then a day later—or was it two? No, I think it was the next day, we passed by there. Old Unc said: "You children might as well see it; look and remember.

There were dead people all over, mostly women and children, in a ravine near a stream called Chankpe-opi Wakpala, Wounded Knee Creek. The people were frozen, lying there in all kinds of postures, their motion frozen too. The soldiers, who were stacking up bodies like firewood, did not like us passing by. They told us to leave there, double-quick or else. Old Unc said: "We'd better do what they say right now, or we'll lie there too."

So we went on toward Pine Ridge, but I had seen. I had seen a dead mother with a dead baby sucking at her breast. The little baby had on a tiny beaded cap with the design of the American flag.

Index

Robert Detweiler received his master's and doctoral degrees from the University of Florida and studied theology at the University of Hamburg. He has published extensively on the intersection of religion, literature, and culture in such works as *Art/Literature/Religion: Life on the Borders, The Daemonic Imagination: Sacred Text and Secular Story,* and the award-winning *Breaking the Fall: Religious Readings of Comtemporary Fiction.* He is professor of comparative literature at Emory University, Atlanta, and was honored by a 1994 festchrift, *In Good Company.*